BY DAN JENKINS

NOVELS
FAST COPY
LIFE ITS OWNSELF
BAJA OKLAHOMA
LIMO (with Bud Shrake)
DEAD SOLID PERFECT
SEMI-TOUGH

NONFICTION
"YOU CALL IT SPORTS, BUT I SAY
IT'S A JUNGLE OUT THERE"
FOOTBALL (photographs by Walter Iooss Jr.)
SATURDAY'S AMERICA
THE DOGGED VICTIMS OF INEXORABLE FATE
THE BEST 18 GOLF HOLES IN AMERICA

SCREENPLAYS
DEAD SOLID PERFECT (with Bobby Roth)
BAJA OKLAHOMA (with Bobby Roth)

SONGS
"BAJA OKLAHOMA" (with Willie Nelson)

DAN

A FIRESIDE BOOK
Published by Simon & Schuster Inc.
New York London Toronto Sydney Tokyo Singapore

JENKINS

"You Call It Sports, But I Say It's a Jungle Out There"

Fireside

Simon & Schuster Building
Rockefeller Center
1230 Avenue of the Americas
New York, New York 10020

First Fireside Edition, 1990

FIRESIDE and colophon are registered trademarks
of Simon & Schuster Inc.

Manufactured in the United States of America

10   9   8   7   6   5   4   3   2   1   Pbk.

Library of Congress Cataloging in Publication Data

Jenkins, Dan.
    You call it sports, but I say it's a jungle out there / Dan
Jenkins.
        p.   cm.
    1. Sports. 2. Football. 3. Golf. I. Title.
GV707.J46   1989
796—dc20   89-35857
                                                               CIP
ISBN 0-671-69021-3
    0-671-72498-3 Pbk.

(Continued on page 367)

For all the poets who've had their funniest leads rewritten by imbeciles, their best quotes killed by quote Nazis, their favorite kicker lines chopped off by mysterious phantoms, and their expense accounts chewed on by eunuchs who've never been to Beverly Hills.

CONTENTS

"You Call It Sports, but I Say It's a Jungle Out There"

IN ALL MY YEARS OF COVERING SPORTS, I CAN HONESTLY TELL YOU I've never heard any athlete say, "We're going to beat the apple-walnut pie out of those strawberry sundaes," but on more than one occasion I've heard a football coach say something like, "I'll tell you one goddamn thing—we're about two niggers away from winnin' this fuckin' conference."

I think that about sums it up. Real sports is not for kids.

But then, of course, I never thought I was writing for kids.

For whom I have always written has yet to be determined, but there's a Congressional committee looking into it.

This book is not my life in sports. It is, to date, so to speak, my life *around* sports—when I wasn't in a convivial saloon, or on a plane, or arguing with room service, all of which have taken up as much time as my typewriter.

The astute observer may discover that the book is a bit lopsided with stories on football and golf. That's because those sports are the ones that have always interested me the most, and not just because of their gambling possibilities.

I should caution that this book is deep in places. Many of the stories were written when I was in the depths of despair, if not over some silly action on the part of the NCAA, or NFL, or PGA, or some other alphabet, then occasionally over my low blood count, which knows nothing of math.

Many of the characters in the book are living while most of the dead ones are still dead, as far as I know.

In the football section, you may stumble across two or three charts, or lists. I hope you will enjoy them and perhaps learn something from them, or at least be kind to them, because the research was a hell of a lot of trouble.

The title comes from a day in my lurid past. Back in 1953, fresh out of college, I was working for a paper in my old hometown of Fort Worth, Texas, when Ben Hogan returned from Scotland after winning the British Open to go along with The Masters and U.S. Open titles he had won earlier in the year—an unprecedented Triple Crown.

Hogan was given a tickertape parade through the streets of downtown Fort Worth and I covered it for the front page of the paper, writing some kind of lead that said:

"Ben Hogan came home today and had to play through a fairway of confetti."

But that's not exactly what ran in the paper.

Since I was writing for the front, my copy had to pass through the hands of a cityside editor.

When the paper came out, my lead read:

"Ben Hogan, champion golfer, came home today and . . ."

Which was as far as I read before I went over to speak to the editor.

"*Champion golfer?*" I said to him in disbelief.

He said, "Yes, well, we have to let our readers know it's about sports, don't we?"

"Fine," I said. "You call it sports but I say it's a jungle out there."

A considerable amount of the material in the book is new, and some of the previously published pieces have been reworded, to give them that ever-popular timeless quality. This means they are part of the stuff I was given the opportunity to write for *Playboy, Sports Illustrated,* and *Golf Digest* magazines, as well as various and sundry newspapers in Various, Texas, and Sundry, Florida.

My wife and daughter and two sons wish to thank those publications here and now for hiring me in the first place, and also for their generous reprint permission.

I wanted to thank the editors, too, but I couldn't get anybody on the phone. They were all out on bombing raids.

Some of them will be dancing at the Savoy tonight and some of them will still be in Germany.

D. J.

FOOTBALL

What Is It?

FOOTBALL IS THE NEAREST THING WE HAVE TO THE CHRISTIANS AND the lions, but this is not to say that all of the Christians are white and all of the lions are black, or that all of the Christians carry a 3.2 average in the core curriculum, or that all of the blacks don't have anything to do in the off-season but steal the radio out of your Mercedes.

Men understand football. It's war without death. It's my school against your school, my town against your town, my state against your state, and if my team loses the big game, I'll either get drunk for a week or kill myself.

Women have a hard time with football, except that they know people are hitting each other, so I will explain it.

The guys aren't fags. The reason they are always patting each other on the ass is because it's tradition.

And the quarterback is not trying to grab the center's dick when he sticks his hands under his ass. He's waiting for the football to be snapped so he can give it to a black guy who will run for a touchdown in front of 80,000 people, although the NCAA rules don't permit him to have any spending money for cheeseburgers.

Football is the supreme test of bravery in sports, but there used to be more fear involved. That's when the players didn't wear face masks.

Many impressive academic institutions have football stadiums that hold over 80,000 people, but these schools say they are interested in academics first and football second.

Contrary to popular belief, you can't be dumb and play football well, except if you're a defensive lineman. Then all you have to do is hit somebody.

It is also true that a much higher percentage of football players graduate from college than the rest of the student body as a whole.

College football, therefore, is not a proving ground for the National Football League, which is also not as much fun as it used to be because there are too many incomplete passes and too many stupid calls by the officials.

Otherwise, football is social. Old school colors breed tail-gate parties, and star players often marry Homecoming Queens.

Later they get divorced and go to separate tail-gate parties where they can root for their team's black guys to outrun the other team's black guys.

Birth of a Sportswriter

THE COLLEGE FOOTBALL SEASON OF 1938, AS IT HAPPENED, TURNED out to be the thing that made me decide to become a sportswriter, for I was already learning at the tender age of 8 that I was never going to make it as a G-man, aviator, ambulance driver, sword fighter, trapeze artist, cowboy, or doughboy knocking out German machine-gun nests.

I was realizing all this by then because I was skinny and had morbid fears of height, speed, and danger.

Anyhow, 1938 was the year that the university in my hometown of Fort Worth, Texas, produced a dazzling, world-beating football team that ultimately won the National Championship. This accomplishment encouraged me to conclude that, despite the breathtaking boredom of the place into which I had been born, I was suddenly and arrogantly living in the sports capital of the universe.

My granddad Pap and Uncle Mack and Cousin Sid had hinted at this a couple of seasons earlier, when Sam Baugh was slinging touchdown passes for the Texas Christian University Horned Frogs, a nickname I didn't think was eccentric or amusing until later in life.

But now it was '38 and a little guy named Davey O'Brien, only 5-7 and 152 pounds, was slinging even more touchdown passes for TCU, as well as darting around on broken-field scampers and tossing tricky laterals all over the field, and the Frogs were tromping over every opponent with utter disdain.

Sometimes they did it without Utter Disdain, who would be resting on the sideline while Remarkable Ease, slower but just as effective, took over.

At the start of the season, my relatives took me out to TCU stadium, a concrete edifice holding 30,000 and looking to me at the time like the largest structure on earth, where I watched the Horned Frogs tromp over Centenary and Arkansas, and then with various relatives and neighborhood friends, I listened intently on the radio as they tromped over Texas A&M at College Station and over Temple and Marquette in the fiercely exotic locales of Philadelphia and Milwaukee.

The Associated Press and the Williamson Rankings, the two most respected rating systems of the era, ran every Tuesday in the *Fort Worth Star-Telegram,* and the relatives would shout obscenities at them over breakfast, lunch, and dinner.

After five impressive victories, the Frogs had been able to climb no higher than fourth in the polls, while, in the meantime, Pitt, the defending national champion, rolling along nicely with Marshall Goldberg and its "dream backfield," seemed to have a death grip on number one.

The sixth week brought the Saturday of the gigantic struggle between undefeated TCU (5–0) and undefeated Baylor (4–0) in Fort Worth, a battle of passing brilliance between O'Brien and Baylor's "Bullet" Bill Patterson, who was destined to become a hero of the East-West game.

On the warm, dry Saturday of October 29, I attended the pregame parade, where I applauded the TCU Swing Band and sneered at a grizzly in a cage being towed by a Baylor truck.

Later, on the grass of the north end zone, surrounded by relatives and a sellout crowd, I watched with awe and frequently with my own eyes as O'Brien hurled three touchdown passes and perpetrated magicianlike laterals to a trailing halfback named Earl Clark and a trailing fullback named Connie Sparks after squirting through the line for 10, 20, 30 yards behind the blocking of his all-American center, Ki Aldrich, and his all-American tackle, I. B. Hale, and TCU demolished the Bears by the stunning score of 39–7.

To this day, I have still not seen football played with such skill, verve, and daring.

The Frogs soared to number two in the polls after the Baylor slaughter and there was much joy around the breakfast, lunch, and dinner table, but then God smiled even more favorably on TCU. A week later on the Saturday the Frogs were whipping Tulsa handily, the invincible Pitt Panthers were shocked, upset, and otherwise stupefied by Carnegie Tech, 20–10.

TCU vaulted to number one and plans were set in motion to paint every house in Fort Worth purple.

It was at that point that a terrible thing happened. God frowned on Fort Worth. Even though the Frogs soundly defeated Texas the following Saturday, Notre Dame remained undefeated and the polls catered to the popularity of the Irish. "IRISH WREST NUMBER-ONE RANKING FROM FROGS."

"Northern sons of bitches," an uncle or cousin commented.

O'Brien and the Frogs finished their perfect season (10–0) with delicious victories over Rice and SMU, and the relatives were resigned to settling for number two when fate stepped in again.

Notre Dame had one last game to play, on December third, and, happily, it was against USC out on the Coast, a very good USC team that had a Grenny Lansdell and an Ambrose Schindler to make mischief for the Irish. That was the best day of radio listening in the history of Fort Worth, for the Trojans crushed Notre Dame, 13–0. We had only to wait for Tuesday's newspaper to receive the blissful news—and we were rewarded with a screaming headline that read: "FROGS FAR AHEAD IN FINAL GRID POLLS."

A few days later, O'Brien became a unanimous all-American quarterback, as well as the winner of the Heisman, Maxwell, and Walter Camp trophies as the best player in the land; and a few weeks later, the Horned Frogs whipped up on Carnegie Tech in the Sugar Bowl, 15–7, to justify the integrity of the A.P. and Williamson polls.

Finally, an 8-year-old kid decided to become a sportswriter, if for no reason other than to help combat Notre Dame's clout in the polls in future years.

Actually, in all the years since then, he has not had much luck in that endeavor, but he still has 1938 to fondle.

Recruiting Diary

THANKS TO CHECKBOOK JOURNALISM, I AM IN POSSESSION OF A recruiting diary that was kept by Bubba Don Supples, an assistant football coach at Jesus and God University, and I am herewith going to publish some excerpts from it, because not only do they tell the whole story of the university's efforts to recruit Maxell Washington, the best running back in the country, they leave no doubt in my mind that college sports are getting cleaner.

I'll start with Bubba Don's first entry in March and then just skip around, hitting a few of the high spots.

March 1: Well, it's time to make the big push on Maxell Washington. This kid can turn our whole program around. It's like I said to coach Tooler: If we get Maxell Washington, you can dust off the trophy shelf—this fucker will put a six-pack of Heismans on it.

I mean, shit. He's 6'3", 237 pounds, runs the 40 in 4.2, and he's got more want-to than any kid I've seen since "Mule Dick" McClinton outrun his clap and took us to the Persimmon Bowl.

The kid will do anything you ask of him. If you say, "Maxell, I want you to jump into that puddle of slop right there," he'll jump. If you say, "Maxell, I want you to run over there to Egypt and knock down them pyramids," he'll do it.

Character is what I'm talking about. You can't teach it.

I think we got the inside track on Maxell. His brother, Dolby, played for us, and me and his daddy was teammates on the Packers. Treble Washington was a great cornerback.

Taking all of them to dinner tonight. Pizza Hut or Dairy Queen. Ain't much else to do here in Loweetha, Texas.

March 2: We got trouble. Maxell and Dolby and Treble come to the Pizza Hut in a new Porsche.

I said, "Maxell, where'd you get that car?"

He said, "I'm not at liberty to say."

I said, "Maxell, they's rules against that shit. Did you get it from Oklahoma? Notre Dame? Florida State? Who?"

He said, "I definitely didn't get it from Oklahoma or Notre Dame or Florida State."

"Did you get it from Texas A&M?"

He said, "I'm not at liberty to say."

Called coach Tooler. He said it wasn't no big problem. He would talk to Mr. Simpson about a Rolls-Royce.

March 7: By God, Mr. Simpson is a man of action—and the best contributor we have. He give us our weight room and our Astroturf.

When Maxell wanted his Rolls-Royce to be bright blue instead of white, Mr. Simpson had it painted for him in three days.

March 10: Real good party on Mr. Simpson's yacht. Maxell had never seen an ocean before. He asked if it was the same ocean that boats sail on. I said as far as I knew, it was.

Maxell asked what it took to get a yacht like Mr. Simpson's. Mr. Simpson said it would take a national championship before Maxell's eligibility was up.

Treble Washington asked Mr. Simpson if he would throw in an airplane if Maxell won *two* national championships for us.

Mr. Simpson laughed and said, "Shit, if he wins two national championships, we'll rename the goddamn library after him!"

I love Mr. Simpson. There's no better friend of college football. "Stud Muffin" Simpson was a great player here.

March 14: I think Maxell is leaning toward us, but I'm a little worried after last night. He started asking about pussy.

Called coach Tooler. Coach said pussy was no problem.

March 19: Took Maxell on a tour of the Pi Nu sorority house today. That's where he'll live if he signs with us. I thought Maxell would be impressed, but he said he had visited Westwood and it looked to him like we was a little light on blondes and tits.

March 22: Bound to happen. We've run into a package deal. Maxell's brother, Dolby, wants a job on our coaching staff, and Maxell's daddy, Treble, thinks he ought to be on the board of directors of one of Mr. Simpson's corporations at a salary that would match coach Tooler's.

They're all talking it over. I put in my two cents. I said it's a small price to pay for what we'll get in return.

March 25: Time to bring in our big gun. The chancellor. He's a good old boy who loves his football. Brought him in because Maxell wanted to talk about grades.

Chancellor guaranteed Maxell he would make passing grades.

Maxell said he didn't want to have to go to no classes to make his grades.

Chancellor asked Maxell if he would go to each class one time.

Maxell said that sounded real hard, especially during football season.

Chancellor asked Maxell if he could get to any classes in the spring.

"That's when I rest up my brain," Maxell said, frowning.

I thought the chancellor was gonna blow the deal, but he agreed to no classes.

March 28: I knew it would all come down to salary—and thank goodness Mr. Simpson is a smart businessman. Maxell asked for $125,000 a year for four years.

Naturally, we don't have that in our athletic budget, so it was up to Mr. Simpson.

Mr. Simpson come up with the plan.

Pretty doggone astute, if you ask me.

Mr. Simpson said he would cough up that amount of money only if it was a donation he could write off on his taxes.

That's when he pointed out that Jesus and God University is affiliated with the Church of Ezekiel and Them, which is across the street from our campus.

Mr. Simpson said he would make the donation to the church, and the preachers could handle the payroll to Maxell and any others on our team who needed money.

This way, he said, the NCAA couldn't never find out nothing because a church don't have to open up its books to nobody.

Coach Tooler and the chancellor said they didn't hear this conversation—they didn't know nothing about it—but they said it sounded like a hell of an idea.

April 1: Today is the happiest day of my life. Maxell signed with us, and I'll tell you what—it's all over but the winning around this place.

Beware: Hypocrites on Campus

IT DOESN'T MUCH MATTER WHETHER THE NCAA STANDS FOR Nerds, Clods, and Androids, or Nitwits, Clowns, and Assholes. They all fit.

Here's what an NCAA committeeman, a member of the infrastructure, likes to do: grasp at the millions of dollars in football bowl money with one hand while frantically fanning himself with the other as he expresses concern over the "cult of winning" and the "call of professionalism" in college football.

An NCAA committeeman, a member of the infrastructure, likes to go to meetings and stay in a lavish hotel suite, expenses paid, and vote for something like Proposition 48, or Proposal 42, or anything that means a black kid can't have a scholarship unless he can quote from Turgenev, and a white kid would be better off if he went to Franklin & Marshall instead of Alabama.

An NCAA committeeman, a member of the infrastructure, is generally the president of a university that hasn't won a football game since 1973, or some pipe-smoking twit who thinks John Barth is witty. And what he enjoys doing is putting a big block of cheese, known as revenue, on the floor and telling the college football player, known as the mouse, that if he takes a bite of it, he's a moral and ethical failure.

Today, there are more than 800 member institutions of the NCAA who are getting away with telling the 108 universities that play major college football what to do, and how.

Nothing has ever made less sense in sports.

But for whatever reasons, the 108 major universities refuse to bolt from the organization and set up their own group, something like the College Football Association, even though they know the odds are heavily against their ever being able to form their own division within the NCAA, a division in which they can make their own realistic rules and police themselves more intelligently.

The NCAA hierarchy likes to say to everybody, "We are you. Look in the mirror. What you see is the NCAA."

Bullshit.

The NCAA is the infrastructure of an out-of-control bureaucracy, a small group of nerds, clods, androids, nitwits, clowns, and assholes who have kissed ass for years in order to get on those committees.

The result is that Alabama and Auburn can't tell each other what to do but the University of Connecticut can tell them *both* what to do.

How? Because the bigtime schools are outnumbered 4 to 1 by the pipsqueaks on all legislation.

There *are* members of the infrastructure who realize that if it weren't for college football most endowments would look like fossils, but they don't want to admit it.

They like to pretend that they're only interested in the "education" of the "scholar-āthlete."

Thus, a kid on a football scholarship is not allowed to have a part-time job to earn cheeseburger money, he is only allowed to put 80,000 people in the stadium on Saturdays.

And if he accepts any favors, large or small, from "overzealous alumnuses," he runs the risk of seeing his school put on probation, receiving sanctions, or even getting the "death penalty," which means no football program for two years—that thing SMU received in 1987.

None of this would hold up in a court of law, of course, but I dare say nobody is ever going to challenge it until the NCAA tries to strap this shit on somebody like Notre Dame, which will never happen.

Questions the so-called "educators" choose to ignore are why did Michigan build a stadium that holds 101,000, why did Stanford build a stadium that holds 90,000, and why did Yale build a stadium that holds 75,000?

I only chose those three examples because they are "great institutions of learning" and obviously have the most copies of Tolstoy in their libraries.

From time to time, I like to remind the NCAA hypocrites that the Ivies didn't deemphasize football until they had given us Walter Camp, Amos Alonzo Stagg, Fritz Pollard, Clint Frank, Albie

Booth, Charley Brickley, Sid Luckman, and so forth; until Yale had won 14 national championships and turned out over 90 all-Americans and produced two Heisman Trophy winners; until every Ivy League school had an endowment that was bigger than the Third World; until they had given us legends, loyalties, pageantry, and purpose.

It's tempting to say that the only thing they've given us since deemphasis is Timothy Leary.

What is endangered by all this mucking around on the part of the hypocrites is the athletic scholarship, something we must never lose.

What in God's name is the big deal if only 95 kids out of a total enrollment of from 6,000 to 50,000 students get a chance to go to college because they excel in football?

No university is a "football factory," and never has been.

Take away the athletic scholarship and one day there'll be nothing left in the world but technological experts, MBAs, and computer freaks who fuck up our credit ratings.

If the hypocrites were as concerned about "cleaning up" college football as they are about staying in their hotel suites and getting on committees, they could do two things that would eliminate most of the "evils" in the sport immediately.

1. Make freshmen ineligible again, as they were for about 100 years. This would again permit the first-year "scholar-athlete" to find out where the classrooms are. It would also mean that those mercenary kids who aren't interested in education at all could go straight to the pros.

2. Allow spending money, varying amounts on a "need basis," and subsidized by the "overzealous alumnuses" *above* the table, for the athlete who can't have a part-time job because it's against the naive rules.

But no. Rather than do these things, the hypocrites prefer to cling to an amateur ideal that hasn't existed since long before Knute Rockne invented recruiting.

Besides, they would lose too many committees of nerds and nitwits.

So I see the future: Oklahoma and Nebraska are meeting at Norman to decide who's No. 1. The Sooners have armed themselves with copies of *Finnegans Wake*. The Cornhuskers have copies of *The Magic Mountain*.

The players take turns reading aloud. Last team awake wins.

During a crucial time-out, Barry Switzer says, "Awright, men, let's go out there and win one for Hans Castorp!"

I'd like to propose a new NCAA—the National Collegiate Alumni Association. There would only be delegates from the schools that play major college football. We would be dedicated to building wings on libraries and fine-arts and science complexes, but only if our schools have a competitive football program.

I have the battle cry: "Eighty thousand people never filled a stadium to watch a fucking math quiz!"

Cupid's Playground

HELPED ALONG BY HOLLYWOOD, THERE WAS A MORE ROMANTIC TIME in our history, when an athlete wanted to excel because of love and the girl next door. Whether it was because the girl next door had big tits, we never questioned.

Remember those days?

Curly, State's star quarterback and all-round good person, gets kidnapped by unshaven gamblers on the eve of State's big game against Normal.

Woe is coach Goldie Bricks, who is tough as bricks but has a heart of gold.

The coach goes to Betty Jean, Curly's girlfriend, who happens to be the sweetheart of Sigma Chi and lives in a little white house only a half block off Flirtation Walk.

"Curly's been kidnapped," the coach says to Betty Jean, who's helping her mother bake a cake.

"Oh, no!" Betty Jean cries out, almost dropping the mixing bowl. "We can't win the game against Normal without Curly!"

"Our kids will give it all they've got, but it sure would make it easier if we had Curly in there so we could hup the ball to him."

Betty Jean says she bets those unshaven gamblers are holding Curly in the old haunted house on the outskirts of town.

"Could be," says the coach, who has to leave now and go to the stadium, because Normal is kicking off to State.

"Bozo and I will go find Curly," Betty Jean says.

Bozo is Curly and Betty Jean's trusty sidekick, the pudgy fellow who plays a hot clarinet when everybody dances at the malt shop.

Betty Jean and Bozo go to the haunted house. Bozo distracts the unshaven gamblers by playing the *Washington and Lee Swing* on his clarinet, while Betty Jean unties Curly.

Curly and Betty Jean race for the jalopy while Bozo fends off the unshaven gamblers with his clarinet.

"Don't worry about me," Bozo yells. "Get Curly to the game!"

"Bozo's a good egg," Curly says, as Betty Jean drives recklessly through town.

They get to the stadium at the start of the fourth quarter. State is two touchdowns behind.

"You know what, Betty Jean?" Curly asks, smiling. "I'm going to win this game for *you*."

"No, Curly," says Betty Jean, giving him a kiss. "You're going to win it for all of us—for everybody who believes in love . . . friendship . . . loyalty . . . and America!"

Down on the sideline, as Curly slips into his football suit, Betty Jean slips into her cheerleader's uniform.

Curly trots onto the field. The crowd roars. State's band strikes up the fight song, which sounds remarkably like the Alabama fight song, and Betty Jean sings, "Fight on, fight on,/Fight on, men./Remember the Rose Bowl;/We'll win then!"

State lines up in the Notre Dame box formation. Curly says, "Forty-seven . . . twenty-three . . . sixteen . . . hike!"

Curly runs 79 yards for a touchdown.

Mysteriously, State gets the ball back.

Curly says, "Sixty-two . . . thirty-seven . . . nineteen . . . hike!"

Curly runs 88 yards for a touchdown.

And State gets the ball back.

Apparently, under the unique rules of this era, a team gets the ball back every time it scores a touchdown.

State is on its own one-yard line and there is time for only one more play. In the huddle, Curly looks at his teammates and says, "K-F-seventy-nine."

Hippo, a burly lineman, says, "Gosh, Curly, that's awful risky, isn't it?"

"It's our only chance," Curly replies.

Curly takes the snapback, throws a pass to himself, runs 30 yards, pitches a lateral to himself, runs 30 more yards, pitches another lateral to himself, and goes the rest of the way—a 99-yard touchdown play.

Up in the stands, Bozo, his head bandaged and his arm in a sling, waves his clarinet jubilantly.

Happy fans swarm the field and carry Curly and Betty Jean from the stadium to the malt shop on the campus drag. There, Bozo is playing the clarinet, coach Goldie Bricks is on piano, Hippo is blowing trumpet, and everybody is singing a medley of college songs.

Meanwhile, in a quiet corner, Curly and Betty Jean sip from the same chocolate malt out of two straws.

"I love this country," Curly says.

"And I love you," Betty Jean says, smiling sweetly.

Things are a little different today, of course.

When Curly tests positive for steroids on the eve of the big game, Betty Jean dashes over to the athletic dorm in the Porsche her daddy bought her.

"What are we going to do?" she asks Dion Leon, the all-American linebacker, who's snorting a line of coke as he talks on the phone to his agent.

Dion can't be bothered, so Betty Jean races up to the six-room suite that's shared by Rusty Hackle, the all-American running back, and four nude, sex-crazed sorority girls, who are nibbling on him.

Rusty can't be bothered, either, so Betty Jean seeks out Kinky Leaper, the split end, who hasn't been to a class in three years but has twice made the scholastic all-American team.

"Curly's tested positive," Betty Jean says.

"Better him than me," says Kinky, who takes a hit off a joint that looks like a cigar as he lies in his indoor hammock and watches three surf movies on three VCRs.

"What do you think we ought to do?" Betty Jean asks.

Kinky shrugs and says, "I don't know about you, but I'm gonna put Normal in a teaser with Auburn and bet the Under."

Kinky rolls out of the hammock, unzips his jeans, and takes out Wilbur. "So, uh . . . is Curly still your old man or what?"

"Screw him," says Betty Jean, lurching for Wilbur.

Later, they're sitting in a bar having their fourth margarita.

Kinky says, "What do you want to do now, bitch?"

"I don't give a shit, asshole," Betty Jean says. "Why don't we suck up some more rocket fuel and go piss on a graveyard?"

The Coach Speaketh

COLLEGE FOOTBALL COACHES HAVE A LANGUAGE OF THEIR OWN, ONE that can only be understood by sportswriters usually, apart from one or two people on an island in the Netherlands Antilles.

What follow are the statements that most college coaches make to the alumni with their translations in parentheses, courtesy of a world-weary listener:

I've never had a reception like this anywhere, and if your enthusiasm carries over into the season, we'll win our share of games.

(Which one of you rich pricks is going to help me recruit that Swahili over in East Texas?)

I left a great school to come here but I've never backed off from a challenge yet.

(I think I'm going to like the oil business.)

I want the kids to think of me as their father. If they have any problem, big or small, I want them to come to me first.

(Until their eligibility is up.)

My obligation is not only to this university but to everybody connected with it. I'll go anywhere to make a speech and make new friends for this team, this faculty, this administration, this town.

(For a $3,000 fee, plus expenses.)

These kids were pretty good football players at one time. We're going to find out what happened to them.

(The guy who was here ahead of me couldn't coach a bunch of Mexicans in a bean-eating contest.)

I managed to get every assistant coach I went after, and I don't know anybody who's got a more capable or more loyal staff than I do.

(The first one of those assholes who screws up is out of here on a flatbed truck.)

I've told these kids that when we go out there for two-a-days, everybody is starting out equal.

(Except for the first team and they're so far ahead of everybody else, it makes my ass hurt.)

It's time for college coaches to understand that we're in the entertainment business. That's why I'm going to open up our offense.

(Anybody with sense knows you win with defense. I'll castrate the first quarterback who throws a pass inside his own 30-yard line.)

I know we've got some big-name teams on our future schedules, but we can't do anything about it, and personally I think those teams will help get us ready for this tough conference we're in.

(The athletic director who scheduled all this Oklahoma and USC shit ought to have his pecker cut off. I've been in touch with Lamar and Louisiana Tech.)

I don't ever want to hear the word steroid in my presence.

(But I'll drive a stake through the heart of any lineman who don't come back next year weighing 280 or over.)

In 30 years of coaching, on all levels, I've never had a punt blocked.

(One of you recruiters better go out and get me one of them barefooted sons of bitches who can kick it over the iron curtain.)

I want to make it clear to everybody that the kids we recruit are coming here to get an education first and play football second.

(Except from September through December when my job is on the line.)

One of the first things I'm going to do is change the uniforms. I've researched it and discovered that our school colors are actually burnt maroon and royal gray.

(No wonder they couldn't win here. They been dressing like peppermint sticks.)

Nobody was more pleased than the coaching staff when the chancellor announced plans for a new science building.

(That phony cocksucker made a promise to me that we'd get an athletic dorm, a weight room, artificial turf, and new stadium lights before those silly jerks got a new building.)

We could have had that kid but we couldn't live with his SAT scores.

(The little shitass wanted a BMW and two wardrobes, one for fall and one for spring.)

I understand the intent behind the NCAA rule. It's a good rule.

(It's a crock of shit. If I want to give a kid some spending it ain't nobody's business but my own.)

The press has a job to do like everybody else.

(There's one particular sportswriter in this town who's gonna get his baby kidnapped if he don't get off my butt.)

I'm not saying we'll win any championships, but in a year or two I'll bet we have a say in who does.

(If the alumni can buy me them Swahilis I want. Otherwise, it's been nice knowing you.)

The Names of the Game

AS ON A PERSONAL CHECK, NAMES ARE IMPORTANT IN FOOTBALL. Names very often make the football player. Could Doak Walker, for instance, have been an interior decorator? No. Could Bronko Nagurski have made pottery in Santa Fe? No. Could Johnny Lujack have shot James Cagney in an old movie? Of course.

Great names have been synonymous with great players since the first three all-America teams were selected, starting in 1889, and were dominated by a guard named Pudge Heffelfinger from Yale.

Each season when the all-America selections come out, I eagerly look for someone who might unseat a member of my All-Time Mobster Team or my All-Time Socialite Team.

The All-Time Mobster Team lines up as follows:

Ends: Harold "Brick" Muller, California, '21, '22; James "Froggy" Williams, Rice, '49.

Tackles: Wilbur "Fats" Henry, Washington & Jefferson, '17, '18, '19; Frank "Bruiser" Kinard, Ole Miss, '36, '37.

Guards: Clarence "Biggie" Munn, Minnesota, '31; Harry "Blackjack" Smith, USC, '38, '39.

Center: Adolph "Germany" Schulz, Michigan, '07.

Backs: Clarence "Ace" Parker, Duke, '36; Ernie "Pug" Rentner, Northwestern, '31; "Bullet Bill" Dudley, Virginia, '41; and Banks McFadden, Clemson, '39.

As for the All-Time Socialite Team, there are so many splendid candidates, I'm forced to go with a modern 22-man squad. Play them as you wish on offense or defense, depending on their Wall Street connections.

Ends: L. Caspar Wister, Princeton, '06; Huntington Hardwick, Harvard, '14; Gaynell Tinsley, LSU, '35, '36; Gerald Dalrymple, Tulane, '30, '31.

Tackles: Lucius Horatio Biglow, Yale, '06, '07; Percy North-croft, Navy, '08; D. Belford West, Colgate, '16, '19; Truman Spain, SMU, '35.

Guards: Endicott Peabody III, Harvard, '41; Seraphim Post, Stanford, '28; T. Truxtun Hare, Penn, '97, '98, '99, 1900; Marshall Robnett, Texas A&M, '40.

Centers: Winslow Lovejoy, Yale, '24; Peter Pund, Georgia Tech, '28.

Backs: Gaylord Stinchcomb, Ohio State, '20; Morley Drury, USC, '27; Foster Rockwell, Yale, '02, '04; W. Earl Sprackling, Brown, '10; Andrew Oberlander, Dartmouth, '25; Jay Berwanger, Chicago, '34, '35; Chalmers Elliott, Michigan, '47; and Creighton Miller, Notre Dame, '43.

I name Morley Drury captain of this team since he was known as "the noblest Trojan of them all."

Because names aren't what they used to be, neither is football writing, as I observe it.

A name could once make a story, but nowadays it's often the name of a player's agent or lawyer, and touchdowns have become less important than contract negotiations.

All too often in this day and time I find myself picking up a newspaper to read:

"Emmerson Falls, who only makes $300,000 this season, with $400,000 due within two years, picked off a pass in the second quarter. The pass was thrown by Phil Stum, who is worried about infringement clauses on his licensing agreements, according to Nobby Shanker, his agent."

And this:

"Tony Faucet took a pitchout and ran toward the sideline, thinking about what his lawyer, Slippy Durham, had mentioned to him in regard to joint ventures and percentages of the gross receipts."

In this age of business news football, let's join a huddle now, where Joe Wyoming is calling a play:

"I'd like to consider a post pattern, but you receivers will have 10 business days to exercise your right of refusal.

"If this becomes the case, Herschel, I'd like to discuss an off-tackle arrangement. You would agree to discharge your obligation as a self-employed person, including all trademarks, trade names, and copyrights, and naturally this would be confined to the off-tackle area.

"I'm a little unclear as to what happens in the case of an audible, particularly if the play results in presenting you in a bad light, or embarrassing you, or damaging your reputation as a ball-carrier.

"You're probably governed by the laws of the State of Texas, or perhaps Delaware, if that's where you're incorporated, so you may want to consult your attorney before the snap.

"Since we're in a two-minute situation, I think I ought to touch on the field-goal possibility. The kicker, as I see it, would agree to furnish a place kick of whatever length is necessary to score three points. The kicker has no right to privacy in this endeavor and may be held responsible to indemnify the head coach, general manager, or owner for any losses or damages, plus legal fees, that might result from a miss.

"This, of course, assumes that no person, firm, or corporation interferes in any way with the kicker's performance."

Names used to make news in football. Today they make margin calls.

Beyond the Fridge

PRO FOOTBALL IN THE 1980S ACHIEVED A NEW DIMENSION WITH THE rise to prominence of a Chicago Bear named William "Refrigerator" Perry, ex-Clemson, magna cum lunch meat.

He gave every other team in the NFL a reason to go searching for a "conversation topic" to put on its roster.

I expected the Dallas Cowboys to take the lead in this, for the

Cowboys are known as the great innovators in the game. It was Dallas, after all, that first implanted an electronic brain in a mannequin, gave it a snapbrim hat, and assigned it coaching responsibilities.

Sure enough, I discovered by tapping into the Cowboys' computer that they had a number of engaging prospects they were looking at. Among the most prominent were:

Bob "Barcalounger" Bates, running back, Fashion-in-Furniture Institute, Heel Point, North Carolina.

A modular, sectional, reclining ball-carrier, Bates stands 3'6" and weighs 409 pounds. Once, in a single off-tackle play, he carried five defenders across a hardwood floor. "I love Naugahyde," says Bates. "It smells like victory."

Clarence "Chevy Pickup" Scroggins, quarterback, Consolidated Technical High School, Justice, Texas.

A fully loaded signal caller and thrower with a V8 engine, rally wheels, power stride, and power vision, Scroggins skipped a college career to go straight into the pros, where he felt there would be more accent on cruise control. His high school coach, Olds Toronado, says Scroggins was the smartest quarterback he's ever had on the squad. "We had no problem with the state's No Pass–No Play rule. Clarence made straight A's in Fender, Headlight, and Dashboard."

Raymond "Betamax" Barnes, running back, Affordable Baptist, Lordsburg, Virginia.

Potentially the most exciting runner in the country. He has blinding speed in the fast-forward position but is just as quick when you put him in rewind.

Dale "Louver Drape" Lawrence, defensive end, Central Florida FM & Patio, Flamingo, Florida.

He would be the thinnest player in America at 6'6" and 82 pounds but his size frequently worked to his advantage in college. On end sweeps, for example, Lawrence can hardly be seen at all; and yet, as swiftly as you can yank on a cord, he can shut off the light on an offense. "Vertically speaking," says one opponent, "he's the most unique player I've ever encountered."

Leotis "Lease/Buy" James, quarterback, Oklahoma State, Nebraska, Iowa, Texas A&M, Florida, SMU, and Temple.

A multitalented runner, passer, and Grand Prix driver, James announced his intention to enter Oklahoma State while sitting on the hood of an orange BMW. Subsequently, he announced his plans to transfer to Nebraska while sitting on the hood of a red Porsche.

James's final collegiate press conference was held in the cargo deck of the *Q. E. II,* where all of his automobiles were assembled. "I'm turning pro," he said. "Everybody kept promising a leather interior but all I ever saw was velour."

Floyd "Fireplace" Granger, linebacker, Mount River Union, St. Dawdle, Minnesota.

He's not tall at 2'9" but his rough-hewn exterior makes him almost impossible to move. Granger's coach, Brick Mortar, says, "What we did was put him in the middle and dare 'em to run at him."

Sidney "Stock Fund" Dillon, offensive lineman, West Loop J. C., Chicago.

A high-yield, high-quality blocker, Dillon first caught the attention of pro scouts in a game in which he seemed to gain weight in each quarter. He started one particular game at 222½ and closed at 257¼. His coach, Al Keogh, says, "You don't get any negative fluctuation with Sid in the lineup. He'll compound your nose-guard on a long-term basis."

Vinny "Vacuum Cleaner" Gambino, defensive end, Intercoastal J. C., Jacksonville, Florida.

After all of the dope scandals in professional sports, nobody ever expected to see another powerhead vacuum with two-motor power, suction control, stand-up speed, and unlimited bag capacity, but then Vinny came along.

"Look at it this way," he said to his agent. "With me on the team, nobody else has got a cocaine problem."

The Mary Tyler Zebra Show

PRO FOOTBALL'S REPLAY GUY, THE "ELECTRONIC OFFICIAL," WHO has yet to see what America sees, inspires a television series that would send a network's ratings through the roof of a domed stadium, if not through the top of Brent Musburger's ego.

Call it *The Mary Tyler Zebra Show,* or *Jeers,* or *All in the Fumbles.*

In the pilot episode, a fumble is scooped up by a defensive player who carries the ball into the end zone for a touchdown.

Two zebras signal a touchdown, but two others throw their flags.

The referee calls a meeting.

In real life, you can't hear what goes on in these meetings, but that's the charm of the show. Well, that, plus a subplot about a zebra's love affair with his numbered account in Switzerland.

At the meeting, we hear the ref say to the umpire, "What have we got, Charley?"

"Touchdown, defense."

The ref turns to the back judge.

"No touchdown," says the back judge. "The guy was down."

The ref calls in the head linesman.

"How'd you see it, Fritz?"

"See what?"

"The play. Was it a fumble or not?"

"Gee, Frank, I don't know. I was looking at those cheerleaders over there."

The referee decides they better ask upstairs.

The umpire beeps on his pager to establish contact with the zebra in the booth.

Robert, the electronic official, is spreading caviar on party rye when he hears:

"Ground to booth . . . come in, Robert."

"Yes?" says Robert with a certain amount of irritation in his voice. "What is it *this* time?"

"How'd you see it, Robert?" the umpire asks.

"The field goal was good."

"What field goal?"

"The one the Dolphins just kicked."

"What game are you watching, Robert?"

"Dolphins-Patriots. What game do you think I'm watching?"

"Well," says the umpire, "we were sort of hoping it was the Cowboys-Giants here at the Meadowlands."

"All anybody has to do is *tell* me," Robert says, switching channels on his TV set.

Down on the field, the referee looks at the umpire. "Eddie, are you sure it wasn't a fumble?"

"The ground can't cause a fumble," the umpire says.

"What do you mean?"

"It's the rule. The ground can't cause a fumble. The guy didn't lose the ball till he hit the ground."

The ref looks frustrated.

"Let me get this straight," the ref says. "You're telling *me*, a man who's worked eight Super Bowls, that a ball carrier gets tackled, hits the ground, loses the football, but it's *not* a fumble?"

The umpire spits, looks off, and says, "The ground can't cause a fumble."

"Well, that's the goddamndest thing I've ever heard of," says the ref. "Back when I played, the ground was the main thing that *could* cause a fumble."

The head linesman asks for calm.

"Gentlemen," he says, "I think we'd better consider what a touchdown would do at this point. It would put the Cowboys up by fourteen. Is that what we really want with six minutes left?"

"Good point," says the back judge. "My next door neighbor has the Giants with seven and a half. Right now, he's ahead. I don't want to sway anybody, but he's a fine fellow with a family and he's been hoping to buy one of those G.E. no-frost refrigerators with an ice cube dispenser. This game could do it for him."

"Oh, yeah?" says the field judge. "Well, my next door neighbor is a fine fellow too. He bet the Over and I'd like to put this thing out of reach for him."

Back upstairs, Robert hollers into his walkie-talkie. "Booth to ground—I just saw the replay, Eddie!"

"Good," says the umpire. "What is it?"

"I can't tell."

"You can't tell? Jesus, Robert!"

"Don't snap at me, Eddie. I've looked at it from all angles. I think you can call it a fumble if you like, but I think you can get away with not calling it a fumble. What I mean is, it's sort of up to you guys."

The referee snatches the walkie-talkie from the umpire. "Listen to me carefully, Robert. I'm calling it no fumble, do you read? The ground can't cause a fumble."

"Since when?"

"Just shut up and listen," snarls the ref. "We never talked, okay? Our communications broke down. Is that clear?"

"Whatever you say, Frank."

"We never talked, right?"

"Not a syllable. No one has called me all day."

The episode ends as Robert spreads more caviar on a piece of rye and switches his TV to a movie.

Letter From an NFL Owner

DEAR TEAM MEMBER:

Sorry I've allowed another great season in the National Football League to draw so near without letting you hear from your owner, who only happens to be your biggest fan; but, as many of you know—or perhaps have read in the columns—Clarissa and I ran into a good bit of trouble redecorating the beach house in Fiji.

Clarissa shares my enthusiasm for the coming season, by the way. In fact, at this very moment, my wife is working on some ideas about the new fabric for the walls of our sky box. I might add that she also has some thoughts in regard to improving our halftime entertainment. It's pretty exciting stuff. Without going into any detail, I'll only mention two things: piano concertos and dissident poetry!

Now I want to say something to you that I know you've heard before but can't be repeated too often. This team is a family! And I intend to stand by an oath I took, which is to meet each and every one of you personally before the end of the season, travel permitting.

I've already had the pleasure of knowing some of you, of course. I speak of those interior linemen who worked at my grandfather's steel plant during the off season, the two quarterbacks who came to our hunt ball in Virginia, and the charming little place kicker who was kind enough to head up the janitorial staff at the family estate in Key Biscayne. (If you're reading this, Raoul, I haven't forgotten my promise to help out with your citizenship papers.)

To all of our rookies, let me say welcome! And let me say a special welcome to those half dozen who were in the fraternity house with me a couple of years ago. I make no apologies for the fact that I exercised a certain amount of influence at the NFL draft. Size, speed, and drug tests are important, as our coaches argued, but I firmly believe that a bunch of guys who've creeped some brews together will be more likely to hang in there when the going gets tough. I often think about the things I learned of character, loyalty, and teamwork, in those pledge days when I had to get naked and slide headfirst down those hallways of barbecue sauce and live minnows.

I mentioned the coaches. I think you'll like the new ones. They should be arriving in camp almost any day. I'm happy to announce that Coach Brains Temple, our new head man, is bringing his whole staff with him, including Bag Man Bailey, his top talent scout and offensive coordinator, a man who has perhaps gained more notoriety than the others. Together, as I'm sure you're aware, Coach Temple and his assistants were responsible for six probation sentences and the loss of more than 700 scholarships at four universities in the Big Eight and the Southwest Conference alone. I don't see how any staff can come more highly recommended.

A word about the new stadium. While it is located across the state line, we're still going to be representing this community, the same faithful community that supported the team when my father moved the franchise from the Midwest, which was after he bought out his narrow-minded partner and shifted the club from its original location up East.

There's no question that those of you who make your homes in this community are going to be slightly inconvenienced by the 125-mile drive to the new stadium, but most of the friends Clarissa and I have spoken to about it seem to feel that it will be worth the trouble to have a modern facility with a dome and a north end zone leading directly into the shopping mall and lake-front condo development.

I'm sure a few of you are concerned about the change of our nickname and logo. Believe me, nobody will miss the old Fighting Auks more than I. The name has served us well through three cities, after all, and I'll certainly never forget the season during my senior year of prep school when I was the Auk on the sidelines in my costume with the webbed feet and little wings.

Times change, however, and I agree with Clarissa that the team will have a greater appeal to the new breed of pro football fans with our new name. I think the Happy Shoppers has a certain ring to it. I think it will strike fear into the hearts of our less sophisticated foes and, frankly, I'm counting the minutes until the grubby bargain-seekers among our opponents see the Happy Shoppers roar onto the field in our new helmets with the proud and familiar Gucci stripe sweeping across the proud and familiar Vuitton pattern!

I want to take this opportunity to express my deepest sympathy to those of you whose agent/managers died in the crash of one of our private jets. It was a terrible tragedy and I suppose it will be months before we know the exact cause. It was doubly unfortunate, because I think the meeting we had scheduled would have been very productive. I believe we could have ironed out most of our contractual differences.

It goes without saying that I will be pleased to meet with all of your new agent/managers when you have finished selecting them.

Lastly, I want to say to the veterans on the team that I greatly appreciate the support you showed my father, both in your depositions and in your personal testimony, during his trial. While I know that many of you benefited from his inside stock tips, I'm certain that friendship was your real motivation.

As you might imagine, my father has had a very difficult time dealing with confinement. But things are looking up. He's working in the kitchen now and has made numerous friends, mostly ex-bankers and real-estate developers. He thinks there's a very good chance in the next several months that a few of them will be given occasional weekends off to play golf in various member-guest golf tournaments around the state of Texas. That would be good. Although I haven't actually been able to get out there to visit him, I'm sure he could use some sun.

Well, I see my pep talk is getting a little long, and I am due for a board meeting at the yacht club. Let's get tough and have a heck of a year, men. And remember—you've got a pal in the front office!

Go, Shoppers!
Bucky

Farewell, Pro Football

THE LAST TIME I BOTHERED TO COUNT, THERE WERE ONLY 4,317 reasons why college football is a better game than pro football — better tasting, less filling, and even serious enough at times to make you throw your body in front of a moving vehicle if the little animal on your blazer doesn't beat the little animal on somebody else's blazer.

I won't list all of the reasons at this time, just the most important.

- As of a few hours ago, college players had not yet learned how to drop passes with shocking consistency or slip down and lose yardage when it's third-and-two near the goal line.
- The University of Alabama, to cite one example, has never moved its franchise from Tuscaloosa, Alabama, to South Bend, Indiana, because of poor attendance. By the same token, Notre Dame has refused to move from South Bend, Indiana, to Palo Alto, California, in order to have sky boxes for its best friends. If pro football owners couldn't move their teams to new cities or new stadiums every so often, they would all have to make do on an income of only $100 million a year.
- College teams sensibly play football from September through

November, whereas the NFL plays from early August until all the winter snow has melted in Aspen and Sun Valley.

- In college football, more often than not, a penalty for offensive holding is not left to the whim of a zebra who's having a bank note called in on him.
- No coach in college football has ever worn a hat like Tom Landry's.
- Athletes still make up the team in college football. This is the opposite of pro football, where the "team" consists of the owner, general manager, and coaching staff. Players are the hired help, who get traded, worn out, or cut by the "team."
- That I know of, no college team plays its home games in another state, unlike the New York Giants and New York Jets, who play in New Jersey. Oklahoma, for example, has never played a home game in Kansas.
- College teams almost never play a game on Monday night. Instead, college players play with Chi Omegas and Tri Delts on Monday nights, and sometimes on Friday nights.
- Bobby, Sonny, Billy, Jake, and Alex—as in Layne, Jurgensen, Kilmer, Scott, and Hawkins—don't play pro football anymore. A sad thing, because they were the last guys who never knew what "closing time" meant but still got the job done on Sundays. Pro football in recent years has mostly been played by Bill Walsh, in all 22 positions.
- College football has a rowdy, romantic history. It goes back 50 years before Knute Rockne, a fact that often catches young sports editors by surprise. The essential history of pro football begins with Arthur Godfrey and peaked with a Miller Lite commercial.
- College football thrives on Notre Dame-USC, Texas-OU, Ohio State-Michigan, Stanford-Cal, Georgia-Florida, Alabama-Auburn, etc. Pro football thrives on Summerall-Madden.
- College football has luscious cheerleaders, marching bands, rousing fight songs. Pro football has bimbos on the sideline, factory workers in the stands, and 539 television time-outs.
- The college game produces coaching giants—Bear Bryant, Barry Switzer, Darrell Royal, John McKay, Woody Hayes, Joe Paterno, Ara Parseghian, and Bob Devaney, to name only a few of the modern ones. All you can come up with in the pros are Vince Lombardi and Tom Landry's computer, unless you want to count Brent Musburger.
- The Super Bowl is not *Masterpiece Football*. In the first 23 Super Bowls, there were actually two football games—Dallas-

Pittsburgh (21–17, Steelers) and 49ers-Cincinnati (20–16, San Francisco). The colleges average three Poll Bowls a season.

It is for this reason that no sportswriter ever looks back on any great Super Bowl plays.

What we look back on is that night on Bourbon Street when two of our brethren got into a bidding war for a flower girl, and the winner watched her go down on room service for the next three days. Or the network pal who couldn't finish what he started with a tattooed debutante, and shouted to a friend who was urging him to hurry up: "Gimme a break, I gotta read the fucking instructions." Or the woefully hungover author in the Miami press box who swallowed a pill to assist him with a deadline story and 30 minutes later, still staring at a blank piece of paper, was heard to shout, "Kick in, you son of a bitch—you've never taken this long before!"

My own memory of covering Super Bowls is that 7,000 sportswriters converge on an American city, stay drunk for a week, mostly interview each other, and a zebra wins the game.

The Super Bowl is the sportswriter's reward for having put up with the crashing, incessant, incredible boredom of covering pro football all season.

He gets to enjoy a drunken week in a warm climate where there's absolutely no news whatsoever to report.

Here are condensed versions of all the stories he files:

NEW ORLEANS—The two Super Bowl teams practiced offense and defense today. They will probably do it again tomorrow.

NEW ORLEANS—Both coaches said breaks would decide Sunday's Super Bowl, unless they don't.

NEW ORLEANS—Injuries could play a big part in Sunday's Super Bowl, or not.

NEW ORLEANS—An NFL spokesman confirmed today that the Super Bowl halftime show will be more spectacular than ever, but he refused to comment on the rumor that part of the pageant will be the actual hijacking of an airliner.

NEW ORLEANS—Commissioner Pete Rozelle said today at his annual Super Bowl press conference that the NFL will definitely expand to 40 teams by the year 2010. Mentioned as possible franchises were Tokyo, Berlin, Perth, Manila, Tehran, Tripoli, Baghdad, Oakland, and Baltimore.

I covered my first Super Bowl in New Orleans. I don't remember who played or who won, but I remember the Absynthe House bar.

It was daylight on the morning of the game and a pal from *Newsweek* was ordering another round.

"Jesus Christ," I said. "I've got to get some sleep. I've had two hundred J&Bs and smoked fourteen cartons of Winstons."

The guy looked at me incredulously and said, "I didn't know we came down here to try to quit smoking."

The Old Fordham Halfback

HE DOESN'T HAVE A NICKNAME, SUCH AS OSCAR OR EMMY, WHICH IS probably just an oversight of the years, like some of the Sam Baughs and Jim Browns who never won him. He is only 18 inches tall. He weighs only 50 pounds. He costs only $452. He is, in fact, just an old Fordham halfback, a dark brown hunk of sculpture running and stiff-arming across a slab of ebony—and a bit ill-proportioned at that, considering that his head is too large, his shoulders are narrow, and his legs are short. For all of this, however, few relics in college football cause more melodrama than the Heisman Memorial Trophy, an award that is supposed to go to the outstanding player in the country each year, and sometimes does.

To be sure, there have been those seasons when a player was so magnificent week after week that the selection of the Heisman winner was the worst-kept secret in America. Most often, though, it comes down to which campus has put forth the biggest effort in terms of publicity and ballyhoo on behalf of its treasured candidate, who is usually a ball-carrier or passer.

The battle for the Heisman begins in the spring and continues every week of the fall, and it is generally waged by campus publicity men with the help of provincial writers and broadcasters. The flacks have taken to mailing out brochures and weekly stats and news features on their stars. As Tony Kornheiser of *The Washington*

Post remarked in 1988, "If this is Tuesday, it must be Troy Aikman Day in my mailbox."

There are roughly 1,000 Heisman voters, but a few dead guys still receive ballots, as do a number of journalists who have changed jobs and haven't seen a college game in years.

I used to get a ballot every three years even though I was covering a game every Saturday, and usually a game involving a serious candidate. At the same time, I knew Thoroughbred racing writers and guys who covered bowling and stock car racing who never failed to get a ballot.

Nonetheless, the war is taken in bitter seriousness.

Very early each season one begins to hear game announcers on the radio huckstering for their hometown heroes.

"Tulane comes out of the huddle," an announcer will say, "and there's big Jock McStrap, our great right tackle, standing down there looking pretty mean. Boy, does he swallow up a ball carrier! He's going for the Heisman, you know."

Then the color man is chimed in with the play-by-play genius and we hear the following:

"During this time-out, Ray, let's just take a minute or two to chat about big Jock McStrap. You've played the game, Ray, and been around it a long time, as all of our good fans know. Have you *ever* seen a better all-around football player than big Jock?"

"Well, there've been a lot of great ones, Fred, but to answer your question as honestly as I know how—I haven't."

"He's got it all, hasn't he?"

"Well, the thing about Jock is, he's not just big, he's mobile. And he's not just fast, he's alert. And he's not just tough, he's got instinct. And he's not just tall, he's rangy. And he's not just ———"

"What about that *grade* average?"

"Well, that's right. You see a lot of kids play this game and fall down in the classroom. But they tell me big Jock's carrying a three point oh, and you never can underestimate intelligence in any walk of life, I like to say."

"We certainly know he comes from good football stock, don't we?"

"Well, that's another thing, Fred. His father used to be president of this great university, as you know. His uncle, of course, is on the board of trustees. His mother was the first lady airline pilot. I'll tell you, I like Thoroughbreds. I like to say you can't underestim———"

"Not a bad discus thrower, either, by the way."

"Well, there's something else. Arm strength and balance. Which reminds me of the day the Rock and I were ———"

"Pretty good catcher on the baseball team last spring."

"Well, it's those hands of his, of course, as I've mentioned on other broadcasts, and those strong shoulders and ———"

"I don't suppose, Ray, that we can mention it too often about big Jock's fondness for the fine arts. Rare to find a kid as ferocious on the football field who finds time to paint and play the violin and write poetry, wouldn't you say?"

"Well, you think about how he combines all this with his interest in campus politics and boys clubs and working in the ghettos, it's ———"

"You know, Ray, I was down on the field chatting with Jock just before the kickoff today and I asked him about the Heisman Trophy and how he honestly felt about all of the publicity he's getting. I don't suppose I'll be talking out of school, so to speak, to repeat what he told me here on the air. He said, 'Fred, it's an honor that every college football player would like to win, but I'll be truthful with you. If I were fortunate enough to be awarded that great trophy, I'd consider it a *team* award.' I think that says quite a lot for Jock McStrap, Ray."

"Well, you see, you're talking about character now. I ———"

"Of course, last week, Ray, when my wife, Nancy, and I were having dinner with Jock and his family before the Kansas State game, the game where he made those thirty-seven unassisted tackles, I recall asking him how he felt about having to play a big game like that on two bandaged knees, and he said, 'Fred, when I go on the field with this bunch of great guys, I don't feel anything but pride.' I think that says something else about Jock McStrap, Ray."

"Well, there again, pride is something ———"

"I see time's back in, Ray, and we've got a ball game on our hands. I see big Jock down there on all fours waiting to meet the Tulane charge and, heh, heh, *sort out* another ball carrier. We'll be right back with play-by-play action after this message from one of our sponsors."

The Heisman is presented by the Downtown Athletic Club of New York and named for John W. Heisman, who was a coach in ancient days whose lasting contribution to the game—before the trophy—was the invention of the center snap. No one knows why or how all of this glory came to the award. It wasn't due to John W.'s coaching record at Auburn, Clemson, Georgia Tech, Penn, Washington and Jefferson, and Rice. And in no way could it be due to the influence of the club itself. The club is a 35-story building in lower Manhattan that rattles and creaks with 4,000 members, 450 employees, four bowling alleys, six squash courts, a gym, a swimming pool, and is absolutely unheard of and unthought about by nonmembers between Heisman award dinners.

The trophy was designed by a sculptor named Frank Eliscu who originally used an NYU halfback, Ed Smith, as a model. Smith was an old high school friend of Eliscu's. Evidently, NYU halfbacks didn't know how to stiff-arm properly because several Fordham players were later used as models after the DAC asked Fordham coach Jim Crowley, once a Four Horseman at Notre Dame, to inspect Eliscu's work and make suggestions.

The finished work, high-top shoes, leather helmet, and all, is just an old Fordham halfback, is what it comes down to.

Today, however, it is the ultimate prize for a gridiron individual, and has always been regarded as a more precious trophy than the Camp or Maxwell awards, which followed the Heisman by two years.

In the old days, the winner was told about it ahead of the banquet, but now TV has taken over. The Heisman has become another of those "May-I-have-the-envelope-please" affairs. This means that the four runners-up get to sit there on camera and despise the recipient, who frequently owes it all to publicity.

The list of Heisman losers is almost as impressive as the list of winners. Judge for yourself:

	THE HEISMAN WINNERS	SOME NOTABLE LOSERS
1935	JAY BERWANGER Chicago	BOBBY WILSON SMU
1936	LARRY KELLEY Yale	SAM BAUGH TCU
1937	CLINT FRANK Yale	MARSHALL GOLDBERG Pitt
1938	DAVEY O'BRIEN TCU	SID LUCKMAN Columbia
1939	NILE KINNICK Iowa	JOHN KIMBROUGH Texas A&M
1940	TOM HARMON Michigan	FRANKIE ALBERT Stanford
1941	BRUCE SMITH Minnesota	BILL DUDLEY Virginia

	THE HEISMAN WINNERS	SOME NOTABLE LOSERS
1942	FRANK SINKWICH Georgia	GLENN DOBBS Tulsa
1943	ANGELO BERTELLI Notre Dame	OTTO GRAHAM Northwestern
1944	LES HORVATH Ohio State	BOB FENIMORE Oklahoma State
1945	DOC BLANCHARD Army	HARRY GILMER Alabama
1946	GLENN DAVIS Army	CHARLEY TRIPPI Georgia
1947	JOHNNY LUJACK Notre Dame	DOAK WALKER SMU
1948	DOAK WALKER SMU	NORM VAN BROCKLIN Oregon
1949	LEON HART Notre Dame	CHARLIE JUSTICE North Carolina
1950	VIC JANOWICZ Ohio State	KYLE ROTE SMU
1951	DICK KAZMAIER Princeton	BABE PARILLI Kentucky
1952	BILLY VESSELS Oklahoma	PAUL CAMERON UCLA
1953	JOHN LATTNER Notre Dame	DICKY MOEGLE Rice
1954	ALAN AMECHE Wisconsin	HOWARD CASSADY Ohio State
1955	HOWARD CASSADY Ohio State	JIM SWINK TCU
1956	PAUL HORNUNG Notre Dame	JIM BROWN Syracuse
1957	JOHN DAVID CROW Texas A&M	CLENDON THOMAS Oklahoma
1958	PETE DAWKINS Army	RANDY DUNCAN Iowa
1959	BILLY CANNON LSU	DON MEREDITH SMU
1960	JOE BELLINO Navy	BILLY KILMER UCLA
1961	ERNIE DAVIS Syracuse	JAMES SAXTON Texas
1962	TERRY BAKER Oregon State	JERRY STOVALL LSU

	THE HEISMAN WINNERS	SOME NOTABLE LOSERS
1963	ROGER STAUBACH Navy	BILLY LOTHRIDGE Georgia Tech
1964	JOHN HUARTE Notre Dame	DICK BUTKUS Illinois
1965	MIKE GARRETT USC	BOB GRIESE Purdue
1966	STEVE SPURRIER Florida	GARY BEBAN UCLA
1967	GARY BEBAN UCLA	O. J. SIMPSON USC
1968	O. J. SIMPSON USC	LEROY KEYES Purdue
1969	STEVE OWENS Oklahoma	ARCHIE MANNING Ole Miss
1970	JIM PLUNKETT Stanford	JOE THEISMANN Notre Dame
1971	PAT SULLIVAN Auburn	ED MARINARO Cornell
1972	JOHNNY RODGERS Nebraska	BERT JONES LSU
1973	JOHN CAPELLETTI Penn State	ROOSEVELT LEAKS Texas
1974	ARCHIE GRIFFIN Ohio State	ANTHONY DAVIS USC
1975	ARCHIE GRIFFIN Ohio State	JOE WASHINGTON Oklahoma
1976	TONY DORSETT Pitt	RICKY BELL USC
1977	EARL CAMPBELL Texas	TERRY MILLER Oklahoma State
1978	BILLY SIMS Oklahoma	CHUCK FUSINA Penn State
1979	CHARLES WHITE USC	BILLY SIMS Oklahoma
1980	GEORGE ROGERS South Carolina	HERSCHEL WALKER Georgia
1981	MARCUS ALLEN USC	DAN MARINO Pitt
1982	HERSCHEL WALKER Georgia	ERIC DICKERSON SMU
1983	MIKE ROZIER Nebraska	BERNIE KOSAR Miami

THE HEISMAN WINNERS	SOME NOTABLE LOSERS
1984 DOUG FLUTIE	ROBBIE BOSCO
Boston College	Brigham Young
1985 BO JACKSON	JAMELLE HOLIEWAY
Auburn	Oklahoma
1986 VINNY TESTAVERDE	D. J. DOZIER
Miami	Penn State
1987 TIM BROWN	STEVE WALSH
Notre Dame	Miami
1988 BARRY SANDERS	RODNEY PEETE
Oklahoma State	USC

The weight that publicity men have had on the selection is most likely exaggerated. But this doesn't keep the campus flacks from thinking they sometimes win for their boys. The most notable jobs seem to have been done at Notre Dame, naturally.

Among those feats are these: Leon Hart becoming only the second lineman ever to win, Angelo Bertelli taking the trophy in 1943 when he played only five games (he got called to duty by the Marines at mid-season), and John Huarte, a total unknown at the season's beginning, winning over such supercandidates in 1964 as Joe Namath, Tucker Frederickson, Gale Sayers, Craig Morton, Jerry Rhome, and Dick Butkus.

But the best of all was Paul Hornung. He won over perhaps more supercandidates than Huarte as the Notre Dame mystique was utterly baffling. Here, around the country, were such stalwarts as Jim Brown at Syracuse, Johnny Majors at Tennessee, Tommy Mc-Donald and Jerry Tubbs at Oklahoma (which also happened to be in the midst of Bud Wilkinson's 47-game win streak), and Jim Swink and Del Shofner and John Crow down in the Southwest. Meanwhile, Hornung's Notre Dame team was getting clobbered: 0–40 by Oklahoma, 14–47 by Michigan State, 7–33 by Navy, and 8–48 by Iowa. It finished with a dazzling 2–8 record.

But Hornung had Notre Dame and Charlie Callahan going for him.

Callahan was the publicity man in South Bend then, and he knew where the power was. Big cities. Radio. Television. Syndicated columnists. Notre Dame was terrible, he admitted, but, gee, this Hornung was great, week after week, fighting all the odds. Golden Boy. All that.

In later years, Charlie liked to reminisce about his conquest like a prize-fight manager. "That was the year Harold Keith at

Oklahoma made the mistake of trying to sell an interior lineman—
Tubbs. He didn't switch his emphasis to McDonald until mid-
season, but it was too late."

Charlie explained, "The East went for Jim Brown, the South for
Majors, Tubbs, McDonald, Swink, and all of those cut each other
up. I had the Midwest to myself, and enough pieces of other sections to skim by."

Callahan was so proud of the victory that he sent for Hornung
in class to tell him personally. But as Paul walked across the South
Bend campus, past the golden dome and Moses, and headed toward
Charlie's small cluttered office, the publicity man placed a long
distance call to Paul's mother in Louisville, Kentucky, and he had
her waiting on the phone when Hornung strolled in, wondering
what Callahan wanted.

Charlie just sat there without looking up, casually pretending
to be sorting through the debris on his desk. He handed the receiver
to Hornung and mumbled something.

"Here," Callahan said. "Tell your mother you just won the
Heisman."

That is my second favorite Heisman story. My favorite con-
cerns Les Horvath, the Ohio State tailback who won the award on
the Buckeyes' "civilian" team of 1944.

It seems that Horvath and his wife moved out to Los Angeles in
about 1947, soon after World War II in any case, and Horvath's wife
noticed this ugly statue being unpacked and placed on the living
room mantel.

"What's that thing?" she asked. "Out. Get it out of here."

Horvath explained that it was among his most prized possessions. He explained what it was. What he had done a few years
before to win it. Couldn't he just leave it there for the time being? If
she really disapproved, he would move it to another room. Fine.

A couple of nights later the Horvaths happened to have dinner
at the home of the Tom Harmons, and Horvath's wife noticed that a
Heisman Trophy adorned Harmon's mantel. And two nights later
they happened to have dinner with the Glenn Davises, and Horvath's wife noticed that another Heisman Trophy had adorned that
mantel as well.

Driving home that evening she turned to Les and said:

"You know that thing you want to keep in the living room? I
wish you would tell me what's so special about it. Everybody we
know has one."

They're Number One!

EVERY YEAR IN THE MONTH OF DECEMBER I LOOK FORWARD TO watching various clowns employed by the TV networks cross their eyes, blow spit bubbles, and start to clamor for a play-off to decide the national champion of college football. It's not because they want to see a true national champion determined (as they lie through their teeth) but because they can envision a game played sometime in January that would attract 400 beer, car, hamburger, and diet soda commercials. TV people have always had the good of sports at heart, as we know.

The simplest plan put forth annually by the network clowns is to take the two top-rated teams (on somebody's computer) *after* the New Year's bowl games and let them play a national championship game.

Well, if the NCAA ever approves this idea, I think it ought to be called the Budweiser-Mobil-Mazda-McMuffin Bowl—or maybe just the Greed Bowl.

The fact is, there is only one type of college football play-off that would be fair, proper, and sensible. It would have to include all of the major conference champions, co-champions, tri-champions, outstanding runners-up, and deserving independents, which means it would have to begin after the 11-game regular season and go on almost as long as pro football, which, when I last looked, was a combination of wrestling, fumbling, and flag-dropping.

Since the NFL has already crashed through my boredom threshold and now threatens to bore the cosmos, I would hate to see it happen to the college game. Also, this kind of play-off would almost certainly destroy the bowl games that have contributed so much to the rich, lusty history of college football.

But a shorter playoff plan would be even worse—four teams, let's say (chosen by God knows who) competing in a phony TV series for the Brent Musburger Trophy.

What's wrong with the way things have been for the past 60 years? What we've lived with are the polls.

I say the polls are great. They create fun, suspense, debates, divorces, not to mention silly hats, and, by and large, they've honored the most deserving teams throughout the years.

And so what if we occasionally have a season where two or three teams lay claim to the mythical national championship? All we're talking about are a few extra bumper stickers.

When it comes to college football polls I happen to be a scholar, so I will share some knowledge with you.

Polls come from ratings systems and the first ratings system was invented by a man named Frank Dickinson, an economics professor at the University of Illinois in the mid-1920s. He devised a mathematical formula for selecting the nation's top teams. In 1929, a market researcher named Dick Dunkel in Springfield, Ohio, came up with another formula, and in 1932, a geologist in New Orleans named Paul Williamson came up with yet another. The rankings of these three men were syndicated in newspapers across the country and were accepted as law by the fans.

Today, of course, there are more polls than you can shake a jockstrap at. Every publication except *Rod & Gun* seems to be naming a national champion. *I* could name a national champion if I wanted to publish my own pamphlet.

Fortunately, you don't need to pay any attention to most of the polls. The NCAA, right for once, recognizes only those national champions that have been selected by a total of eight reputable selectors since ratings systems began.

Those authorities are the Dickinson System (1924–1940); the Dunkel Index (1929–1987); the Williamson Rankings (1932–1963); the Associated Press (1936–1988); the Helms Athletic Foundation (1942–1982, with predated selections for earlier years); the United Press International (1950–1988); the Football Writers Association of America (1954–1988); and the National Football Foundation and Hall of Fame (1959–1988).

This seems like a good time to get them all under one roof. After a good deal of backbreaking research on my part, what now follows is a handy chart to fondle, caress, and win bets with—a list of the only "official" national champions in the modern history of college football:

YEAR	TEAM, RECORD	COACH, Star players	POLLS WON
1924	NOTRE DAME, 10-0	KNUTE ROCKNE "Four Horsemen": Harry Stuhldreher Don Miller Jim Crowley Elmer Layden	**
1925	ALABAMA, 10-0	WALLACE WADE Pooley Hubert, qb Johnny Mack Brown, hb	*
	DARTMOUTH, 8-0	JESSE HAWLEY Andy Oberlander, hb	*
1926	STANFORD, 10-0-1	POP WARNER Ted Shipkey, e	*
	ALABAMA, 9-0-1	WALLACE WADE Hoyt Winslett, e	*
1927	ILLINOIS, 7-0-1	BOB ZUPPKE Russ Crane, g	**
1928	GEORGIA TECH, 10-0	BILL ALEXANDER Warner Mizell, hb Peter Pund, c	*
	USC, 9-0-1	HOWARD JONES Russ Saunders, fb	*
1929	NOTRE DAME, 9-0	KNUTE ROCKNE Frank Carideo, qb Jack Cannon, g	**
1930	NOTRE DAME, 10-0	KNUTE ROCKNE Frank Carideo, qb Marchy Schwartz, hb Marty Brill, hb	**
1931	USC, 10-1	HOWARD JONES Gus Shaver, qb Orv Mohler, hb Erny Pinckert, hb	***
1932	USC, 10-0	HOWARD JONES Cotton Warburton, hb Ford Palmer, e Ernie Smith, t	***
	MICHIGAN, 8-0	HARRY KIPKE Harry Newman, qb Fred Petoskey, e	*

YEAR	TEAM, RECORD	COACH, Star players	POLLS WON
1933	USC, 10-1-1	HOWARD JONES Cotton Warburton, hb Homer Griffith, qb Aaron Rosenberg, g	*
	MICHIGAN, 7-0-1	HARRY KIPKE Stan Fay, qb Frank Wistert, t	**
	OHIO STATE, 7-1	SAM WILLAMAN Dick Heekin, hb	*
1934	ALABAMA, 10-0	FRANK THOMAS Dixie Howell, qb Don Hutson, e Riley Smith, hb Bear Bryant, e	**
	MINNESOTA, 8-0	BERNIE BIERMAN Pug Lund, hb Frank Larson, e	**
1935	TCU, 12-1	DUTCH MEYER Sam Baugh, qb Jimmy Lawrence, hb Darrell Lester, c	*
	SMU, 12-1	MATTY BELL Bobby Wilson, hb Harry Shuford, fb Truman Spain, t	*
	PRINCETON, 9-0	FRITZ CRISLER Pepper Constable, hb John Weller, g	*
	MINNESOTA, 8-0	BERNIE BIERMAN Glenn Seidel, hb Dick Smith, t	*
1936	LSU, 9-1-1	BERNIE MOORE Gaynell Tinsley, e Bill Crass, fb	*
	MINNESOTA, 7-1	BERNIE BIERMAN Andy Uram, hb Julie Alfonse, hb Bud Wilkinson, fb	****
1937	CALIFORNIA, 10-0-1	STUB ALLISON Sam Chapman, fb Vic Bottari, hb	**

YEAR	TEAM, RECORD	COACH, Star players	POLLS WON
	PITTSBURGH, 9-0-1	JOCK SUTHERLAND Marshall Goldberg, hb Bill Daddio, e	***
1938	TCU, 11-0	DUTCH MEYER Davey O'Brien, qb Ki Aldrich, c I. B. Hale, t	****
	TENNESSEE, 11-0	BOB NEYLAND George Cafego, hb Bowden Wyatt, e	*
	NOTRE DAME, 8-1	ELMER LAYDEN Bob Saggau, hb Ed Beinor, t	*
1939	TEXAS A&M, 11-0	HOMER NORTON John Kimbrough, fb Joe Boyd, t Marshall Robnett, g	****
	USC, 8-0-2	HOWARD JONES Grenny Lansdell, qb Ambrose Schindler, fb Harry Smith, g	*
1940	STANFORD, 10-0	CLARK SHAUGHNESSY Frankie Albert, qb Fred Meyer, e Chuck Taylor, g	*
	TENNESSEE, 10-1	BOB NEYLAND Bob Suffridge, g Johnny Butler, hb	**
	MINNESOTA, 8-0	BERNIE BIERMAN George Franck, hb Bruce Smith, hb	**
1941	MINNESOTA, 8-0	BERNIE BIERMAN Bruce Smith, hb Dick Wildung, t	***
	TEXAS, 8-1-1	DANA X. BIBLE Pete Layden, qb Jack Crain, hb Mal Kutner, e	*
1942	GEORGIA, 11-1	WALLY BUTTS Frank Sinkwich, qb Charley Trippi, hb Lamar Davis, e	*

YEAR	TEAM, RECORD	COACH, Star players	POLLS WON
	OHIO STATE, 9-1	PAUL BROWN Les Horvath, hb Paul Sarringhaus, hb	**
	WISCONSIN, 8-1-1	HARRY STUHLDREHER Pat Harder, fb Elroy Hirsch, hb Dave Schreiner, e	*
1943	NOTRE DAME, 9-1	FRANK LEAHY Angelo Bertelli, qb Creighton Miller, hb	****
1944	ARMY, 9-0	EARL BLAIK Glenn Davis, hb Doc Blanchard, fb Arnold Tucker, qb Barney Poole, e	****
1945	ARMY, 9-0	EARL BLAIK Glenn Davis, hb Doc Blanchard, fb Arnold Tucker, qb Dewitt Coulter, t John Green, g	****
1946	GEORGIA, 11-0	WALLY BUTTS Charley Trippi, hb Johnny Rauch, qb Reid Moseley, e	*
	ARMY, 9-0-1	EARL BLAIK Glenn Davis, hb Doc Blanchard, fb Arnold Tucker, qb Hank Foldberg, e	*
	NOTRE DAME, 8-0-1	FRANK LEAHY Johnny Lujack, qb George Connor, t George Strohmeyer, c	***
1947	MICHIGAN, 10-0	FRITZ CRISLER Bob Chappius, hb Bump Elliott, hb	**
	NOTRE DAME, 9-0	FRANK LEAHY Johnny Lujack, qb George Connor, t Bill Fischer, g	***

YEAR	TEAM, RECORD	COACH, Star players	POLLS WON
1948	MICHIGAN, 9-0	BENNIE OOSTERBAAN Charley Ortmann, hb Leo Koceski, hb Dick Rifenburg, e Al Wistert, t	****
1949	NOTRE DAME, 10-0	FRANK LEAHY Bob Williams, qb Emil Sitko, hb Leon Hart, e Jim Martin, t	****
1950	TENNESSEE, 11-0	BOB NEYLAND Hank Lauricella, hb Andy Kozar, fb Bud Sherrod, e	*
	OKLAHOMA, 10-1	BUD WILKINSON Billy Vessels, hb Leon Heath, fb Jim Weatherall, t Frank Anderson, e	****
1951	MARYLAND, 10-0	JIM TATUM Jack Scarbath, qb Ed Modzelewski, fb	*
	TENNESSEE, 10-1	BOB NEYLAND Hank Lauricella, hb Ted Daffer, g	***
	MICHIGAN STATE, 9-0	BIGGIE MUNN Al Dorow, qb Bob Carey, e Don Coleman, t	*
1952	MICHIGAN STATE, 9-0	BIGGIE MUNN Don McAuliffe, hb Leroy Bolden, hb Billy Wells, hb	*****
1953	MARYLAND, 10-1	JIM TATUM Bernie Faloney, qb Dick Bielski, fb Stan Jones, t	**
	NOTRE DAME, 9-0-1	FRANK LEAHY John Lattner, hb Ralph Guglielmi, qb	***
1954	OHIO STATE, 10-0	WOODY HAYES Howard Cassady, hb Dave Leggett, qb Jim Parker, g	***

YEAR	TEAM, RECORD	COACH, Star players	POLLS WON
	UCLA, 9-0	RED SANDERS Primo Villanueva, hb Bob Davenport, fb Rommie Loudd, e	****
1955	OKLAHOMA, 11-0	BUD WILKINSON Tommy McDonald, hb Jimmy Harris, qb Bo Bolinger, g	******
1956	OKLAHOMA, 10-0	BUD WILKINSON Tommy McDonald, hb Jimmy Harris, qb Jerry Tubbs, c	******
1957	AUBURN, 10-0	SHUG JORDAN Tommy Lorino, hb Billy Atkins, fb Jimmy Phillips, e Jackie Burkett, c Zeke Smith, g	***
	OHIO STATE, 9-1	WOODY HAYES Bob White, fb Jim Houston, e	**
	MICHIGAN STATE, 8-1	DUFFY DAUGHERTY Walt Kowalczyk, hb Jim Ninowski, qb Dan Currie, c	*
1958	LSU, 11-0	PAUL DIETZEL Billy Cannon, hb Warren Rabb, qb Johnny Robinson, hb Max Fugler, lb	*****
	IOWA, 8-1-1	FOREST EVASHEVSKI Randy Duncan, qb Curt Merz, e	*
1959	SYRACUSE, 11-0	BEN SCHWARTZWALDER Ernie Davis, hb Ger Schwedes, hb Dick Easterly, qb Fred Mautino, e	******
	OLE MISS, 10-1	JOHNNY VAUGHT Jake Gibbs, qb Charley Flowers, fb	*

YEAR	TEAM, RECORD	COACH, Star players	POLLS WON
1960	WASHINGTON, 10-1	JIM OWENS Bob Schloredt, qb George Fleming, hb	*
	OLE MISS, 9-0-1	JOHNNY VAUGHT Jake Gibbs, qb Bobby Crespino, hb Jim Dunaway, t	***
	MINNESOTA, 8-1	MURRAY WARMATH Sandy Stephens, qb Roger Hagberg, fb Bobby Bell, t	***
1961	ALABAMA, 11-0	BEAR BRYANT Pat Trammell, qb Mike Fracchia, fb Lee Roy Jordan, lb	******
	OHIO STATE, 8-0-1	WOODY HAYES Bob Ferguson, fb Paul Warfield, hb Bob Vogel, t	*
1962	USC, 11-0	JOHN MCKAY Pete Beathard, qb Hal Bedsole, e Willie Brown, hb	******
	ALABAMA, 10-1	BEAR BRYANT Joe Namath, qb Lee Roy Jordan, lb	*
1963	TEXAS, 11-0	DARRELL ROYAL Duke Carlisle, qb Tommy Nobis, lb Ernie Koy, hb Tommy Ford, hb Scott Appleton, t	*******
1964	ARKANSAS, 11-0	FRANK BROYLES Fred Marshall, qb Ken Hatfield, hb Bobby Crockett, e Ronnie Caveness, lb	**
	ALABAMA, 10-1	BEAR BRYANT Joe Namath, qb Steve Bowman, hb Wayne Trimble, db	**

YEAR	TEAM, RECORD	COACH, Star players	POLLS WON
	NOTRE DAME, 9-1	ARA PARSEGHIAN John Huarte, qb Jack Snow, e	*
	MICHIGAN, 9-1	BUMP ELLIOTT Bob Timberlake, qb	*
1965	MICHIGAN STATE, 10-1	DUFFY DAUGHERTY Steve Juday, qb Clinton Jones, hb Bubba Smith, e	*****
	ALABAMA, 9-1-1	BEAR BRYANT Steve Sloan, qb Paul Crane, c Steve Bowman, hb Ray Perkins, e	**
1966	NOTRE DAME, 9-0-1	ARA PARSEGHIAN Terry Hanratty, qb Jim Seymour, e Nick Eddy, hb	******
	MICHIGAN STATE, 9-0-1	DUFFY DAUGHERTY Jimmy Raye, qb Clinton Jones, hb Bubba Smith, de George Webster, lb	**
1967	USC, 10-1	JOHN MCKAY O. J. Simpson, hb Steve Sogge, qb Ron Yary, t Mike Battle, db	*****
	NOTRE DAME, 8-2	ARA PARSEGHIAN Terry Hanratty, qb Jim Seymour, e Mike McCoy, t	*
1968	OHIO STATE, 10-0	WOODY HAYES Rex Kern, qb Jim Otis, fb Jack Tatum, db Jim Stillwagon, g	******
1969	TEXAS, 11-0	DARRELL ROYAL James Street, qb Steve Worster, fb Jim Bertelsen, hb Cotton Speyrer, e Bob McKay, t	******

YEAR	TEAM, RECORD	COACH, Star players	POLLS WON
1970	NEBRASKA, 11-0-1	BOB DEVANEY Jerry Tagge, qb Jeff Kinney, hb Johnny Rodgers, hb	****
	TEXAS, 10-1	DARRELL ROYAL Eddie Phillips, qb Steve Worster, fb Cotton Speyrer, e	**
	OHIO STATE, 9-1	WOODY HAYES Rex Kern, qb John Brockington, hb Jack Tatum, db Jim Stillwagon, g	*
1971	NEBRASKA, 13-0	BOB DEVANEY Jerry Tagge, qb Jeff Kinney, hb Johnny Rodgers, hb Rich Glover, g Larry Jacobson, t	******
1972	USC, 12-0	JOHN MCKAY Anthony Davis, hb Sam Cunningham, fb Mike Rae, qb Lynn Swann, e	******
1973	NOTRE DAME, 12-0	ARA PARSEGHIAN Tom Clements, qb Dave Casper, e Eric Penick, hb	****
	ALABAMA, 11-1	BEAR BRYANT Richard Todd, qb Wilbur Jackson, hb	*
	OKLAHOMA, 10-0-1	BARRY SWITZER Steve Davis, qb Joe Washington, hb Tinker Owens, e	*
1974	OKLAHOMA, 11-0	BARRY SWITZER Steve Davis, qb Joe Washington, hb LeRoy Selmon, t	***
	USC, 10-1-1	JOHN MCKAY Pat Haden, qb Anthony Davis, hb J. K. McKay, e	****

YEAR	TEAM, RECORD	COACH, Star players	POLLS WON
1975	OKLAHOMA, 11-1	BARRY SWITZER Steve Davis, qb Joe Washington, hb Tinker Owens, e	******
	OHIO STATE, 11-1	WOODY HAYES Archie Griffin, hb Pete Johnson, fb	*
1976	PITTSBURGH, 12-0	JOHNNY MAJORS Tony Dorsett, hb Matt Cavanaugh, qb Randy Holloway, t	*****
	USC, 11-1	JOHN ROBINSON Ricky Bell, fb Vince Evans, qb Randy Simmrin, e	*
1977	NOTRE DAME, 11-1	DAN DEVINE Joe Montana, qb Ken MacAfee, e Vagas Ferguson, hb Bob Golic, lb Ross Browner, e	******
1978	USC, 12-1	JOHN ROBINSON Charles White, hb Paul McDonald, qb	**
	OKLAHOMA, 11-1	BARRY SWITZER Billy Sims, hb Thomas Lott, qb	**
	ALABAMA, 11-1	BEAR BRYANT Jeff Rutledge, qb Tony Nathan, hb Barry Krauss, lb Marty Lyons, t	****
1979	ALABAMA, 12-0	BEAR BRYANT Major Ogilvie, hb E. J. Junior, de David Hannah, t	******
1980	GEORGIA, 12-0	VINCE DOOLEY Herschel Walker, hb Buck Belue, qb Lindsay Scott, e	*****
	OKLAHOMA, 10-2	BARRY SWITZER J. C. Watts, qb David Overstreet, hb	*

YEAR	TEAM, RECORD	COACH, Star players	POLLS WON
1981	CLEMSON, 12-0	DANNY FORD Homer Jordan, qb Cliff Austin, hb Terry Kinard, db	*****
	PENN STATE, 10-2	JOE PATERNO Curt Warner, hb Todd Blackledge, qb	*
1982	SMU, 11-0-1	BOBBY COLLINS Eric Dickerson, hb Craig James, hb	*
	PENN STATE, 11-1	JOE PATERNO Curt Warner, hb Todd Blackledge, qb	******
1983	MIAMI, 11-1	HOWARD SCHNELLENBERGER Bernie Kosar, qb Alonzo Highsmith, hb Eddie Brown, wr	*****
1984	BRIGHAM YOUNG, 13-0	LAVELL EDWARDS Robbie Bosco, qb Glen Koslowski, wr Jim Herrmann, t	****
	FLORIDA, 9-1-1	GALEN HALL Kerwin Bell, qb Neal Anderson, hb John L. Williams, hb Lorenzo Hampton, hb	*
1985	OKLAHOMA, 11-1	BARRY SWITZER Jamelle Holieway, qb Keith Jackson, e Spencer Tillman, hb Brian Bosworth, lb	*****
1986	PENN STATE, 12-0	JOE PATERNO D. J. Dozier, hb Shane Conlan, lb	****
	OKLAHOMA, 11-1	BARRY SWITZER Jamelle Holieway, qb Keith Jackson, e Lydell Carr, fb	*
1987	MIAMI, 12-0	JIMMY JOHNSON Steve Walsh, qb Michael Irvin, e Mel Bratton, fb Bennie Blades, cb	*****

YEAR	TEAM, RECORD	COACH, Star players	POLLS WON
1988	NOTRE DAME, 12-0	LOU HOLTZ Tony Rice, qb Mark Green, hb Mike Stonebreaker, lb Frank Stamms, t Ned Bolcar, lb	*****

Play as many games with the chart as you like but here are a few facts: In the long history of polls, only 38 schools have won any kind of national championship, and only 22 schools have won two or more. Notre Dame leads with 15, as you might guess. USC has 11. Oklahoma and Alabama have 10 each. That's how it stood through 1988.

Notre Dame, again as you might suspect, is the only school to win national championships in all seven decades.

There are some interesting streaks for coaches.

Minnesota's Bernie Bierman won five over a period of eight years, from 1934 through 1941.

USC's Howard Jones won four over six years, from 1928 through 1933.

Notre Dame's Frank Leahy won five over 11 years, from 1943 through 1953.

Oklahoma's Barry Switzer has won seven in the 16 years he's coached, at this writing, from 1973 through 1988.

Bear Bryant at Alabama is the only other coach to accumulate seven national championships.

As for those several seasons when there is more than one claimant for the national title—when the polls differed—everybody would do well to remember the words of Bryant. He once said, "All you need to win is one, then your fans can play like they won 'em all."

Ancient History

FOR MY MONEY, THE FIRST SPORTSWRITER WHO WAS WORTH HIS weight in pens, scrolls, or typewriter ribbons was a fellow named Caspar Whitney, who for a brief time edited a journal called *The Week's Sport,* who later wrote for *Harper's Weekly,* and who sat up on his hind legs one day in 1889 and chose the first mythical national champion in college football, which happened to be Princeton, and also selected the first all-America team, which happened to include Yale's Amos Alonzo Stagg at end and Yale's Pudge Heffelfinger at guard.

Is it safe to say that Caspar Whitney started something?

Over the next 45 years, until polls, the matter of naming a national champion was in the hands of one Eastern writer or another, many of whom would ask Walter Camp, "the father of American football," about it, and all of whom might best have been named Special (Spec) Interest and Regional (Reggie) Emphasis.

Caring historians generally regard two lists of these early-day champions as being "official." One was published by the Spalding Guide in 1934 and the other by the Helms Athletic Foundation in 1942. The custodians of these institutions delved back in history and studied results and strengths of schedules and selected national champions on a predated basis.

Here are the national champions of the pre-poll years, as ordained by the Spalding Guide and the Helms Athletic Foundation, and artfully assembled by your genial host:

YEAR	TEAM, RECORD	COACH, Star players
1889	PRINCETON, 10-0	(NO COACH) Edgar Allan Poe, hb Hector Cowan, t
1890	HARVARD, 11-0	GEORGE STEWART Marshall Newell, t John Corbett, hb

YEAR	TEAM, RECORD	COACH, Star players
1891	YALE, 13-0	WALTER CAMP Pudge Heffelfinger, g Frank Hinkey, e Thomas McClung, hb
1892	YALE, 13-0	WALTER CAMP Frank Hinkey, e Vance McCormick, hb
1893	PRINCETON, 11-0	(NO COACH) Tom Trenchard, e Biffy Lea, t Philip King, fb
	YALE, 10-1	BILL RHODES Frank Hinkey, e Bill Hickok, g Frank Butterworth, hb
1894	YALE, 16-0	BILL RHODES Frank Hinkey, e Frank Butterworth, hb
	PENN, 12-0	GEORGE WOODRUFF George Brooke, hb Charley Gelbert, e
1895	PENN, 14-0	GEORGE WOODRUFF George Brooke, hb Charley Gelbert, e
	YALE, 13-0-2	JOHN HARTWELL Sam Thorne, hb Fred Murphy, t
1896	LAFAYETTE, 11-0-1	DR. S. B. NEWTON Fielding H. Yost, t George Barclay, hb
	PRINCETON, 10-0-1	(NO COACH) Addison Kelly, hb Bill Church, t
1897	PENN, 15-0	GEORGE WOODRUFF T. Truxtun Hare, g John Outland, t
	YALE, 9-0-2	FRANK BUTTERWORTH Charles DaSaulles, hb Gordon Brown, g
1898	HARVARD, 11-0	CAMERON FORBES Charley Daly, hb John Hallowell, e

YEAR	TEAM, RECORD	COACH, Star players
	PRINCETON,	(NO COACH)
	11-0-1	Lew Palmer, e
		Ben Dibblee, hb
1899	HARVARD,	BEN DIBBLEE
	10-0-1	Charley Daly, hb
	PRINCETON,	(NO COACH)
	12-1	Arthur Poe, e
		Art Hillebrand, t
1900	YALE,	MALCOLM MCBRIDE
	12-0	Perry Hale, hb
		George Chadwick, hb
		Herman Olcott, e

It was here, and not a moment too soon, that Fielding H. Yost at Michigan let it be known that some pretty good football was being played outside the East.

"Hurry Up" Yost, he was called, and his teams were known as the "Point-a-Minute" Wolverines.

YEAR	TEAM, RECORD	COACH, Star players
1901	HARVARD,	BILL REID
	12-0	Ed Bowditch, e
		Bob Kernan, hb
	MICHIGAN,	FIELDING H. YOST
	11-0	Willie Heston, hb
1902	MICHIGAN,	FIELDING H. YOST
	11-0	Willie Heston, hb
	YALE,	JOE SWAN
	11-0-1	Tom Shevlin, e
		Foster Rockwell, hb
1903	PRINCETON,	DOC HILLEBRAND
	11-0	Dana Kafer, hb
		John DeWitt, t
1904	PENN,	CARL WILLIAMS
	12-0	Andy Smith, hb
		Frank Pickarski, g
1905	CHICAGO,	AMOS ALONZO STAGG
	10-0	Walter Eckersall, qb
	YALE,	JACK OWSLEY
	10-0	Tom Shevlin, e
		Guy Hutchinson, hb

YEAR	TEAM, RECORD	COACH, Star players
1906	PRINCETON, 9-0-1	BILL ROPER Edward Dillon, hb Caspar Wister, e
1907	YALE, 9-0-1	BILL KNOX Ted Coy, fb T. A. D. "Tad" Jones, hb
1908	PENN, 11-0-1	SOL METZGER Bill Hollenback, fb Hunter Scarlett, e
1909	YALE, 10-0	HOWARD JONES Ted Coy, fb John Reed Kilpatrick, e
1910	HARVARD, 8-0-1	PERCY HAUGHTON Percy Wendell, hb Bob Fisher, g
1911	PRINCETON, 8-0-2	BILL ROPER Hobey Baker, hb Sanford White, e
1912	HARVARD, 9-0	PERCY HAUGHTON Charley Brickley, hb Stan Pennock, g
1913	HARVARD, 9-0	PERCY HAUGHTON Charley Brickley, hb Eddie Mahan, fb
	CHICAGO, 7-0	AMOS ALONZO STAGG Paul Des Jardien, c

Other strangers now appear, as if the rabble is running through the streets and no ivy-covered campus is safe from harm.

YEAR	TEAM, RECORD	COACH, Star players
1914	ARMY, 9-0	CHARLEY DALY Louis Merillat, e John McEwan, c
	ILLINOIS, 7-0	BOB ZUPPKE Perry Graves, e Bart Macomber, hb
1915	CORNELL, 9-0	AL SHARPE Charley Barrett, hb
	PITT, 8-0	POP WARNER Bob Peck, c Jack Herron, e

YEAR	TEAM, RECORD	COACH, Star players
1916	ARMY,	CHARLEY DALY
	9-0	Elmer Oliphant, fb
	PITT,	POP WARNER
	8-0	Bob Peck, c
		Jock Sutherland, g
1917	GEORGIA TECH,	JOHN HEISMAN
	9-0	George Strupper, hb
		Joe Guyon, t
		Bum Day, c
1918	PITT,	POP WARNER
	6-1	Tom Davies, hb
		Len Hilty, t
1919	NOTRE DAME,	KNUTE ROCKNE
	9-0	George Gipp, fb
	HARVARD,	BOB FISHER
	9-0-1	Edward Casey, fb
	ILLINOIS,	BOB ZUPPKE
	6-1	Bob Fletcher, hb
		Charles Carney, e
1920	CALIFORNIA,	ANDY SMITH
	9-0	Brick Muller, e
	NOTRE DAME,	KNUTE ROCKNE
	9-0	George Gipp, fb
	PRINCETON,	BILL ROPER
	6-0-1	Donald Lourie, hb
		Stan Keck, t
1921	LAFAYETTE,	JOCK SUTHERLAND
	9-0	Frank Schwab, g
	CORNELL,	GIL DOBIE
	8-0	Ed Kaw, hb
		George Pfann, hb
	IOWA,	HOWARD JONES
	7-0	Aubrey Devine, hb
		Gordon Locke, hb
1922	PRINCETON,	BILL ROPER
	8-0	Herb Treat, t
	CORNELL,	GIL DOBIE
	8-0	Ed Kaw, hb
		George Pfann, hb
1923	ILLINOIS,	BOB ZUPPKE
	8-0	Red Grange, hb

So much for the prepoll years.

One of the things all this research does is tell us who the great coaches were. No coach has ever been accused of achieving greatness if he didn't win two or more national championships.

This is the law of the press, don't argue.

As it happens, I've just concluded a stroll through the lists of *all* the national champions, from 1889 through 1988, so here are the greatest coaches who ever barked at a player or a sportswriter:

COACHES OF NATIONAL CHAMPIONS
(2 or more)

7—HOWARD JONES	1909, Yale
	1921, Iowa
	1928, USC
	1931, USC
	1932, USC
	1933, USC
	1939, USC
7—BEAR BRYANT	1961, Alabama
	1962, Alabama
	1964, Alabama
	1965, Alabama
	1973, Alabama
	1978, Alabama
	1979, Alabama
7—BARRY SWITZER	1973, Oklahoma
	1974, Oklahoma
	1975, Oklahoma
	1978, Oklahoma
	1980, Oklahoma
	1985, Oklahoma
	1986, Oklahoma
6—WOODY HAYES	1954, Ohio State
	1957, Ohio State
	1961, Ohio State
	1968, Ohio State
	1970, Ohio State
	1975, Ohio State
5—KNUTE ROCKNE	1919, Notre Dame
	1920, Notre Dame
	1924, Notre Dame
	1929, Notre Dame
	1930, Notre Dame

5—FRANK LEAHY	1943, Notre Dame
	1946, Notre Dame
	1947, Notre Dame
	1949, Notre Dame
	1953, Notre Dame
5—BERNIE BIERMAN	1934, Minnesota
	1935, Minnesota
	1936, Minnesota
	1940, Minnesota
	1941, Minnesota
4—POP WARNER	1915, Pitt
	1916, Pitt
	1918, Pitt
	1926, Stanford
4—BOB NEYLAND	1938, Tennessee
	1940, Tennessee
	1950, Tennessee
	1951, Tennessee
4—JOHN MCKAY	1962, USC
	1967, USC
	1972, USC
	1974, USC
4—BOB ZUPPKE	1914, Illinois
	1919, Illinois
	1923, Illinois
	1927, Illinois
4—BILL ROPER	1906, Princeton
	1911, Princeton
	1920, Princeton
	1922, Princeton
4—ARA PARSEGHIAN	1964, Notre Dame
	1966, Notre Dame
	1967, Notre Dame
	1973, Notre Dame
3—DARRELL ROYAL	1963, Texas
	1969, Texas
	1970, Texas
3—BUD WILKINSON	1950, Oklahoma
	1955, Oklahoma
	1956, Oklahoma
3—RED BLAIK	1944, Army
	1945, Army
	1946, Army

3—DUFFY DAUGHERTY	1957, Michigan State
	1965, Michigan State
	1966, Michigan State
3—JOE PATERNO	1981, Penn State
	1982, Penn State
	1986, Penn State
3—PERCY HAUGHTON	1910, Harvard
	1912, Harvard
	1913, Harvard
3—GEORGE WOODRUFF	1894, Penn
	1895, Penn
	1897, Penn
2—DUTCH MEYER	1935, TCU
	1938, TCU
2—WALLY BUTTS	1942, Georgia
	1946, Georgia
2—JIM TATUM	1951, Maryland
	1953, Maryland
2—JOHNNY VAUGHT	1959, Ole Miss
	1960, Ole Miss
2—BIGGIE MUNN	1951, Michigan State
	1952, Michigan State
2—FRITZ CRISLER	1935, Princeton
	1947, Michigan
2—BOB DEVANEY	1970, Nebraska
	1971, Nebraska
2—WALLACE WADE	1925, Alabama
	1926, Alabama
2—CHARLEY DALY	1914, Army
	1916, Army
2—JOCK SUTHERLAND	1921, Lafayette
	1937, Pitt
2—HARRY KIPKE	1932, Michigan
	1933, Michigan
2—FIELDING H. YOST	1901, Michigan
	1902, Michigan
2—BILL RHODES	1893, Yale
	1894, Yale
2—AMOS ALONZO STAGG	1905, Chicago
	1913, Chicago
2—JOHN ROBINSON	1976, USC
	1978, USC

2—GIL DOBIE	1921, Cornell
	1922, Cornell
2—WALTER CAMP	1891, Yale
	1892, Yale

There is another school of thought put forth by Old Grads that holds that national championships have too often been left up to whim, prejudice, and luck, and that another way to judge coaches is on how many undefeated teams they produced. The theory here is that an undefeated team can make an Old Grad as happy as a good stock tip and entice him to make just as large a financial contribution to the university as a national championship.

To satisfy this clamor before it begins, I felt it wise to provide yet another pile of research, which is not available at your neighborhood supermarket. Hence:

COACHES OF UNDEFEATED TEAMS (REGULAR SEASON)
(2 or more)

12—GIL DOBIE	1908, WASHINGTON, 6-0-1
	1909, WASHINGTON, 7-0
	1910, WASHINGTON, 6-0
	1911, WASHINGTON, 7-0
	1912, WASHINGTON, 6-0
	1913, WASHINGTON, 7-0
	1914, WASHINGTON, 6-0-1
	1915, WASHINGTON, 7-0
	1916, WASHINGTON, 6-0-1
	1921, CORNELL, 8-0
	1922, CORNELL, 8-0
	1923, CORNELL, 8-0

Although he still holds the major college record of going nine straight seasons without a defeat while he was at the University of Washington, he was known as "Gloomy Gil" Dobie. It must have been those ties, or the fact that some of his opponents had names like Puget Sound and Rainer Valley Athletic Club.

9—BOB NEYLAND	1927, TENNESSEE, 8-0-1
	1928, TENNESSEE, 9-0-1
	1929, TENNESSEE, 9-0-1
	1931, TENNESSEE, 9-0-1

	1932, TENNESSEE, 9-0-1
8—BEAR BRYANT	1938, TENNESSEE, 10-0
	1939, TENNESSEE, 10-0 (Lost Rose Bowl)
	1940, TENNESSEE, 10-0 (Lost Sugar Bowl)
	1951, TENNESSEE, 10-0 (Lost Sugar Bowl)
	1956, TEXAS A&M, 9-0-1
	1961, ALABAMA, 10-0
	1964, ALABAMA, 10-0 (Lost Orange Bowl)
	1966, ALABAMA, 10-0
	1971, ALABAMA, 11-0 (Lost Orange Bowl)
	1973, ALABAMA, 11-0 (Lost Sugar Bowl)
	1974, ALABAMA, 11-0 (Lost Sugar Bowl)
	1979, ALABAMA, 11-0

As shrewd as Bryant and Neyland were, you'd think they might have had better luck in choosing bowl opponents.

8—FIELDING H. YOST	1901, MICHIGAN, 10-0
	1902, MICHIGAN, 11-0
	1903, MICHIGAN, 11-0-1
	1904, MICHIGAN, 10-0
	1910, MICHIGAN, 3-0-3
	1918, MICHIGAN, 5-0
	1922, MICHIGAN, 6-0-1
	1923, MICHIGAN, 8-0
7—FRANK LEAHY	1940, BOSTON COLLEGE, 10-0
	1941, NOTRE DAME, 8-0-1
	1946, NOTRE DAME, 8-0-1
	1947, NOTRE DAME, 9-0
	1948, NOTRE DAME, 8-0-1
	1949, NOTRE DAME, 10-0
	1953, NOTRE DAME, 9-0-1
7—BERNIE BIERMAN	1929, TULANE, 9-0 (Lost Rose Bowl)
	1931, TULANE, 11-0 (Lost Rose Bowl)
	1933, MINNESOTA, 4-0-4
	1934, MINNESOTA, 8-0
	1935, MINNESOTA, 8-0
	1940, MINNESOTA, 8-0
	1941, MINNESOTA, 8-0

7—RED BLAIK	1937, DARTMOUTH, 7-0-2
	1944, ARMY, 9-0
	1945, ARMY, 9-0
	1946, ARMY, 9-0-1
	1948, ARMY, 8-0-1
	1949, ARMY, 9-0
	1958, ARMY, 8-0-1
6—HOWARD JONES	1909, YALE, 10-0
	1921, IOWA, 7-0
	1922, IOWA, 8-0
	1928, USC, 9-0-1
	1932, USC, 9-0
	1939, USC, 7-0-2
6—POP WARNER	1915, PITTSBURGH, 9-0
	1916, PITTSBURGH, 8-0
	1917, PITTSBURGH, 9-0
	1920, PITTSBURGH, 6-0-2
	1924, STANFORD, 7-0-1 (Lost Rose Bowl)
	1926, STANFORD, 10-0
6—JOE PATERNO	1968, PENN STATE, 10-0
	1969, PENN STATE, 10-0
	1973, PENN STATE, 11-0
	1978, PENN STATE, 11-0 (Lost Sugar Bowl)
	1985, PENN STATE, 11-0 (Lost Orange Bowl)
	1986, PENN STATE, 11-0
6—WOODY HAYES	1954, OHIO STATE, 10-0
	1961, OHIO STATE, 8-0-1
	1968, OHIO STATE, 10-0
	1970, OHIO STATE, 9-0 (Lost Rose Bowl)
	1973, OHIO STATE, 9-0-1
	1975, OHIO STATE, 11-0

By the way, there's no alphabetical order to any of this. Only a fool would expect such diligence.

5—KNUTE ROCKNE	1919, NOTRE DAME, 9-0
	1920, NOTRE DAME, 9-0
	1924, NOTRE DAME, 9-0
	1929, NOTRE DAME, 9-0
	1930, NOTRE DAME, 10-0

5—BUD WILKINSON	1949, OKLAHOMA, 10-0
	1950, OKLAHOMA, 10-0 (Lost Sugar Bowl)
	1954, OKLAHOMA, 10-0
	1955, OKLAHOMA, 10-0
	1956, OKLAHOMA, 10-0
5—ANDY SMITH	1920, CALIFORNIA, 8-0
	1921, CALIFORNIA, 9-0
	1922, CALIFORNIA, 9-0
	1923, CALIFORNIA, 9-0-1
	1924, CALIFORNIA, 8-0-2
5—WALLACE WADE	1925, ALABAMA, 9-0
	1926, ALABAMA, 9-0
	1930, ALABAMA, 9-0
	1938, DUKE, 9-0 (Lost Rose Bowl)
	1941, DUKE, 9-0 (Lost Rose Bowl)
5—JOCK SUTHERLAND	1921, LAFAYETTE, 9-0
	1927, PITTSBURGH, 8-0-1 (Lost Rose Bowl)
	1929, PITTSBURGH, 9-0 (Lost Rose Bowl)
	1932, PITTSBURGH, 8-0-2 (Lost Rose Bowl)
	1937, PITTSBURGH, 9-0-1
5—PERCY HAUGHTON	1908, HARVARD, 9-0-1
	1910, HARVARD, 8-0-1
	1912, HARVARD, 9-0
	1913, HARVARD, 9-0
	1914, HARVARD, 7-0-2
5—DR. HENRY WILLIAMS	1900, MINNESOTA, 9-0-1
	1903, MINNESOTA, 11-0-1
	1904, MINNESOTA, 12-0
	1911, MINNESOTA, 6-0-1
	1915, MINNESOTA, 6-0-1
5—WALTER CAMP	1888, YALE, 13-0
	1891, YALE, 13-0
	1892, YALE, 13-0
	1893, STANFORD, 8-0-1
	1895, STANFORD, 4-0-1
4—DARRELL ROYAL	1962, TEXAS, 9-0-1 (Lost Cotton Bowl)
	1963, TEXAS, 10-0
	1969, TEXAS, 10-0
	1970, TEXAS, 10-0 (Lost Cotton Bowl)

4—JOHN MCKAY	1962, USC, 10-0
	1968, USC, 9-0-1 (Lost Rose Bowl)
	1969, USC, 9-0-1
	1972, USC, 11-0
4—AMOS ALONZO STAGG	1899, CHICAGO, 12-0-2
	1905, CHICAGO, 10-0
	1908, CHICAGO, 5-0-1
	1913, CHICAGO, 7-0
4—BOB ZUPPKE	1914, ILLINOIS, 7-0
	1915, ILLINOIS, 5-0-2
	1923, ILLINOIS, 8-0
	1927, ILLINOIS, 7-0-1
4—JOHN HEISMAN	1905, GEORGIA TECH, 5-0-1
	1915, GEORGIA TECH, 7-0-1
	1916, GEORGIA TECH, 8-0-1
	1917, GEORGIA TECH, 9-0
4—FRANK THOMAS	1934, ALABAMA, 9-0
	1936, ALABAMA, 8-0-1
	1937, ALABAMA, 9-0 (Lost Rose Bowl)
	1945, ALABAMA, 9-0
4—DAN MCGUGIN	1904, VANDERBILT, 8-0
	1910, VANDERBILT, 8-0-1
	1921, VANDERBILT, 7-0-1
	1922, VANDERBILT, 8-0-1
4—BILL ROPER	1906, PRINCETON, 9-0-1
	1911, PRINCETON, 8-0-2
	1920, PRINCETON, 6-0-1
	1922, PRINCETON, 8-0
4—BENNIE OWEN	1911, OKLAHOMA, 8-0
	1915, OKLAHOMA, 10-0
	1918, OKLAHOMA, 6-0
	1920, OKLAHOMA, 6-0-1
4—JOHNNY VAUGHT	1952, OLE MISS, 8-0-2 (Lost Sugar Bowl)
	1960, OLE MISS, 9-0-1
	1962, OLE MISS, 9-0
	1963, OLE MISS, 7-0-2
4—CHARLEY MORAN	1909, TEXAS A&M, 7-0-1
	1918, CENTRE, 4-0
	1919, CENTRE, 9-0
	1921, CENTRE, 10-0

3—BARRY SWITZER	1973, OKLAHOMA, 10-0-1
	1974, OKLAHOMA, 11-0
	1987, OKLAHOMA, 11-0 (Lost Orange Bowl)
3—BOB DEVANEY	1965, NEBRASKA, 10-0 (Lost Orange Bowl)
	1970, NEBRASKA, 10-0-1
	1971, NEBRASKA, 12-0
3—FRITZ CRISLER	1933, PRINCETON, 9-0
	1935, PRINCETON, 9-0
	1947, MICHIGAN, 9-0
3—JIM TATUM	1951, MARYLAND, 9-0
	1953, MARYLAND, 10-0 (Lost Orange Bowl)
	1955, MARYLAND, 10-0 (Lost Orange Bowl)
3—CHARLEY DALY	1914, ARMY, 9-0
	1916, ARMY, 9-0
	1922, ARMY, 8-0-2
3—HARRY KIPKE	1930, MICHIGAN, 8-0-1
	1932, MICHIGAN, 8-0
	1933, MICHIGAN, 7-0-1
3—DANA X. BIBLE	1917, TEXAS A&M, 9-0
	1919, TEXAS A&M, 10-0
	1927, TEXAS A&M, 8-0-1
3—GEORGE WOODRUFF	1894, PENNSYLVANIA, 12-0
	1895, PENNSYLVANIA, 14-0
	1897, PENNSYLVANIA, 15-0
3—JOHN WILCE	1916, OHIO STATE, 7-0
	1917, OHIO STATE, 8-0-1
	1920, OHIO STATE, 7-0 (Lost Rose Bowl)
3—RAY MORRISON	1923, SMU, 9-0
	1926, SMU, 8-0-1
	1929, SMU, 6-0-4
3—FRANK CAVANAUGH	1920, BOSTON COLLEGE, 8-0
	1926, BOSTON COLLEGE, 6-0-2
	1929, FORDHAM, 7-0-2
3—JUMBO STIEHM	1913, NEBRASKA, 8-0
	1914, NEBRASKA, 7-0-1
	1915, NEBRASKA, 8-0

3—PAPPY WALDORF	1948, CALIFORNIA, 10-0 (Lost Rose Bowl)
	1949, CALIFORNIA, 10-0 (Lost Rose Bowl)
	1950, CALIFORNIA, 9-0-1 (Lost Rose Bowl)

Hey, Pappy. Had a little trouble in Pasadena, huh?

2—JIMMY JOHNSON	1986, MIAMI, 11-0 (Lost Fiesta Bowl)
	1987, MIAMI, 11-0
2—FRANK BROYLES	1964, ARKANSAS, 10-0
	1965, ARKANSAS, 10-0 (Lost Cotton Bowl)
2—MATTY BELL	1935, SMU, 12-0 (Lost Rose Bowl)
	1947, SMU, 9-0-1
2—BOBBY DODD	1951, GEORGIA TECH, 10-0-1
	1952, GEORGIA TECH, 11-0
2—CARL SNAVELY	1939, CORNELL, 8-0
	1948, NORTH CAROLINA, 9-0-1 (Lost Sugar Bowl)
2—SHUG JORDAN	1957, AUBURN, 10-0
	1958, AUBURN, 9-0-1
2—FRANK HOWARD	1948, CLEMSON, 10-0
	1950, CLEMSON, 8-0-1
2—CLARK SHAUGHNESSY	1925, TULANE, 9-0-1
	1940, STANFORD, 9-0
2—BIGGIE MUNN	1951, MICHIGAN STATE, 9-0
	1952, MICHIGAN STATE, 9-0
2—DUFFY DAUGHERTY	1965, MICHIGAN STATE, 10-0 (Lost Rose Bowl)
	1966, MICHIGAN STATE, 9-0-1
2—MIKE DONAHUE	1913, AUBURN, 8-0
	1914, AUBURN, 7-0-1
2—JESSE HAWLEY	1924, DARTMOUTH, 7-0-1
	1925, DARTMOUTH, 8-0
2—FRANK KUSH	1970, ARIZONA STATE, 10-0
	1975, ARIZONA STATE, 11-0
2—FRANCIS SCHMIDT	1929, TCU, 9-0-1
	1932, TCU, 10-0-1
2—ANDY KERR	1927, WASHINGTON & JEFFERSON, 7-0-2
	1932, COLGATE, 9-0

2—DR. EDDIE ANDERSON	1935, HOLY CROSS, 9-0-1
	1937, HOLY CROSS, 8-0-2
2—HENRY FRNKA	1942, TULSA, 10-0 (Lost Sugar Bowl)
	1943, TULSA, 6-0-1 (Lost Sugar Bowl)
2—BO SCHEMBECHLER	1971, MICHIGAN, 11-0 (Lost Rose Bowl)
	1973, MICHIGAN, 10-0-1 (Lost Rose Bowl)
2—FRED AKERS	1977, TEXAS, 11-0 (Lost Cotton Bowl)
	1983, TEXAS, 11-0 (Lost Cotton Bowl)

The hope here is that all of this material will help you win a few bets in saloons, and I would suggest that the best way to enjoy each and every chart, or list, is to curl up in a Rose Bowl blanket in front of a cozy fire.

Incidentally, since quarterbacks often make the coaches what they are, here's my favorite football trivia question: How many quarterbacks have ever won a national championship in college and an NFL championship or Super Bowl in the pros?

Just three.

Sam Baugh with TCU and the Washington Redskins.

Joe Namath with Alabama and the New York Jets.

Joe Montana with Notre Dame and the San Francisco 49ers.

Trust me on this. Shove it in with both hands if the question ever comes up.

POLL BOWLS

What Are They?

A POLL BOWL IS A CRUCIAL SHOWDOWN, A BATTLE OF GIANTS, A Big Shootout.

It is sometimes a Game of the Year, occasionally a Game of the Decade, and in rare instances a Game of the Century.

This is all generally decided by sportswriters, who have never played in a Game of the Year, a Game of the Decade, or a Game of the Century.

Poll Bowls never die. They are burned into the memories of the winners and losers forever.

In Poll Bowls, people with names like Thorpe, Grange, Harmon, Doak, Lujack, O.J., and so forth get to do amazing things and become immortal.

Schools win national championships in Poll Bowls.

Schools lose national championships in Poll Bowls.

Poll Bowls encourage witty T-shirts, buttons, and bumper stickers.

A Poll Bowl between Notre Dame and USC once drew 112,000 people in Chicago's Soldier Field, and this was 20 years and a World War before television, which did not invent football *or* Poll Bowls.

By and large, Poll Bowls cause sportswriters to choke up at their typewriters on deadline, but not all of them. Some of them turn cynical and say, "It's only a game."

But it's not. It's a Poll Bowl. Which means it's more important than life or death. We're talking about football here.

Fit to Be Tied

FOR 58 MINUTES IN EAST LANSING, MICHIGAN, ON THE OVER-wrought Saturday of Nov. 19, 1966, the savages of Notre Dame and Michigan State pounded each other into enough mistakes to fill Bubba Smith's uniform, but the chaotic deadlock that destiny seemed to be demanding had a strange, noble quality to it. Suddenly, then, it no longer did, for the Fighting Irish decided to tie one for the Gipper.

One makes such a remark at the risk of having his car bombed. No fans are as passionate as Notre Dame's, or quite as insufferable. They are generally overbearing in victory and malicious in defeat. It is as if they actually believe that phony old saying, "We didn't lose the game, we just ran out of time."

Quite surprising, therefore, that on this momentous occasion, it was Notre Dame that ran out the time.

You could forget everything else that happened under the cold, dreary sky of the Spartans' stadium, all of the thudding in the line that caused five fumbles, four interceptions, 25 incompletions, assorted bobbles, confusing time-outs, sideline arguments, and a total of 20 rushing plays that lost yardage, and you could forget the few good plays, the passes that connected. Put the Nation's No. 1 team, Notre Dame, on its own 30-yard line, first down, plenty of time left to throw the ball, momentum going. A No. 1 team, especially Notre Dame, would try *something* to win the game, wouldn't it?

Notre Dame did not. The Irish let the air out of the game, rode out the clock. The Irish ran into the line and settled for a final score of 10 to 10.

"We couldn't believe it," said George Webster, Michigan State's tough roverback. "When they came up for their first play we kept hollering, 'Watch the pass, watch the pass.' But they ran. We knew the next one was a pass for sure. But they ran again. We were stunned. Then it dawned on us. They were settling for ten to ten."

Bubba Smith had hollered, "Come on, sissies. You gonna quit?" And he had yelled at Ara Parseghian, the Notre Dame coach, in the same manner. So had the other Spartan defenders.

Parseghian had made the decision to end the so-called Game of the Decade this way. His players had only followed instructions, some of them reluctantly.

"We'd fought hard to come back from ten points down and tie it up," Ara argued later. "I didn't want to risk giving it to them cheaply. One reckless pass and it could have cost us the game. I wasn't going to do a jackass thing like throw it away at this point."

Thus ended a game that had been blown up for weeks into the biggest collegiate spectacle in 20 years. Notre Dame had won eight games, lost none, and was rated No. 1. Michigan State had won nine games, lost none, and was rated No. 2. The last game to create such a prekickoff frenzy had also involved Notre Dame. That was in 1946 · at Yankee Stadium when the Irish met Army. That Game of the Decade had also brought together undefeated, untied teams with tickets going for $100, and it had been full of as many fluky things as this one. It too had ended in a tie, 0 to 0, with both teams claiming No. 1, and it had left thousands dissatisfied and somewhat bewildered by the fact that such folklore characters as Johnny Lujack and George Connor, and Glenn Davis and Doc Blanchard, had not been able to perform the one remarkable deed that would have decided it.

Like that one years before, the East Lansing game was decided a bushel of times, it seemed, as the two national powers heaped heroics onto boners, and vice versa—as Michigan State surged to a 10–0 lead and as Notre Dame struggled back to the indecisive tie that was earned but unapplauded.

The game was marked by all of the brutality you somehow knew it would be when such animals were to be present as Michigan State's 6-foot-7, 285-pound Bubba Smith, "the intercontinental ballistic Bubba," as Spartan rooters referred to him, a creature whose play at defensive end had long ago encouraged students to wear buttons that said KILL, BUBBA, KILL.

Bubba killed, all right. He killed Notre Dame's talented sophomore quarterback, Terry Hanratty, early in the first quarter. Hanratty's passing to another whiz of a sophomore, Jim Seymour, had whirled Notre Dame into No. 1 in the first place. They had become known as the Baby Bombers. But now Hanratty was just another injured player, thanks to Bubba. As Terry had slid off right tackle on a keeper play, Bubba had whomped him in the left shoulder and separated it. It looked as if Hanratty had been smacked by a giant swinging green door.

"That didn't help us any," Bubba said later. "It just let 'em put in that Coley O'Brien, who's more slippery and faster than Hanratty. He gave us more trouble. Hanratty sits there and waits to throw, and that's what our defense wanted. We knew we could get to him."

Given a choice, of course, Ara Parseghian would have preferred to play the rest of the game with Hanratty at quarterback. He could throw deep better than O'Brien, although O'Brien threw well enough to gain the tie. Ara not only would have liked to have had Hanratty but his all-America halfback, Nick Eddy, and his center, George Goeddeke, as well. Like Hanratty, Goeddeke, a fine blocker, went out with a first-quarter injury, compliments of Bubba. It was an ankle. But Eddy, a great broken field runner, never even got in the game. The Grand Trunk got Eddy.

The Grand Trunk was not another nickname for Bubba Smith. It was the railroad train that Notre Dame took from South Bend to East Lansing the day before the game. When the train arrived, Eddy slipped off the steps—hardly a tribute to his cutting and swerving—and fell onto an already injured shoulder. He was out. And sophomore Bob Gladieux was told in a doomsday Parseghian voice that he would start the biggest game of 1966 at left half.

As Notre Dame still lives with the tie, it has not forgotten these injuries and the alibis they strongly suggest. Still, as Michigan State coach Duffy Daugherty said, the Irish do not exactly substitute with girls from Sweet Briar. O'Brien and Gladieux could play for most anybody, he said. And even Parseghian admitted, "Considering everything, I thought they played super."

Indeed they did. They weren't in the game very long before they got Notre Dame untracked. On a marvelously executed play, O'Brien, a young man who requires two insulin shots a day for diabetes, shot a 34-yard spiral to Gladieux for a touchdown in the second quarter. Gladieux was cutting behind a defender right at the goalpost and never broke stride. Until that play, which narrowed the score to 10–7, Notre Dame was not even on the field.

The combination of Eddy's injury, which everyone tried to keep secret, and the mounting pressure of the game made Notre Dame an extraordinarily grim-looking group when the Irish arrived in East Lansing. Usually loose and smiling, the Irish marched into the Jack Tar Hotel beneath a marquee that said WELCOME TO THE BIG ONE with frozen, dedicated expressions that for some indescribable reason did not suggest confidence. Jim Seymour, the startling young pass catcher and friendly, outgoing personality of other Saturdays, was rigid, quiet, and uncommunicative. In the battle itself Seymour was double covered so well all day that he was scarcely noticeable. He had one decent chance at a pass but dropped it.

For a long while, it seemed the two teams would never calm down and look like the No. 1 and the No. 2 that they were supposed to be. Of the four passes Terry Hanratty tried before his shoulder met Bubba Smith, three were atrociously off target, one of them a routine screen that darted into the turf. The runners, meanwhile, went nowhere, primarily because of Bubba and George Webster of the Spartans, and of Kevin Hardy and Jim Lynch of the Irish. When Notre Dame failed to get off a punt because of a poor snapback, Michigan State countered with a fumble, a delay penalty, a clip, and interference on a fair catch. It looked like the big intramural game at Dartmouth.

Near the end of the first quarter, Michigan State finally got around to looking like a football team. Jimmy Raye, the Spartans' skittery quarterback, a junior out of South Carolina, a kid who wore a mustache, let sail a long pass to Gene Washington, a tall black kid from LaPorte, Texas. Washington took the pass over his shoulder and fell out of bounds at the Notre Dame 31, a 55-yard play. Nine ground plays later, Regis Cavendar plunged over and it was 7–0, Spartans.

Early in the second quarter, Michigan State scored again. Jimmy Raye slipped outside on a 30-yard keeper, and he hit Washington again for 17 yards. Two passes and a sweep failed, so Dick Kinney, the Spartans' barefoot place kicker, booted a field goal. It was 10–0, Spartans.

This had to stop, the Irish felt. So Johnny Ray, Notre Dame's defensive coach, gathered his troops around him on the sideline. "Forget everything I told you all week," he said. "You're not getting out of your tracks. Just start hitting people."

They did. And Michigan State didn't cross Notre Dame's 47-yard line the rest of the day.

It was late in the third quarter that Coley O'Brien revved up the tying drive. He hit passes over the middle and out in the flats, and short, stabbing runs by Larry Conjar, the fullback, Rocky Bleier, a halfback, and O'Brien himself moved the ball to Michigan State's 10-yard line. There, it was third and three—the kind of play that made Ara Parseghian chew his gum on the sideline like a rabbit. The call was a pass, but George Webster and Bubba Smith applied so much pressure on O'Brien he did well to scamper back

to the line of scrimmage. The Irish thus cashed in on a field goal by
Joe Azzaro.

By now, with a slow kind of subtlety, the look of the game had
changed. Michigan State, certainly the better team in the first half,
did not seem so sure anymore. Notre Dame had fought back. It was
all even. And now some freaky break would decide it, and surely
the wrong team would win. Whoever it was would be wrong. You
knew that.

Right away, the play that *should* have turned the game did in
fact happen. Jimmy Raye, escaping a rush, threw a wild pass—the
Spartans were gambling, unlike the Irish—and Notre Dame's safety,
Tom Schoen, stole it. He rambled back 31 yards with it to the
Spartans' 18-yard line. At this point, anyone who thought Ara
would try anything other than three line plunges and a winning
field goal should have been locked up in intensive care.

The Irish did run on first down. Larry Conjar made two yards.
Fine. Second down at the 16. But now what was this? Here was Dick
Haley, a substitute halfback, taking a pitchout and going wide to the
left and drifting backward. And here came Bubba Smith and another Spartan, Phil Hoag, rumbling through to smother him for an
eight-yard loss. So it was third down back on the 24. O'Brien failed
with a pass, then, and it was fourth down and Joe Azzaro's kick had
to travel 42 yards. It was wide to the right, and the swoon of relief in
Spartan Stadium made the structure lean a little.

Notre Dame had got the big break and blown it.

"That Haley play," said Parseghian. "That was just leakage. We
leaked a guy through, blew an assignment." He stared at the dressing room floor. "Damn."

Then he defended his decision to run out the clock, and lob-
bied for the national championship. "When you go into a game
Number One and you only get tied, you can't lose it," he said.

Duffy Daugherty had a different idea. He said Michigan State
ought to be No. 1 and he would give Notre Dame 1-A.

Later on, a third opinion came from Bear Bryant, whose splendid Alabama team wound up the season 11-0, the only unblem-
ished squad in the country.

"I have a lot of seniors on this team," Bear said. "Most of 'em are
too little to play pro ball. They'll be going into business or into the
service. I hope I've taught 'em not to play for a tie."

And it was only a few days later that Bear had a second
thought.

Notre Dame had won most of the polls, so Bear said:

"Ara must have done the right thing, playin' for that old tie. All I've got is the best football team in the country, but he's got Number One."

Lights, Camera, Football!

IT WAS, OF COURSE, TOO HOLLYWOOD FOR BELIEF. THAT UCLA'S glamorous quarterback, Gary Beban, and USC's glamorous half-back, O. J. Simpson, could emerge in the same city, in the same conference, as the best players of 1967, was improbable enough. That they could also wind up battling for the national championship, the Rose Bowl bid, and the Heisman Trophy, all on one unbearable Saturday afternoon, was strictly from the studio lots.

The event belonged on an MGM sound stage with everybody singing *Buckle Down, John Heisman.*

But there it was that Saturday, the Trojans against the Bruins before 93,000 in the Los Angeles Memorial Coliseum and millions more on ABC-TV's national telecast—a game played for more trophies, titles, and prestige than any single college contest ever.

Of course, the game would have been immense, dramatic, historical, all of that, if it had matched total strangers under those same conditions. And it was equally true that almost every USC-UCLA game is worthwhile. But to bring two such dedicated enemies, two universities so close in proximity (10 miles) yet galaxies apart in image and attitude, down to so desperate an hour made the attraction all the more dazzling.

Consider first the ironies and contrasts of the campuses. Here sat UCLA, a sprawling state institution with an enrollment of 29,000 students of varying backgrounds, colors, politics, and ideals, and with generous portions of everything from hippies to Harlows, located right where, according to USC, it does not belong. UCLA is on a lovely rise called Westwood, just beneath the elegant neighborhood of Bel Air, a five-minute Mercedes ride from the dining, drinking, and shopping splendors of Beverly Hills.

And over there sat USC, older by far, the smug, conservative, private school, with all of its scrubbed, predominantly white, Protestant, slow-smiling, basically upper-middle-class types. Just look where it is, laughs UCLA — practically in the middle of Watts, for God's sake. Southern Cal's campus is in fact flanked by rows of condemned paint stores, auto parts companies, and junk shops, and only a few moments from the disenchantment of downtown L.A.

To the USC man, UCLA would never represent more than it was in its beginning, a preparatory facility for teachers, a school unhappily named Los Angeles State Normal in its infancy, a school that turned to basketball when it couldn't hack it at football, a school that deserves such card tricks as "FUCLA," the poor school, the school that gave us Tokyo Rose.

At the same time, UCLA finds it difficult to be troubled by anything those Wasps at USC think. UCLA is so vast that half of the campus could protest the world's wrongdoings and the other half wouldn't know it.

Long before Gary Beban and O. J. Simpson, there were sports heroes on both campuses, particularly at USC. In the 1920s and 1930s, USC was turning out such immortals as Morley Drury, Erny Pinckert, Orv Mohler, Gus Shaver, Johnny Baker, Cotton Warburton, Harry "Blackjack" Smith, Grenny Lansdell, Ambrose Schindler, and Antelope Al Krueger. In the meantime, UCLA produced Kenny Washington and Jackie Robinson — yep, he was a football star first — and then Bob Waterfield in the 1940s. But it wasn't until Red Sanders turned the Bruins into a national power in the 1950s that the Trojans had to take UCLA seriously, every season.

As for the coaches in this year's Game of the Century, USC's John McKay and UCLA's Tommy Prothro, they were as different as the campuses they represented.

Prothro was bigger, taller, older, and had been a head coach five years longer than McKay. He was more secretive. McKay was generally open and friendly, a wisecrack artist in his profession. It was easy to imagine Prothro as a rancher. It was just as easy to imagine McKay, a careful dresser who leaned toward sun-bleached slacks, as a golf pro. Among their colleagues, Prothro most closely resembled Alabama's Bear Bryant in drawl, manner, and attitude. Quick, talkative, and well organized in the contemporary, gray-flannel way, McKay was similar to Texas's Darrell Royal.

There was an equally distinct difference between the two players who had brought their teams to high national ranking—the halfback, Simpson, who rolled right over you, and the quarterback, Beban, who rolled around you.

For the seven and a half games of the season that Orenthal James Simpson had been whole, he had seemed to possess the finest combination of speed and power within the memory of any pro scout. He rushed for 1,238 yards in that span, and until his mishap in the Oregon game—a sprained instep that knocked him off his feet and onto crutches—he was a good bet to break the NCAA yardage record (which he would, indeed, break a year later). Not only did he crash repeatedly into stacked defenses and still wedge his way out and slice and dart for yardage, he caught passes and threw them at the least expected moments.

Coaches, scouts, and writers tried to figure out all season who it was Simpson's running style reminded them of. He exhibited the raw burst of speed that Mel Renfro had in college and some of the deceptive moves of Gale Sayers. But he also slammed in there and broke tackles like Jim Brown. Given daylight, he slid through with the nifty balance of Jon Arnett.

Gary Beban, the UCLA answer to Orange Juice, was one of those athletes who did things with infuriating ease. He passed with classic form, and he ran gracefully, almost in slow motion except that he managed to turn the corners and slide through. When his passes were in the air, the ball somehow looked longer, and the spiral was perfect, as if Beban had figured out exactly how many rotations it should make. His ball handling was superb, his faking even better. But above everything else, Beban had poise.

Prothro often said that Beban could beat you with a run, pass, fake, or call, and that his ability to change plays at the scrimmage line was perhaps his finest asset. A familiar sight for three seasons was Beban behind the center, shifting his backs, then checking, raising his head to survey the defense and shouting another play that unfolded perfectly. In the clutch.

Since early in the season when USC and UCLA attained their top-level rankings in the national polls, trying to rate their strengths and deficiencies had been a parlor game. You gave USC a point for offense, UCLA a point for defense. You gave USC strength, but UCLA got quickness. USC had a better blocking line, but UCLA had a better pursuing defense. UCLA had the best passing, but USC had the best receiving. The kicking was even, the coaching was even, and there was no home-field advantage.

So who would win? A day before the game, a man who should be able to judge the situation well, John McKay himself, went to a blackboard and evaluated the two teams, player by player. He had a point grading system for this, and when he was through adding point by point, he totaled the figures for each team. Just like in the Hollywood script, they came out exactly equal. When that happened, McKay stepped back from the blackboard and made the least newsworthy comment of the most exciting football season Los Angeles had ever known:

"It's going to be a helluva game," he said.

In the end, the difference was that this guy with a name like a Russian poet, Zenon Andrusyshyn, couldn't place-kick the ball over this other guy with a name like the president of the Van Nuys Jaycees—Bill Hayhoe. Andrusyshyn would try to side-boot a field goal or extra point for UCLA, and Hayhoe, who happened to be 6'8", would rise up. The ball would go splat, plink, or karang. The last time Hayhoe did it, he tipped the leather just enough to make the Bruins fail on a precious conversion, and USC got away with a 21–20 victory in a spectacle that will be remembered for ages, or at least as long as German-born, Ukrainian, Canadian-bred soccer-style kickers play the game.

Of course, it was not exactly fair to insinuate that Zenon Andrusyshyn, the German-Ukrainian-Canadian, was the goat of the whole desperate afternoon. Though only a sophomore, he was a splendid kicker who boomed punts into the California heavens all day, and it appeared that if the ball were given time to rise, he was capable of place kicking one more than 60 yards. Rather, it was more accurate to give credit to USC's John McKay for one of those little coaching touches that sometimes supplies a subtle edge. This time it proved to be a subtle edge that gave McKay the most important game of his life.

"We knew he kicked it low, so we just put the tallest guy we had in there on defense," said McKay later, in what may have been the happiest dressing room since showers were invented. "We told the kids it wasn't so important that they bust through and make him rush the kicks as it was just getting to the scrimmage line and raising their arms high."

In his wry, twinkling way, McKay then lit a cigar and said, "I call that brilliant coaching."

Although neither O.J. nor Beban was 100 percent perfect physically, both were superb in clutch after clutch. While he practically had to crawl to the sideline no less than five times to regain his breath because of his injured ribs, Beban whirled the Bruins to three touchdowns, passing for more than 300 yards, giving his team a 7–0 lead in the first quarter, a 14–14 tie in the third, and a 20–14 lead in the fourth.

Meanwhile, Simpson, his right foot throbbing inside a shoe with a special sponge cover, wearily hobbled away from piles of brutal tacklers and eventually managed to race for a total of 177 yards, including the touchdowns that put the Trojans ahead 14–7 and finally 21–20.

Had the Heisman Trophy award, therefore, really been decided by a couple of young men named Zenon Andrusyshyn and Bill Hayhoe? As Jim Murray of the *Los Angeles Times* said, "They should send the Heisman out here with two straws."

For almost the first 20 minutes it looked as if UCLA was the only team in the coliseum. The Bruins were a lot quicker in the line, niftier in execution, more confident in their game plan, and more inventive in their attack. Beban had thrown the first of 16 completions to his left end, Dave Nuttall, who would catch seven, and he had gotten 11 big yards on a keeper, and he had led the interference for Greg Jones's blasting 12-yard touchdown run, which put UCLA out front. At the same time, the Trojans had not been able to move. In five possessions they had not scratched out a first down. On his first 10 carries, even behind an occasional and surprising eight-man line that McKay thought would unsettle Prothro, O. J. Simpson had gained only 11 measly yards. He had come no closer to breaking clear than Andy Williams, who was there to sing at halftime.

The situation looked normal; Prothro had McKay's number, just as everyone had been saying at the Daisy, the Factory, La Scala, and Stefanino's before diverting conversation back to who got which part in what TV series. It was normal except for one thing: USC did not have any yards or first downs, but it had seven points.

On the last play of the first quarter, just as it looked like Beban was cranking up the Bruins again, the UCLA quarterback threw a pass at midfield into the wide left flat. The receiver was open, as Bruin receivers were all day, but the ball hung. It may have hung because Beban's side, injured in the Washington game the previous week, prevented him from slinging the ball hard when he had to. It may have hung because he misjudged the risk of an interception. Whatever the reason, USC's Pat Cashman saw it coming. He darted in front of Greg Jones, leaped, and took the ball with nothing but 55 yards of beautiful, unpopulated coliseum turf before him.

While Pat Cashman's interception perked up the USC rooters—

hundreds of whom, like UCLA's, had been in the stands since dawn to get good seats—it did not seem at the time to be all that important; it might hold down the score, maybe. Sure enough, after a wiggly, 42-yard punt return by UCLA's Mark Gustafson, the Bruins were quickly threatening again, with a first down on the 15.

But now a series of strange things happened that changed the game for the rest of the day. In three plays the Bruins got nowhere, and on the third one Beban got the first of the deadly blows in the ribs—this one courtesy of Pat Cashman—that would send him writhing toward the sideline. Andrusyshyn came in and missed a field goal from the 20. The kick was not one of those molested by Bill Hayhoe; Zenon simply side-winded it off to the left. And on USC's first play from its own 20, the game suddenly had another offensive team. Earl "the Pearl" McCullouch started it by streaking down the sideline off a daring reverse for 52 yards. McCullouch then caught a 13-yard pass. And now Simpson was warmed up. From 13 yards out, O.J. burst over guard for the touchdown—one that was especially vital, for it proved to the USC offense that it could move the ball.

Still, if UCLA was impressed it did not act it. The Bruins took the kickoff amid the most noise since D-day, and Beban promptly threw a 48-yard pass to Nuttall. It was first down on the Trojan 15 again. But, just like the time before, USC's defense got riled. Beban was smacked by everybody but Southern California President Norman Topping, one of nine losses he would suffer, and he had to retreat to the bench again. In came Andrusyshyn for the first of two field-goal tries that Bill Hayhoe would block.

As had been said so many times about Beban, he learned from mistakes. He could hardly wait for the second half to start to take advantage of Pat Cashman, who had intercepted him and who had buried his red USC headgear into Beban's lung. With only two minutes gone in the third quarter, Beban laid a perfect 47-yard pass into the hands of halfback George Farmer for the tying touchdown.

"Cashman had been waiting for another of those flat passes, so we sent Farmer straight down, right past him," said Gary afterward. "It balanced out. Cashman's interception was really responsible for our second touchdown." Between this score and the one that put UCLA ahead early in the fourth quarter, Prothro's team blew another excellent opportunity. The combination of a poor punt by USC's Rikki Aldridge, who redeemed himself for this and all other misdeeds of a lifetime by ultimately kicking the game-winning conversion, and a Beban pass put UCLA on the Trojan 17. It was there that Hayhoe, a junior from Van Nuys who weighed 254 along with his 6'8", lumbered through to drop Beban for a whopping loss, and two plays later he blocked another field-goal attempt by the Ukrainian.

"Those things somehow weren't as discouraging then as they are now," said Beban later as he wandered around in the USC locker room, sipping a canned Coke, smiling, and congratulating the Trojans. "We knew we would score again."

They did. Beban hit four passes in a brisk seven-play drive covering 65 yards, the last one going to Nuttall for 20 yards and the touchdown that made it 20–14 with only 11 minutes remaining. Andrusyshyn missed the point because Hayhoe had gotten a finger on it, and while it occurred to everybody in the Western world that this could be a pretty unfortunate point to miss, UCLA still looked like the better team. The Trojans had not seriously threatened. Junior Steve Sogge had given way to senior Toby Page at quarterback, and it was no Los Angeles secret that John McKay's wife, Corky, was a better passer than Page. Nor had O.J. really busted loose.

But now it was time for Simpson to get back in the Heisman derby, thanks to a thing called 23-Blast. UCLA's tough tacklers had been kindly helping O.J. back up on his feet all day, a fine sporting gesture with the subtle design of keeping Simpson from resting. And at last it was time for O.J. to knock them down. And out.

It was third down at his own 36 when Toby Page saw UCLA's linebacker move out, anticipating the play Page had called in the huddle. Page checked signals and called another play at the line. It was 23-Blast. As it unfolded, it looked like a five-yard gain. Guard Steve Lehmer and tackle Mike Taylor cleared O.J. through the hole. Then Simpson veered out toward the left sideline. Oh, well, a 15-yard gain and a first down. But end Ron Drake screened off UCLA's halfback, and the safety sucked over, and, hey, what's this? O.J. angled back to the middle, to his right, and a great glob of daylight became visible. And then he was running like the 9.4 sprinter he is, despite that sore foot and that funny shoe, and there was not anybody down there for the rest of the 64 yards who was about to catch him.

Of the remarkable 1,415 yards Simpson gained that season, those 64 were the most impressive of all, for they came after two hours of the toughest punishment he had endured—and they stretched all the way to No. 1.

About an hour and a half after the game, down in the USC

dressing room, which had finally emptied and grown as quiet as it had been before the kickoff, a brief scene was enacted that served as a fitting epilogue. Dressed now, blazers on, hair combed, refreshed, Gary Beban and O. J. Simpson met, looking like two young men anticipating a fraternity council meeting.

"Gary, you're the greatest," said O.J. "It's too bad one of us had to lose."

"O.J., you're the best," said Beban. "Go get 'em in the Rose Bowl."

O.J. grinned. Presently, he ambled down the hall, through a door, and up a walkway to an exit gate where clusters of USC fans were still gathered. It was roughly, oh, about 64 yards.

Madness in the Ozarks

ALL WEEK LONG IN TEXAS THE PEOPLE HAD SAID THAT HOGS AIN'T nuthin' but groceries, and all week long in Arkansas the people had said that King Kong, meaning Texas' mighty No. 1 football team, ain't nuthin' but a big old monkey. So everybody was in the proper spirit for the President's Game of the Decade and, more important where Texans and Razorbacks were concerned, *their* game of a lifetime. As one fellow modestly put it early in the week, "If the damn game don't hurry up and get here, I'm gone keel myself."

Throughout 100 years of the sport, there had never been a situation quite like it. The fates had dictated that in this very last regular season game of 1969—of a whole century, in fact—two brilliant teams were coming together that were not only undefeated and untied but also were rated No. 1 and No. 2 in the national polls. And if this wasn't enough to drive everyone mad, then President Richard Nixon, an old Whittier College tackle who had never lost his fondness for the game, chose to add the final touch that would.

Nixon announced a week ahead of time that he would attend

the contest down in that thundering zoo of Fayetteville, Arkansas, down in that creaking old stadium that would hold only 44,000 if everybody stood on one foot and didn't bring along their pet pigs in their little red sweaters. And not only was the President going to be in the stadium, he was going to bring along a special plaque that he would present to the winning team, either Darrell Royal's Long-horns or Frank Broyles's Razorbacks, as the national champion that wound up football's first 100 years.

It would be a hellacious football game, to be sure, but for Fayetteville, Arkansas, it would merely be the climax of a week-long metamorphosis—from the nation's No. 2 chicken producer to its sports capital. But the kickoff would come none too soon, for the town's economy was just about to suffer badly.

"I was tryin' to sell a suit today," the manager of a men's store said on Wednesday, "and that feller and me started talkin' about the game, and he walked out and didn't buy a thing."

The poor man stared out of his display window, which was all decorated with the red and white crepe paper of Arkansas, and said, "What's happenin' is, you wake up in the mornin' and your first thought is 'how many days to go?'"

The mania grew like a strawberry rash. Hog fever, they called it. Its symbol was Arkansas' mascot, a rather unhandsome razor-back. Poster likenesses with various exhortations to Hog supremacy appeared in most of Fayetteville's store fronts. Then a large sign went up at the First Baptist Church: ATTENTION DARRELL ROYAL—DO NOT CAST YOUR STEERS BEFORE THE SWINE.

Royal heard about it in Austin and said, "I thought God was neutral?"

"He ought to know this is the Lord's home state," replied Andrew Hall, the First Baptist pastor. "Whoever heard of a Garden of Eden in *Texas?*"

This was the same pastor who had received national attention four years earlier by posting a sign on his church before another big Texas-Arkansas game, a sign that said: FOOTBALL IS ONLY A GAME. SPIRITUAL THINGS ARE ETERNAL. NEVERTHELESS, BEAT TEXAS!

By midweek local newspapers were layers of cartoon ads showing galloping Hogs and moribund Texas Steers. "May the Steers rest in peace with our perpetual care plan. Lots $80 and up. Beat Texas. Forest Park Cemetery," said one notice.

It was extremely difficult at this point to find anyone in the town of 30,000 who did not wear a GO HOGS button of some kind, even elderly ladies and farmers in overalls.

To switch on the radio in one's hotel room or rented car was to hear practically the only song played, a lively Country-Western tune by a group called Cecil Profet and the Buffaloes. Its title: *Short Squashed Texan.* Its refrain:

I'm a short squashed Texan,
I had the Number One crown.
Now people look and say,
That big red pig, he put you down.

To lift the phone was to be greeted in the following manner:
"Beat Texas. Long distance."
"Beat Texas. Reservations desk."
"Beat Texas. First Baptist Church."
"Beat Texas. Holiday Inn."
Compounding the madness, of course, was the President's visit, which would mark the first time in history that a commander in chief had ever been anywhere near Fayetteville.

"I've never seen such tension in the air," said a waitress. "Imagine, almost anyone I wait on could be a secret service man. I just hope I get frisked."

Meanwhile, in Austin one heard that things had been slightly more sophisticated but nonetheless frantic. There had been the usual banners draped across campus buildings, little gems of wisdom which said: STEERS SNOW HOGS AND SKI NO. 1, and HOGS AIN'T NUTHIN' BUT GROCERIES, and BEAT NOTRE DAME (the winner would get to play the Fighting Irish in the Cotton Bowl), and WE'LL HAVE HOG MEAT WITH WORSTERSPEYRER SAUCE, a horrendous pun taking its meaning from two fine Texas players, Steve Worster, a fullback, and Cotton Speyrer, a split end.

Only 5,000 seats were allotted to the University of Texas, which had 40,000 students, but of this number most of the seats went to loyal alumni. There were actually only 312 seats for students wearing the burnt orange.

"It's just as well I'm not going," said a Texas coed. "Arkansas is a hicky place—all they do is sell jelly by the side of the road."

Instant traffic jams were already developing around the Arkansas campus and stadium on Friday afternoon. Students were just driving, going nowhere, honking and hollering, waving beer cans and Confederate flags, their roadsters painted red and white, their hands uplifted in the "V" sign.

I was driving Darrell back to his motel after the Friday workout, and he looked around at all of the Razorback revelry as we moved along, and he started working up his mad for the game; putting on his "game face," as he liked to call it. "Only angry people win football games," he had often said. And he believed that if *he* got angry every Saturday, his team would get angry.

"To hell with Arkansas," he said. "What the heck does this place have? A low per-capita income and pig farmers. . . ." Royal owned resort property in Arkansas and had a number of close friends there, including Frank Broyles, and he liked to go there to spend a week playing golf, but he chose not to think about any of that just now. There was a game to play, a great big fantastic game that had grown into what Duffy Daugherty once said of a big game: "It's not a matter of life and death. It's more important than that."

"Look at that," Darrell said, pointing to a carload of Arkansas fans giving the "V" sign. "They don't know that means peace. A lot of things haven't gotten up here yet."

"This whole week has been fairly colorful," he was told.

"To hell with Arkansas," he said.

It was Texas, trapped in the din and wild speckled red of that stadium, which, as you might guess, almost went to blazes.

For three quarters Arkansas did everything right and Texas did everything wrong. The Razorbacks had a slender, cool quarterback named Bill Montgomery (who came from Texas) and he could pass and run with the best in the country. And what he did was pass and run the Longhorns into a state of utter shock. While a furious Arkansas defense swarmed on Royal's team to cause four fumbles and two interceptions—and create the loudest explosions in the history of Arkansas—Montgomery and his roommate end, Chuck Dicus, combined to build a 14-point lead, which looked like the safest place for any Razorback to be since Orval Faubus rode in a motorcade.

While Texas hadn't been able to drive past Arkansas' 30-yard line, Bill Montgomery, with his father all decked out in red and swallowing tranquilizers in the stands, hurled a 21-yard pass to set up a touchdown in the first quarter, and then hurled a 29-yard touchdown pass to Dicus in the third quarter and it was 14–0.

Texas had known what it was like to trail before, however. It had trailed an equally bitter foe, Oklahoma, by 14 points earlier in the season, and James Street, the Longhorns' miracle-making quarterback who had never lost a game, had managed to bring his team back. "Mr. Excalibur," the fans called Street, whose teammates called him Slick because of his good looks, flashy clothes, and ball-handling. Slick had won 18 straight games for Texas since he had become the quarterback in the third week of his junior season, and he had a way of revving up the team with his jabbering confidence.

His teammates said that in moments of crisis Street would look everyone in the eye in the huddles and say things like "Guts up time . . . Gotta go . . . Gotta get 'em . . . No fumblin' . . . Everbody get his man . . . Suck it up, suck it up . . . Gotta go . . . We're the best. . . ." And he would keep it up until somebody like big Bob McKay, the all-America tackle, would say, "Aw, James, shut up and call the play."

Somehow, some way, in the midst of all of that chaos in the Ozarks, with the season-long battle for No. 1 now shrunk down to the last 15 minutes of the very last game, James Street would find a way for Texas, and pull out a glorious 15–14 victory on a day that would be remembered forever.

Upstairs in the world's most crowded little press box where the President had moved at halftime to chat on national television with ABC's announcers, Chris Schenkel and Bud Wilkinson, a most miserable man stood holding hands, for luck, with a pretty young girl.

He was Jones Ramsey, the good-natured Texas publicity man, and she was Barbara Specht, a lovely blond coed from Texas Tech who had reigned all season as the Centennial Queen of College Football.

Barbara looked as worried and grim as Ramsey. "I hate to be partial," she said. "But after all, I am a Texan. This game just means so much to everybody, I can't stand it."

Ramsey managed a smile and said, "I'll tell you. I'm a coward and I believe in all kinds of jinxes, but maybe James Street doesn't. We still got time."

Along about now, down there at the Arkansas 42-yard line, James Street was drifting back to try a pass. Suddenly, he began to run. He ran through the line, cut to the left, then back to his right, and he was rolling through the Razorbacks' secondary, his white uniform with the burnt orange trim a blur against the bright green Astroturf. Now he was carving an angle across the field, and then turning toward the Arkansas goal—either that, or the presidential helicopter moored on a practice field just outside the end zone. In any case, Street was gone, and nobody was about to catch him. It was the first daylight Texas had seen all afternoon, and Street made the most of it.

Quickly, then, Street lined up his team for an unconventional two-point try after the touchdown. He took the snap, darted to his left, then cut inside and wiggled through a cluster of red jerseys, and flopped over the goal. James Street had personally got Texas eight points. It was 14–8, and as suddenly as anything else, this was the old Texas-Arkansas type of game that everyone knew and loved.

"I was gonna throw a hook," James explained later. "But their linebacker had my eyes fogged. I couldn't see any receivers, so I decided to run. Sure glad."

Although Street's two dazzling plays had certainly put Texas back in the ball game—and Texas' hopes began to glimmer—Arkansas wasn't finished. Bill Montgomery stormed the Razorbacks right back down the field, 73 gnawing yards, to Texas' seven-yard line. The crowd was no more delirious than any normal audience for Willie Nelson. It gave off long choruses of Whoooooo, Pig, Soooooey, the Arkansas yell.

If Arkansas did the right thing now, it was all over. You knew that. It was third down, only 10 minutes to play. Surely the Razorbacks would run into the line, shoving into position for a field goal that would make the score 17–8, a margin too great, no doubt, for the Longhorns to overcome. But Arkansas didn't do that. Weirdly, the call to Montgomery from Arkansas' offensive coach Don Breaux, calling all the plays from a booth upstairs, was a flat pass. And when Texas got a hard rush on Montgomery, he threw late for Chuck Dicus, and Texas' Danny Lester spurted in front of the end to intercept in the end zone. Texas was still alive.

The Longhorns moved the ball but couldn't score on that drive because of a *fifth* fumble, but when they got the ball again 74 yards away from the Arkansas goal and only six minutes left, James Street and Darrell Royal—the whole world, in fact—knew that this would have to be it.

In the press box the partisan announcer from Arkansas said over his P.A. to the writers, "Fellers, if I keep gettin' these yardages and names wrong on the play-by-play, it's just because I'm more nervous than I was on my weddin' day. This shootout, or whatever you want to call it, has made me a wreck."

On the first three plays of the drive Steve Worster, who somehow tore out 94 yards rushing during the day, made six steps, and Ted Koy made one. A fourth down had come up, with three yards needed for new life, and the ball was on Texas' own 43-yard line. Less than five minutes were left. If Texas punted, it might never see the ball again. It had to gamble.

The Longhorns called time-out and Street went to the sideline to confer with Darrell Royal.

"Can you get it on the keep?" asked Royal.

"Yeah," said Street.

"Is Steve tired?" the coach wondered.

"Nobody's tired," said James.

Royal looked up at the scoreboard clock and the down and distance.

James said, "*They're* gettin' tired, Coach. I think we can option 'em."

"Hit Peschel deep," said Royal.

"Huh?" said Street.

"Tight end deep," Royal said.

Street started onto the field, stopped, and came back.

"Are you sure you want to throw, Coach?" he said.

Royal nodded and waved him onto the field, and turned and walked away.

When Street got to the huddle and started jabbering about how this might be Texas' last play of the season, and then called the pass play, saying he thought they could surprise Arkansas with a long bomb to the tight end, Bob McKay shrieked.

"Geeaad, damn, James. You cain't *throw* it that far," he said.

"Gimme some time and I'll get it there," said Street. "Randy," he added, looking his end in the eye, "this is it."

Street tossed the 44-yard spiral perfectly to Randy Peschel, who took the ball in full stride over his shoulder and collapsed out of bounds on Arkansas' 13-yard line. And in two piercing ground plays Texas' Jim Bertelsen barged into the end zone, and then Happy Feller place-kicked the extra point that made it 15–14.

"In a case like that," said Darrell Royal of the desperate pass that Street gambled with, "there's no logic. You don't know what to call. You just suck it up and pick a number. And it doesn't hurt to have James Street playing for you."

Thus, a team had labored all day under more pressure than any No. 1 team ever had, and then with time running out, on alien ground, with few friends about, with a whole century closing in, that team had somehow survived.

James Street made no all-America teams that season, but later on that afternoon in the locker room he shook hands with a President of the United States.

The Cream Gravy Game

IN THE LAND OF THE PICKUP TRUCK AND CREAM GRAVY FOR BREAK-fast, down where the wind can blow through the walls of a diner and into the grieving lyrics of a country song on the jukebox—down there in dirt-kicking Big Eight territory—they played a football game on Thanksgiving Day 1971 that was mainly for the quarter-backs on the field and the self-styled intellectuals everywhere. The spectacle itself was for everybody, for all of those who had been waiting weeks and weeks for Nebraska and Oklahoma to get it on, for all those guys with big stomachs and bigger Stetsons, their faces cracked and burned and aged by the harsh land, and for all of the luscious coeds who danced through the doors of bars near the campus drinking daiquiris out of paper cups, their golden hair flowing down to their waists. But the game of chess that was played by the athletes in the Sooners' chaotic stadium, that was strictly for the cerebral types who will keep playing it into the ages and wondering whether it was the greatest collegiate football battle ever. Under the agonizing conditions that existed, it well may have been.

Quality. That's what the game had more of than anything else. There had been scads of Poll Bowls in the past—games played in brimming-over stadiums for life, limb, and the right to put a "WE'RE NO. 1" bumper sticker on the old camper, but it is impossible to stir the pages of history and find a game in which both teams per-formed so reputably, so courageously, and for so long, throughout a single afternoon.

These were a couple of teams that had demolished every oppo-nent, and each looked unbeatable. Nebraska was the complete team with a balanced attack of rushing and passing and an iron defense. A team of Johnny Rodgers, Jerry Tagge, Jeff Kinney, Rich Glover, Willie Harper, Larry Jacobsen. Oklahoma was all offense, most of it gushing out of its fashionable Wishbone-T—a team of Jack Mildren, Greg Pruitt, Joe Wylie, Jon Harrison.

Nebraska, a muscled-up bully, reflected the personality of its coach, Bob Devaney. It liked to probe and hammer, and hold that line. Oklahoma only wanted the football so it could score on you again. Flashy and swift, Coach Chuck Fairbanks' team was convinced it could simply outpoint you.

By the time they came up to the big game, the records of the two teams caused double-takes and blinking and forehead smoting. Nebraska was averaging 35 points a game, gaining 441 yards a game, and allowing only 6.4 points a game—tops in the U.S. Meanwhile, Oklahoma was averaging 45 points a game, 563 yards a game on offense, and some of the teams the Sooners had destroyed were Texas, USC, and Colorado, which were among the nation's best. The margins by which both were beating opponents were enough to frighten Russia.

NEBRASKA (10-0)	OKLAHOMA (9-0)
34 Oregon 7	30 SMU 0
35 Minnesota 7	55 Pitt 29
34 Texas A&M 7	33 USC 20
42 Utah State 6	48 Texas 27
56 Missouri 0	45 Colorado 17
55 Kansas 0	75 Kansas State 28
41 Oklahoma State 13	43 Iowa State 12
31 Colorado 7	20 Missouri 3
37 Iowa State 0	56 Kansas 10
44 Kansas State 17	

Nebraska thought of itself as a team without stars but stars had emerged. Jerry Tagge, the quarterback, was a star. He was big, strong, smart. He could throw, run, read defenses, lead. Once during the season his tough running back, Jeff Kinney, had said in the huddle, "I'm tired, Tag." Tagge had said, "Shut up. I'll tell you when you're tired."

And then there was Johnny Rodgers, the hummingbird of a halfback and flanker who could beat you catching, running, returning punts, or simply by going in motion. He was a game-breaker, and in Rodgers the Cornhuskers had a quick threat to counterbalance Oklahoma's speed.

Oklahoma's heroes were just as glittering. Jack Mildren was the equal of Tagge, but an even better runner. He was in the process of becoming the first quarterback to gain over 1,000 yards rushing that anyone could remember—but he could also throw. And in Greg Pruitt, the halfback, he had the fleetest accomplice in the land.

Pruitt, usually by taking a wide pitchout from Mildren off the Wishbone's triple option, had already gained 1,423 yards. For Oklahoma, speed was everywhere. Joe Wylie and Roy Bell in the backfield were almost as fast, and so was Jon Harrison, the flanker who could go get the ball wherever Mildren threw it.

Everyone who had played both teams during the season was besieged to make a comparison, but Colorado's assistant athletic director, Fred Casotti, said it the best.

"It depends on how you want to die," said Casotti. "Oklahoma kills you quick, like a dagger in the heart. Nebraska slowly gives you cancer."

This was how it was when the whole world converged on Norman, Oklahoma, that week. National TV. Every sportswriter who could get away from a turkey dinner, from Malibu to Boston. So many pro scouts it looked like an NFL bonus march. And the 63,385 lucky mortals able to get tickets and shove into the Oklahoma stadium.

It was a crazy week in which the Eastern press discovered road houses and rhythm pickers, truck stops and chicken fried steak, an assortment of pubs occupied by cowboys and debutantes, afternoons spent guzzling beer and listening to Charlie Pride and Tammy Wynette on the jukeboxes, listening to how the game was going to be won and lost, days and nights filled with waiting for the kickoff, hearing "dear old Nebraska U." and "Boomer Sooner" ringing across the prairies, days devoted to feeling young again and trying to remember if the coeds were always this beautiful and handled their booze so well.

In essence, what won the game for Nebraska was a pearl of a punt return in the game's first three and a half minutes. Everything else ultimately balanced out, even the precious few mistakes—Oklahoma's three fumbles against Nebraska's one, plus a costly Nebraska offsides, the only penalty in the game.

There was this unending fury of offense from both teams that more or less overwhelmed the defenses, maniacal though they were. But that is how it is with modern college football. You can't take away every weapon. Nebraska and Oklahoma stopped the things they feared most, but in so doing they gave up practically everything else.

From the Oklahoma Wishbone, the Cornhuskers took away the wide pitch to Greg Pruitt, but they gave up Jack Mildren's keepers, Leon Crosswhite's fullback jabs into the middle, and most of all Mildren's passes to Jon Harrison.

To stop Pruitt, Nebraska was forced to cover Harrison one on one, which couldn't be done. He caught four big passes, two of them for shocking touchdowns, as Mildren drilled the ball perfectly and calmly.

From Nebraska's crushing I-Spread and I-Slot attack, Oklahoma took away the passing game, smothering Johnny Rodgers with double and triple coverage, rushing Jerry Tagge relentlessly. But the Sooners had to give up the power running, and that was where Jeff Kinney became an immortal.

So the two teams traded touchdowns evenly from scrimmage, four for four, and Oklahoma added a field goal that kept looking like it might be the real difference. But always there lingered the one thing they had not traded—that sudden, shocking punt return by Johnny Rodgers.

It was one of those insanely thrilling plays in which an athlete, seized by the moment—perhaps even by history—twisted, whirled, slipped, held his balance, spun, darted, curved, and fled all the way to the goal line. Rodgers went 72 yards for that touchdown, the one that grows larger and larger in the minds of all. And afterward, back on the Nebraska bench, Johnny did what most everybody in Norman, Oklahoma, probably felt like doing. He threw up. From exhaustion.

Oklahoma's Joe Wylie had punted the ball high and far, and the Sooners' coverage was down fast, led by Greg Pruitt. It looked as if Rodgers should have signaled for a fair catch, he was so surrounded. But it never entered his mind. It seldom did.

And then, Heavens to Lincoln, if Rodgers didn't catch the ball with Pruitt staring him in the face guard. Pruitt hit him, but not solidly enough. The blow spun Rodgers around at his own 30-yard line, where he planted his left hand on the Tartan Turf to keep from falling. Strangely, Pruitt's lick only turned Rodgers away from the grasp of another lunging Sooner, Ken Jones. Luck? Maybe.

With that, Rodgers set sail to his right, and just as quickly he darted back to the left, seeing some daylight through a whole cluster of wine-colored Oklahoma jerseys. He wiggled, feinted, and turned it on. He was away from the flow of coverage, heading for the left sideline. Up ahead, his friend Joe Blahak inherited the chore of screening off the last man with a chance to make the tackle, the punter, Joe Wylie.

Wylie never had a real chance, although Rodgers was obviously tiring and Wylie was fast. As the stadium thundered and screeched, Blahak bumped Wylie just enough, and from there on Rodgers could have crawled, retching every inch, and still scored.

What the punt return accomplished was monumental to the Nebraska cause. It gave the Cornhuskers an 11-point lead *twice* during the game, at 14–3 in the second quarter and 28–17 late in the third quarter. It forced Oklahoma to struggle uphill all the way.

And when Oklahoma's marvelous Jack Mildren overcame it twice, that bit of genius by Johnny Rodgers always had Nebraska's own brilliant quarterback, Jerry Tagge, in a position to recapture the lead (or the game) with a single drive. Which Tagge coolly did when the scoreboard clock dictated that it was time, finally, and again, for the game to be won or lost by the Nebraska offense.

Upstairs in the press quarters, there were journalists already calling it the greatest game ever played, and it wasn't even over. Up there also, the sports information directors of the two schools, Nebraska's Don Bryant and Oklahoma's Johnny Keith, had been watching it together, trying to joke, trying to enjoy it, trying not to act *that* involved.

"We gave 'em a show, didn't we, Hoss?" said Keith. "Whatever happens now, they'll all know they been to a county fair."

Bryant, who enjoys his nickname of the Fat Fox, said, "I think we wrote 'em a pretty good script."

There were just seven minutes left to play now. Jack Mildren had done all he could. He had dashed for two touchdowns and passed for two more. He had Wishboned 467 yards against the best defense in the land. And he had given his Sooners a 31–28 lead in a game that had every right to be running out of heroics.

But Nebraska still had Jerry Tagge and Johnny Rodgers and Jeff Kinney, and the Nebraska offense was going to keep on coming like the disciplined Prussian army it resembled under Bob Devaney.

Devaney was a calm and likable man and a complete realist. He was one of those coaches who always said about superstitions, "It's bad luck not to have good football players." He had lost his polite cool only once earlier in the game when he turned to his defense on the sideline and said, sarcastically, "Why the hell don't some of you guys give Glover some help once in a while?"

The reference was to Rich Glover, the quick middle guard who seemed to be making every tackle.

But Devaney was calm again now, or so it looked. When that last drive of 74 yards had to be made against Oklahoma—and the clock—Devaney was willing to let Jerry Tagge handle it. With just a little reassurance, now and then.

The day-long pounding had begun to wear down Oklahoma's defense, and Tagge knew it. The ground game had worked throughout the second half with Jeff Kinney banging his way to the 174 yards (and four touchdowns) he would wind up with.

"Nobody said a word in the huddle but me," Tagge remembered later. "We all just knew what had to be done. We never doubted we were going to win the game, one way or another."

The drive required 12 plays and almost six minutes. Tagge would break out of the huddle, go to the line, and frequently call an audible. He would key on the Oklahoma safety and run to the opposite side, while OU played the pass. Kinney made two pounding runs of 17 yards and 13 yards, his jersey looking like confetti, breaking tackles, trampling people.

For Nebraska, there was one moment of pure horror. Nebraska had come up to a third down and eight at the Sooners' 46, behind by three, the clock running, and Oklahoma itching for the ball.

Tagge called a pass right there, and the Oklahoma rush got to him quickly. He had to run for his life, if not the old ball game. He went right, angling, looking, desperate. OU's best defensive end, Ray "Sugar Bear" Hamilton, bore down on him. At the last second, Tagge saw Rodgers squirming between two defenders, kneeling on the artificial turf. Tagge drilled the ball to the Oklahoma 35 and Rodgers somehow caught it. First down. New life. The Prussians were still coming.

Two minutes later it was second down at the Oklahoma six and Tagge, who had been constantly glancing at the clock, called time. He wanted that last chat with his coach. At the sideline, they talked.

"I'll take us in, Coach," said Tagge.

"We're going for the touchdown," Devaney said. "No field goals, no ties."

"We'll get it," Tagge said.

"What's your best play?"

"Off-tackle with Jeff."

"Okay, let's run it with no mistakes."

Nebraska did exactly that. Twice. Jeff Kinney barged for four yards the first time, down to the two. Then he took it over for the touchdown that mercifully ended the afternoon, 35 to 31, Nebraska.

Upstairs in the sophisticated confines of the press box, away from the madness outdoors, Johnny Keith and Don Bryant shook hands.

"If I had to see one of these damn things every week, I'd drown myself in a bucket of cream gravy," said Johnny Keith.

And Nebraska's Don Bryant said, "Wait till I get my hat, I'll go with you."

Memory Lane

THE TRUTH IS, I'VE BEEN A POLL BOWL COLLECTOR ALL MY LIFE, including the ones I never saw, or particularly the ones I never saw.

Nostalgia freak. History junkie.

So what? Everybody needs a hobby.

The result is this trip I'm about to take you on, a journey through the Poll Bowls—the biggest games—that college football has lavished upon mankind.

The journey reasonably begins in 1889, the year the first all-America team was selected, a time when the game was dominated by Yale, Harvard, Princeton, that crowd, those schools that shaped and polished American football, creating all of its rules and strategies through the first three decades of its existence.

What we have here, as selected by a panel of one—me—are the most significant games in the first 120 years of college football, or what Grantland Rice often referred to as "our nation's finest sport," which, of course, it is.

DATE, SITE	OPPONENTS	TOP PLAYERS	RESULT
Nov. 28, 1889 New York City	Yale (14–0) vs. Princeton (8–0)	Amos Alonzo Stagg, e Hector Cowan, t	10–0, Princeton
Nov. 26, 1891 New York City	Yale (12–0) vs. Harvard (12–0)	Pudge Heffelfinger, g Marshall Newell, t	10–0, Yale
Nov. 12, 1894 Trenton, N.J.	Penn (9–0) vs. Princeton (7–0)	George Brooke, hb Biffy Lea, t	12–0, Penn
Nov. 19, 1894 Springfield	Yale (14–0) vs. Harvard (11–0)	Frank Hinkey, e Charley Brewer, hb	12–4, Yale
Nov. 15, 1898 Philadelphia	Penn (10–0) vs. Harvard (8–0)	T. Truxtun Hare, g Charley Daly, qb	10–0, Harvard
Oct. 28, 1899 New York City	Yale (5–0) vs. Columbia (5–0)	Malcolm McBride, hb Harold Weakes, hb	5–0, Columbia

DATE, SITE	OPPONENTS	TOP PLAYERS	RESULT
Jan. 1, 1902 Rose Bowl	Michigan (10–0) vs. Stanford (3–0–3)	Willie Heston, hb Bill Traeger, t	49–0, Michigan
Oct. 31, 1903 Minneapolis	Michigan (7–0) vs. Minnesota (7–0)	Willie Heston, hb Fred Schacht, t	6–6, Tie
Nov. 23, 1905 Chicago	Michigan (12–0) vs. Chicago (9–0)	Germany Schulz, c Walter Eckersall, qb	2–0, Chicago
Nov. 20, 1909 Cambridge	Yale (9–0) vs. Harvard (8–0)	Ted Coy, fb Hamilton Fish, t	8–0, Yale
Nov. 11, 1911 Cambridge	Carlisle (8–0) vs. Harvard (5–1)	Jim Thorpe, fb Percy Wendell, hb	18–15, Carlisle

That's it for the pioneer days. Gus Dorais (the thrower) and Knute Rockne (the catcher) are about to popularize the forward pass, which will be followed by the Golden Age of Sport, Football Division.

DATE, SITE	OPPONENTS	TOP PLAYERS	RESULT
Nov. 1, 1913 West Point	Notre Dame (3–0) vs. Army (4–0)	Gus Dorais, qb Vern Prichard, qb	35–13, N.D.
Nov. 29, 1913 New York City	Army (7–1) vs. Navy (7–0–1)	Louis Merillat, e Babe Brown, g	22–9, Army
Nov. 3, 1916 South Bend	Army (5–0) vs. Notre Dame (4–0)	Elmer Oliphant, fb Stan Cofall, hb	30–10, Army
Nov. 23, 1918 Pittsburgh	Georgia Tech (6–0) vs. Pitt (4–0)	Joe Guyon, t Tom Davies, hb	32–0, Pitt
Nov. 16, 1920 West Point	Notre Dame (4–0) vs. Army (5–0)	George Gipp, fb Bill French, fb	27–17, N.D.
Jan. 1, 1921 Rose Bowl	California (8–0) vs. Ohio State (7–0)	Brick Muller, e Gaylord Stinchcomb, hb	28–0, Cal
Oct. 29, 1921 Cambridge	Centre (7–0) vs. Harvard (5–0–1)	Bo McMillin, hb John Brown, g	6–0, Centre
Jan. 2, 1922 Rose Bowl	California (9–0) vs. Washington & Jefferson (10–0)	Brick Muller, e Russ Stein, t	0–0, Tie
Oct. 29, 1922 Chicago	Princeton (4–0) vs. Chicago (5–0)	Jack Cleaves, hb John Thomas, hb	20–18, Princeton
Nov. 20, 1923 Cambridge	Yale (7–0) vs. Harvard (4–2–1)	Ducky Pond, hb Charles Hubbard, t	13–0, Yale

DATE, SITE	OPPONENTS	TOP PLAYERS	RESULT
Oct. 19, 1924 Champaign, Ill.	Illinois (4–0) vs. Michigan (2–0)	Red Grange, hb Benny Friedman, qb	39–14, Illinois
Nov. 22, 1924 Berkeley	California (8–0) vs. Stanford (7–0)	Tut Imlay, hb Jim Lawson, e	20–20, Tie
Jan. 1, 1925 Rose Bowl	Notre Dame (9–0) vs. Stanford (7–0–1)	"Four Horsemen" Ernie Nevers, fb	27–10, N.D.
Jan. 1, 1926 Rose Bowl	Alabama (9–0) vs. Washington (10–0–1)	Johnny Mack Brown, hb George Wilson, fb	20–19, Alabama
Nov. 27, 1926 Chicago	Army (7–1) vs. Navy (9–0)	Chris Cagle, hb Tom Hamilton, hb	21–21, Tie
Jan. 1, 1927 Rose Bowl	Alabama (9–0) vs. Stanford (10–0)	Hoyt Winslett, e Ted Shipkey, e	7–7, Tie
Oct. 22, 1927 West Point	Army (4–0) vs. Yale (2–1)	Chris Cagle, hb Bruce Caldwell, qb	10–6, Yale
Jan. 1, 1928 Rose Bowl	Pitt (8–0–1) vs. Stanford (7–2–1)	Gibby Welch, hb Biff Hoffman, fb	7–6, Stanford
Nov. 1, 1928 New York City	NYU (5–0) vs. Carnegie Tech (5–0)	Ken Strong, fb Howard Harpster, hb	27–13, NYU
Jan. 1, 1929 Rose Bowl	Georgia Tech (9–0) vs. California (6–1–2)	Warner Mizell, hb "Wrong Way" Riegels, c	8–7, Tech
Nov. 16, 1929 Chicago	Notre Dame (6–0) vs. USC (6–1)	Frank Carideo, qb Russ Saunders, hb	13–12, N.D.
Oct. 15, 1930 Knoxville	Alabama (3–0) vs. Tennessee (3–0)	Johnny Cain, hb Gene McEver, hb	18–6, Alabama
Nov. 22, 1930 Evanston, Ill.	Notre Dame (7–0) vs. Northwestern (7–0)	Frank Carideo, qb Pug Rentner, fb	14–0, N.D.
Nov. 29, 1930 New York City	Notre Dame (8–0) vs. Army (8–0–1)	Marchy Schwartz, hb Ray Stecker, hb	7–6 N.D.
Jan. 1, 1931 Rose Bowl	Alabama (9–0) vs. Washington State (9–0)	Johnny Cain, hb Mel Hein, e	24–0 Alabama

So ends an era. The Four Horsemen. Red Grange. Ernie Nevers. Chris Cagle. All that. So, too, ends the life of Knute Rockne, who died in a plane crash in the spring of '31.

Enter a new age, featuring the rise to national power of teams like USC, and Minnesota. And thanks largely to Slingin' Sam

Baugh at TCU, attention is drawn to a colorful new region, the wide-open, pass-conscious Southwest.

DATE, SITE	OPPONENTS	TOP PLAYERS	RESULT
Nov. 2, 1931 New Haven	Yale (2–1–1) vs. Dartmouth (4–1)	Albie Booth, hb Bill Morton, hb	33–33, Tie
Nov. 16, 1931 Evanston, Ill.	Purdue (8–1) vs. Northwestern (7–0–1)	Roy Horstmann, fb Pug Rentner, fb	7–0, Purdue
Nov. 23, 1931 South Bend	USC (6–1) vs. Notre Dame (6–0–1)	Gus Shaver, qb Marchy Schwartz, hb	16–14, USC
Dec. 7, 1931 New York City	Tennessee (8–0–1) vs. NYU (6–2–1)	Beattie Feathers, hb Bob McNamara, hb	13–0, Tennessee
Jan. 1, 1932 Rose Bowl	USC (9–1) vs. Tulane (11–0)	Erny Pinckert, hb Don Zimmerman, hb	21–10, USC
Nov. 11, 1932 Fort Worth	TCU (7–0–1) vs. Texas (6–1)	Johnny Vaught, g Bohn Hilliard, hb	14–0, TCU
Nov. 19, 1932 Minneapolis	Michigan (7–0) vs. Minnesota (5–2)	Harry Newman, qb Jack Manders, fb	3–0, Michigan
Nov. 24, 1932 Providence	Colgate (8–0) vs. Brown (7–0)	Charley Soleau, qb Bill Gilbane, hb	21–0, Colgate
Jan. 1, 1933 Rose Bowl	USC (9–0) vs. Pitt (8–0–2)	Cotton Warburton, hb Warren Heller, hb	35–0, USC
Nov. 18, 1933 Pittsburgh	Nebraska (6–0) vs. Pitt (6–1)	George Sauer, fb Warren Heller, hb	6–0 Pitt
Nov. 18, 1933 Lafayette, Ind.	Purdue (5–0–1) Iowa (4–2)	Duane Purvis, qb Dick Crayne, hb	14–6, Iowa
Jan. 1, 1934 Rose Bowl	Columbia (7–1) vs. Stanford (8–1–1)	Cliff Montgomery, qb Bobby Grayson, hb	7–0, Columbia
Oct. 20, 1934 Pittsburgh	Minnesota (2–0) vs. Pitt (3–0)	Pug Lund, hb Izzy Weinstock, fb	13–7, Minnesota
Nov. 24, 1934 Houston	Rice (8–0–1) vs. TCU (6–3)	Bill Wallace, hb Sam Baugh, qb	7–2, TCU
Dec. 1, 1934 Philadelphia	Army (7–2) vs. Navy (7–1)	Jack Buckler, hb Buzz Borries, hb	3–0, Navy
Jan. 1, 1935 Rose Bowl	Alabama (9–0) vs. Stanford (9–0–1)	Dixie Howell, qb Bobby Grayson, hb	29–13, Alabama

DATE, SITE	OPPONENTS	TOP PLAYERS	RESULT
Nov. 2, 1935 Columbus, Ohio	Notre Dame (5–0) vs. Ohio State (4–0)	Bill Shakespeare, qb Tippy Dye, qb	18–13, N.D.
Nov. 23, 1935 Princeton	Princeton (7–0) vs. Dartmouth (8–0)	Pepper Constable, hb Frank Nairne, hb	26–6, Princeton
Nov. 30, 1935 Fort Worth	TCU (10–0) vs. SMU (10–0)	Sam Baugh, qb Bobby Wilson, hb	20–14, SMU
Jan. 1, 1936 Sugar Bowl	TCU (11–1) vs. LSU (9–1)	Sam Baugh, qb Abe Mickal, qb	3–2, TCU
Jan. 1, 1936 Rose Bowl	SMU (12–0) vs. Stanford (7–1)	Bobby Wilson, hb Keith Topping, e	7–0, Stanford
Oct. 31, 1936 Evanston, Ill.	Minnesota (4–0) vs. Northwestern (4–0)	Andy Uram, hb Don Heap, hb	6–0, Northwestern
Dec. 12, 1936 San Francisco	Santa Clara (8–0) vs. TCU (7–2–2)	Nello Falaschi, qb Sam Baugh, qb	9–0, TCU
Oct. 16, 1937 New York City	Pitt (3–0) vs. Fordham (3–0)	Marshall Goldberg, hb Alex Wojciechowicz, e	0–0, Tie
Oct. 30, 1937 New Haven	Yale (4–0) vs. Dartmouth (5–0)	Clint Frank, hb Bob MacLeod, hb	9–9, Tie
Jan. 1, 1938 Rose Bowl	Alabama (9–0) vs. California (9–0–1)	Joe Kilgrow, hb Vic Bottari, hb	13–0, Cal
Oct. 29, 1938 Fort Worth	TCU (5–0) vs. Baylor (4–0)	Davey O'Brien, qb Billy Patterson, qb	39–7, TCU
Nov. 5, 1938 Pittsburgh	Pitt (6–0) vs. Carnegie Tech (4–1)	Marshall Goldberg, hb Merlyn Condit, hb	20–10, Carnegie Tech
Nov. 26, 1938 Durham, N.C.	Duke (8–0) vs. Pitt (8–1)	Eric Tipton, fb Marshall Goldberg, hb	7–0, Duke
Dec. 3, 1938 Los Angeles	Notre Dame (8–0) vs. USC (7–2)	Bob Saggau, hb Harry Smith, g	13–0, USC
Jan. 2, 1939 Sugar Bowl	TCU (10–0) vs. Carnegie Tech (7–1)	Davey O'Brien, qb George Muha, hb	15–7, TCU
Jan. 2, 1939 Rose Bowl	Duke (9–0) vs. USC (8–2)	Eric Tipton, fb "Nave to Krueger"	7–3, USC
Oct. 28, 1939 Columbus, Ohio	Cornell (3–0) vs. Ohio State (3–0)	Nick Drahos, t Don Scott, hb	23–14, Cornell
Nov. 11, 1939 Iowa City	Notre Dame (6–0) vs. Iowa (4–1)	Milt Piepul, fb Nile Kinnick, hb	7–6, Iowa

DATE, SITE	OPPONENTS	TOP PLAYERS	RESULT
Nov. 18, 1939 Philadelphia	Michigan (4–2) vs. Penn (4–2)	Tom Harmon, hb Frank Reagan, hb	19–17, Michigan
Dec. 9, 1939 Los Angeles	USC (7–0–1) vs. UCLA (6–0–3)	Grenny Lansdell, qb Kenny Washington, hb	0–0, Tie
Jan. 1, 1940 Sugar Bowl	Texas A&M (10–0) vs. Tulane (8–0–1)	John Kimbrough, fb Bobby Kellogg, hb	14–13, A&M
Jan. 1, 1940 Rose Bowl	USC (7–0–2) vs. Tennessee (10–0)	Grenny Lansdell, qb George Cafego, hb	14–0, USC
Nov. 9, 1940 Minneapolis	Michigan (5–0) vs. Minnesota (5–0)	Tom Harmon, hb Bruce Smith, hb	7–6, Minnesota
Nov. 16, 1940 Boston	Georgetown (7–0) vs. Boston College (7–0)	Augie Lio, g Charley O'Rourke, qb	19–18, B.C.
Nov. 28, 1940 Austin	Texas A&M (8–0) vs. Texas (6–2)	John Kimbrough, fb Pete Layden, qb	7–0, Texas
Jan. 1, 1941 Sugar Bowl	Tennessee (10–0) vs. Boston College (10–0)	Bob Suffridge, g Charley O'Rourke, qb	19–13, B.C.
Jan. 1, 1941 Cotton Bowl	Texas A&M (8–1) vs. Fordham (7–1)	John Kimbrough, fb Steve Filipowicz, qb	13–12, A&M
Nov. 1, 1941 Minneapolis	Minnesota (4–0) vs. Northwestern (3–1)	Bruce Smith, hb Bill deCorrevont, hb	8–7, Minnesota
Nov. 8, 1941 Annapolis	Notre Dame (5–0–1) vs. Navy (5–0–1)	Steve Juzwik, qb Bill Busik, hb	20–13, N.D.
Nov. 15, 1941 Austin	Texas (6–0–1) vs. TCU (5–2)	Jack Crain, hb Emory Nix, qb	14–7, TCU
Jan. 1, 1942 Orange Bowl	Georgia (8–1–1) vs. TCU (7–2–1)	Frank Sinkwich, qb Kyle Gillespie, qb	40–26, Georgia
Oct. 31, 1942 Atlanta	Georgia (6–0) vs. Alabama (5–0)	Frank Sinkwich, qb Russ Craft, hb	20–10, Georgia
Oct. 31, 1942 Madison, Wis.	Ohio State (5–0) vs. Wisconsin (5–0–1)	Les Horvath, hb Elroy Hirsch, hb	17–7, Wisconsin

Hey, there's a war on. The big one. WWII. But football is a morale builder—so call it Army's finest hour, both on the battlefield and in stadiums.

Glenn Davis and Doc Blanchard do so much for morale, Gen. Douglas MacArthur sends a wire to Red Blaik, the Army coach, saying he has stopped the war to celebrate Army's national championship of '44. True story.

DATE, SITE	OPPONENTS	TOP PLAYERS	RESULT
Jan. 1, 1943 Sugar Bowl	Tulsa (10–0) vs. Tennessee (8–1–1)	Glenn Dobbs, qb Bobby Cifers, hb	14–7, Tennessee
Nov. 27, 1943 Great Lakes	Notre Dame (9–0) vs. Great Lakes (9–2)	Creighton Miller, hb Steve Lach, qb	19–14, Great Lakes
Dec. 2, 1944 Baltimore	Army (8–0) vs. Navy (6–2)	Davis & Blanchard Bob Jenkins, hb	23–7, Army
Dec. 1, 1945 New York City	Army (8–0) vs. Navy (7–0–1)	Davis & Blanchard Skip Minisi, hb	32–13, Army

Comes now a postwar boom of super heroes—your Johnny Lujack, your Doak Walker, your "Choo Choo" Justice, your Charley Trippi, your Kyle Rote . . . and the emergence of a bunch of Split-T magicians called the Oklahoma Sooners.

DATE, SITE	OPPONENTS	TOP PLAYERS	RESULT
Oct. 26, 1946 Houston	Texas (5–0) vs. Rice (3–1)	Bobby Layne, qb Virgil Eikenberg	18–13, Rice
Nov. 9, 1946 New York City	Army (7–0) vs. Notre Dame (5–0)	Davis & Blanchard Johnny Lujack, qb	0–0, Tie
Jan. 1, 1947 Sugar Bowl	Georgia (10–0) vs. North Carolina (8–1–1)	Charley Trippi, hb Charlie Justice, hb	20–10, Georgia
Nov. 1, 1947 Dallas	SMU (5–0) vs. Texas (6–0)	Doak Walker, hb Bobby Layne, qb	14–13, SMU
Nov. 29, 1947 Fort Worth	SMU (9–0) vs. TCU (4–3–1)	Doak Walker, hb Lindy Berry, qb	19–19, Tie
Dec. 6, 1947 Los Angeles	Notre Dame (8–0) vs. USC (7–0–1)	Johnny Lujack, qb Don Doll, hb	38–7, N.D.
Jan. 1, 1948 Cotton Bowl	SMU (9–0–1) vs. Penn State (9–0)	Doak Walker, hb Fran Rogel, hb	13–13, Tie
Oct. 23, 1948 Minneapolis	Michigan (4–0) vs. Minnesota (3–1)	Charley Ortmann, hb Leo Nomellini, t	27–14, Michigan
Dec. 4, 1948 Los Angeles	Notre Dame (9–0) vs. USC (6–3)	Billy Gay, hb Jim Powers, qb	14–14, Tie
Jan. 1, 1949 Sugar Bowl	Oklahoma (9–1) vs. North Carolina (9–0–1)	Darrell Royal, hb Charlie Justice, hb	14–6, Oklahoma

DATE, SITE	OPPONENTS	TOP PLAYERS	RESULT
Jan. 1, 1949 Cotton Bowl	SMU (8–1–1) vs. Oregon (9–1)	Doak Walker, hb Norm Van Brocklin, qb	21–13, SMU
Dec. 3, 1949 Dallas	Notre Dame (9–0) vs. SMU (5–3–1)	Emil Sitko, hb Kyle Rote, hb	27–20, N.D.
Oct. 14, 1950 Dallas	Texas (2–0) vs. Oklahoma (2–0)	Bobby Dillon, hb Claude Arnold, qb	14–13, Oklahoma
Nov. 25, 1950 Knoxville	Kentucky (10–0) vs. Tennessee (8–1)	Babe Parilli, qb Hank Lauricella, hb	7–0, Tennessee
Nov. 25, 1950 Norman, Okla.	Oklahoma (8–0) vs. Nebraska (6–1–1)	Billy Vessels, hb Bobby Reynolds, hb	49–35, Oklahoma
Jan. 1, 1951 Cotton Bowl	Texas (9–1) vs. Tennessee (10–1)	Gib Dawson, hb Andy Kozar, fb	20–14, Tennessee
Jan. 1, 1951 Sugar Bowl	Oklahoma (10–0) vs. Kentucky (10–1)	Leon Heath, fb Babe Parilli, qb	13–7, Kentucky
Oct. 20, 1951 Berkeley	California (4–0) vs. USC (4–0)	Johnny Olszewski, fb Frank Gifford, hb	21–14, USC
Oct. 28, 1951 College Station	Baylor (4–0) vs. Texas A&M (4–1)	Larry Isbell, qb Bob Smith, fb	21–21, Tie
Nov. 17, 1951 Columbus, Ohio	Illinois (7–0) vs. Ohio State (4–2–1)	Johnny Karras, hb Vic Janowicz, hb	0–0, Tie
Nov. 24, 1951 Palo Alto	Stanford (9–0) vs. California (7–2)	Gary Kerkorian, qb Johnny Olszewski, fb	20–7, Cal
Jan. 1, 1952 Sugar Bowl	Maryland (10–0) vs. Tennessee (10–0)	Jack Scarbath, qb Hank Lauricella, hb	28–13, Maryland
Nov. 8, 1952 South Bend	Oklahoma (5–0–1) vs. Notre Dame (4–1–1)	Eddie Crowder, qb Ralph Guglielmi, qb	27–21, N.D.
Nov. 15, 1952 Atlanta	Georgia Tech (8–0) vs. Alabama (7–1)	Leon Hardeman, fb Bobby Marlow, hb	7–3, Tech
Nov. 22, 1952 Los Angeles	USC (8–0) vs. UCLA (8–0)	Jim Sears, hb Paul Cameron, hb	14–12, USC
Oct. 17, 1953 Palo Alto	UCLA (4–0) vs. Stanford (2–2)	Paul Cameron, hb Bobby Garrett, qb	21–20, Stanford
Nov. 14, 1953 Madison, Wis.	Illinois (6–0–1) vs. Wisconsin (5–2)	J. C. Caroline, hb Alan Ameche, fb	34–7, Wisconsin
Nov. 21, 1953 South Bend	Notre Dame (7–0) vs. Iowa (5–3)	John Lattner, hb Jerry Reichow, qb	14–14, Tie

DATE, SITE	OPPONENTS	TOP PLAYERS	RESULT
Jan. 1, 1954 Orange Bowl	Maryland (10–0) vs. Oklahoma (8–1–1)	Bernie Faloney, qb J. D. Roberts, g	7–0, Oklahoma
Jan. 1, 1954 Rose Bowl	UCLA (8–1) vs. Michigan State (8–1)	Paul Cameron, hb Billy Wells, hb	28–20, Mich. St.

Sorry to interrupt, but I think I see a Woody Hayes about to kick in at Ohio State, and the end of Oklahoma's 47–game win streak.

DATE, SITE	OPPONENTS	TOP PLAYERS	RESULT
Nov. 20, 1954 Columbus, Ohio	Ohio State (9–0) vs. Michigan (6–2)	Howard Cassady, hb Ron Kramer, e	21–7 Ohio State
Nov. 20, 1954 Los Angeles	UCLA (8–0) vs. USC (8–1)	Primo Villanueva, hb Jon Arnett, hb	34–0, UCLA
Jan. 2, 1956 Orange Bowl	Oklahoma (10–0) vs. Maryland (10–0)	Tommy McDonald, hb Eddie Vereb, hb	20–6, Oklahoma
Jan. 2, 1956 Rose Bowl	UCLA (9–1) vs. Michigan State (8–1)	Bob Davenport, fb Clarence Peaks, hb	17–14, Mich. St.
Oct. 20, 1956 College Station	TCU (3–0) vs. Texas A&M (3–0–1)	Jim Swink, hb John David Crow, hb	7–6, A&M
Nov. 3, 1956 Boulder, Colo.	Oklahoma (5–0) vs. Colorado (5–1)	Tommy McDonald, hb John Bayuk, fb	27–19, Oklahoma
Nov. 10, 1956 Atlanta	Tennessee (6–0) vs. Georgia Tech (6–0)	Johnny Majors, hb Paul Rotenberry, hb	6–0, Tennessee
Jan. 1, 1957 Cotton Bowl	TCU (7–3) vs. Syracuse (7–1)	Jim Swink, hb Jim Brown, hb	28–27, TCU
Jan. 1, 1957 Sugar Bowl	Tennessee (10–0) vs. Baylor (8–2)	Johnny Majors, hb Del Shofner, hb	13–7, Baylor
Nov. 9, 1957 Birmingham	Auburn (6–0) vs. Mississippi State (5–1)	Jim Phillips, e Billy Stacy, qb	15–7, Auburn
Nov. 16, 1957 Houston	Texas A&M (8–0) vs. Rice (4–3)	John David Crow, hb Frank Ryan, qb	7–6, Rice
Nov. 16, 1957 Norman, Okla.	Oklahoma (7–0) vs. Notre Dame (4–2)	Clendon Thomas, hb Nick Pietrosante, fb	7–0, N.D.
Nov. 15, 1958 Iowa City	Iowa (6–0–1) vs. Ohio State (4–1–2)	Randy Duncan, qb Bob White, fb	38–28, Ohio St.
Oct. 31, 1959 Baton Rouge	LSU (6–0) vs. Ole Miss (6–0)	Billy Cannon, hb Jake Gibbs, qb	7–3, LSU

DATE, SITE	OPPONENTS	TOP PLAYERS	RESULT
Nov. 7, 1959 University Park, Pa.	Syracuse (6–0) vs. Penn State (7–0)	Ernie Davis, hb Richie Lucas, qb	20–18, Syracuse
Nov. 14, 1959 Athens, Ga.	Georgia (7–1) vs. Auburn (6–1)	Fran Tarkenton, qb Ed Dyas, fb	14–13, Georgia
Jan. 1, 1960 Cotton Bowl	Syracuse (10–0) vs. Texas (9–1)	Ernie Davis, hb Jack Collins, hb	23–14, Syracuse
Nov. 5, 1960 Durham, N.C.	Navy (7–0) vs. Duke (5–1)	Joe Bellino, hb Tee Moorman, e	19–10, Duke
Nov. 5, 1960 Minneapolis	Iowa (6–0) vs. Minnesota (6–0)	Wilburn Hollis, qb Sandy Stephens, qb	27–10, Minnesota
Nov. 19, 1960 Columbia, Mo.	Missouri (9–0) vs. Kansas (6–2–1)	Mel West, hb John Hadl, qb	23–7, Kansas

Hi. Me again. Incredible dynasties ahead, built by coaches such as Bear Bryant at Alabama, Darrell Royal at Texas, John McKay at USC, and Ara Parseghian at Notre Dame. This isn't going to leave much for anyone else.

Jan. 1, 1961 Rose Bowl	Minnesota (8–1) vs. Washington (9–1)	Sandy Stephens, qb Bob Schloredt, qb	17–7, Washington
Jan. 1, 1962 Sugar Bowl	Alabama (10–0) vs. Arkansas (8–2)	Pat Trammell, qb Lance Alworth, hb	10–3, Alabama
Jan. 1, 1962 Cotton Bowl	Texas (9–1) vs. Ole Miss (9–1)	James Saxton, hb Glynn Griffing, qb	12–7, Texas
Nov. 3, 1962 Baton Rouge	Ole Miss (5–0) vs. LSU (5–0–1)	Glynn Griffing, qb Jerry Stovall, hb	15–7, Ole Miss
Nov. 17, 1962 Atlanta	Alabama (8–0) vs. Georgia Tech (5–2–1)	Joe Namath, qb Billy Lothridge, qb	7–6, Tech
Jan. 1, 1963 Rose Bowl	USC (10–0) vs. Wisconsin (8–1)	Pete Beathard, qb Ron VanderKelen, qb	42–37, USC
Oct. 12, 1963 Dallas	Texas (3–0) vs. Oklahoma (2–0)	Duke Carlisle, qb Jim Grisham, fb	28–7, Texas
Nov. 9, 1963 Austin	Texas (7–0) vs. Baylor (5–1)	Duke Carlisle, qb Don Trull, qb	7–0, Texas
Jan. 1, 1964 Cotton Bowl	Texas (10–0) vs. Navy (9–1)	Tommy Nobis, g Roger Staubach, qb	28–6, Texas

DATE, SITE	OPPONENTS	TOP PLAYERS	RESULT
Oct. 17, 1964 Austin	Texas (4–0) vs. Arkansas (4–0)	Tommy Nobis, g Ken Hatfield, hb	14–13, Arkansas
Nov. 28, 1964 Los Angeles	Notre Dame (9–0) vs. USC (6–3)	John Huarte, qb Craig Fertig, qb	20–17, USC
Jan. 1, 1965 Orange Bowl	Alabama (10–0) vs. Texas (9–1)	Joe Namath, qb Ernie Koy, hb	21–17, Texas
Oct. 16, 1965 Fayetteville	Texas (4–0) vs. Arkansas (4–0)	Marv Kristynik, qb Jon Brittenun, qb	27–24, Arkansas
Oct. 23, 1965 Lafayette, Ind.	Michigan State (5–0) vs. Purdue (4–0–1)	Clinton Jones, hb Bob Griese, qb	14–10, Mich. St.
Oct. 30, 1965 Columbia, Mo.	Nebraska (6–0) vs. Missouri (5–0–1)	Harry Wilson, hb Gary Lane, qb	16–14, Nebraska
Jan. 1, 1966 Orange Bowl	Nebraska (10–0) vs. Alabama (8–1–1)	Bob Churchich, qb Steve Sloan, qb	39–28, Alabama
Oct. 15, 1966 Knoxville	Alabama (3–0) vs. Tennessee (2–1)	Ken Stabler, qb Dewey Warren, qb	11–10, Alabama
Nov. 5, 1966 Jacksonville	Florida (7–0) vs. Georgia (6–1)	Steve Spurrier, qb Kent Lawrence, hb	27–10, Georgia
Nov. 19, 1966 East Lansing	Notre Dame (8–0) vs. Michigan State (9–0)	Coley O'Brien, qb Bubba Smith, de	10–10, Tie
Nov. 18, 1967 Los Angeles	USC (8–1) vs. UCLA (8–0–1)	O. J. Simpson, hb Gary Beban, qb	21–20, USC
Jan. 1, 1969 Rose Bowl	USC (9–0–1) vs. Ohio State (10–0)	O. J. Simpson, hb Rex Kern, qb	27–10, Ohio St.
Nov. 22, 1969 Ann Arbor	Ohio State (8–0) vs. Michigan (7–2)	Rex Kern, qb Don Moorhead, qb	24–12, Michigan
Dec. 6, 1969 Fayetteville	Texas (9–0) vs. Arkansas (9–0)	James Street, qb Bill Montgomery, qb	15–14, Texas
Jan. 1, 1970 Cotton Bowl	Texas (10–0) vs. Notre Dame (8–1–1)	James Street, qb Joe Theismann, qb	21–17, Texas
Nov. 21, 1970 Columbus, Ohio	Michigan (9–0) vs. Ohio State (8–0)	Don Moorhead, qb Rex Kern, qb	20–9, Ohio St.
Jan. 1, 1971 Cotton Bowl	Texas (10–0) vs. Notre Dame (9–1)	Eddie Phillips, qb Joe Theismann, qb	24–11, N.D.
Jan. 1, 1971 Rose Bowl	Ohio State (9–0) vs. Stanford (8–3)	Rex Kern, qb Jim Plunkett, qb	27–17, Stanford

DATE, SITE	OPPONENTS	TOP PLAYERS	RESULT
Nov. 20, 1971 Norman, Okla.	Nebraska (10–0) vs. Oklahoma (9–0)	Jerry Tagge, qb Jack Mildren, qb	35–31, Nebraska
Jan. 1, 1972 Orange Bowl	Nebraska (12–0) vs. Alabama (11–0)	Johnny Rodgers, hb Johnny Musso, hb	38–6, Nebraska
Dec. 2, 1972 Birmingham	Alabama (10–0) vs. Auburn (8–1)	Terry Davis, qb David Langner, cb	17–16, Auburn
Dec. 2, 1972 Los Angeles	USC (10–0) vs. Notre Dame (8–1)	Anthony Davis, hb Eric Penick, hb	45–23, USC
Nov. 24, 1973 Ann Arbor	Michigan (10–0) vs. Ohio State (9–0)	Dennis Franklin, qb Archie Griffin, hb	10–10, Tie
Jan. 1, 1974 Sugar Bowl	Alabama (11–0) vs. Notre Dame (11–0)	Richard Todd, qb Tom Clements, qb	24–23, N.D.
Nov. 23, 1974 Lincoln, Neb.	Oklahoma (9–0) vs. Nebraska (8–2)	Joe Washington, hb David Humm, qb	28–14, Oklahoma
Jan. 1, 1975 Rose Bowl	USC (9–1–1) vs. Ohio State (10–1)	Pat Haden, qb Archie Griffin, hb	18–17, USC
Jan. 1, 1977 Sugar Bowl	Pitt (11–0) vs. Georgia (10–1)	Tony Dorsett, hb Ray Goff, qb	27–3, Pitt
Oct. 8, 1977 Dallas	Oklahoma (4–0) vs. Texas (3–0)	Thomas Lott, qb Earl Campbell, fb	13–6, Texas
Jan. 1, 1978 Cotton Bowl	Texas (11–0) vs. Notre Dame (10–1)	Earl Campbell, fb Joe Montana, qb	38–10, N.D.
Sept. 23, 1978 Birmingham	USC (2–0) vs. Alabama (1–0)	Charles White, hb Tony Nathan, hb	24–14, USC
Nov. 11, 1978 Lincoln, Neb.	Oklahoma (10–0) vs. Nebraska (8–0)	Billy Sims, hb I. M. Hipp, hb	17–14, Nebraska
Jan. 1, 1979 Sugar Bowl	Alabama (10–1) vs. Penn State (11–0)	Jeff Rutledge, qb Chuck Fusina, qb	14–7, Alabama
Oct. 13, 1979 Los Angeles	USC (5–0) vs. Stanford (4–1)	Charles White, hb Turk Schoenart, qb	21–21, Tie
Nov. 29, 1979 Birmingham	Alabama (10–0) vs. Auburn (8–2)	Major Ogilvie, hb Joe Cribbs, hb	25–18, Alabama
Jan. 1, 1980 Orange Bowl	Oklahoma (10–1) vs. Florida State (11–0)	Billy Sims, hb Mark Lyles, hb	24–7, Oklahoma

Oh, by the way. Has anybody noticed there's a Barry Switzer around now? And a Joe Paterno? My guess is, there's a Miami Hurricane coming along, and who knows, maybe even a Notre Dame again.

DATE, SITE	OPPONENTS	TOP PLAYERS	RESULT
Nov. 8, 1980 Jacksonville	Georgia (8–0) vs. Florida (6–1)	Herschel Walker, hb Wayne Peace, qb	26–21, Georgia
Nov. 28, 1981 Pittsburgh	Pitt (10–0) vs. Penn State (9–1)	Dan Marino, qb Curt Warner, hb	48–14, Penn St.
Jan. 1, 1982 Orange Bowl	Clemson (11–0) vs. Nebraska (9–2)	Homer Jordan, qb Mike Rozier, hb	22–15, Clemson
Sept. 25, 1982 University Park, Pa.	Penn State (3–0) vs. Nebraska (2–0)	Todd Blackledge, qb Turner Gill, qb	28–21, Penn St.
Jan. 1, 1983 Cotton Bowl	SMU (10–0–1) vs. Pitt (9–2)	Eric Dickerson, hb Dan Marino, qb	7–3, SMU
Jan. 1, 1983 Sugar Bowl	Georgia (10–1) vs. Penn State (10–1)	Herschel Walker, hb Todd Blackledge, qb	27–23, Penn St.
Jan. 1, 1984 Cotton Bowl	Texas (11–0) vs. Georgia (10–1)	Jerry Gray, db John Lastinger, qb	10–9, Georgia
Jan. 1, 1984 Orange Bowl	Nebraska (12–0) vs. Miami (10–1)	Turner Gill, qb Bernie Kosar, qb	31–30, Miami
Nov. 24, 1984 Miami	Miami (8–3) vs. Boston College (9–2)	Bernie Kosar, qb Doug Flutie, qb	47–45, B.C.
Jan. 1, 1986 Orange Bowl	Oklahoma (10–1) vs. Penn State (11–0)	Lydell Carr, fb D. J. Dozier, hb	25–10, Oklahoma
Jan. 1, 1987 Fiesta Bowl	Miami (11–0) vs. Penn State (11–0)	Vinny Testaverde, qb Shane Conlan, lb	14–10, Penn St.
Oct. 3, 1987 Tallahassee	Miami (2–0) vs. Florida State (4–0)	Michael Irvin, e Danny McManus, qb	26–25, Miami
Nov. 26, 1987 Lincoln, Neb.	Oklahoma (10–0) vs. Nebraska (10–0)	Charles Thompson, qb Steve Taylor, qb	14–7, Oklahoma
Jan. 1, 1988 Orange Bowl	Miami (11–0) vs. Oklahoma (11–0)	Steve Walsh, qb Rickey Dixon, db	20–14, Miami
Oct. 15, 1988 South Bend	Miami (4–0) vs. Notre Dame (5–0)	Steve Walsh, qb Tony Rice, qb	31–30, N.D.

DATE, SITE	OPPONENTS	TOP PLAYERS	RESULT
Nov. 26, 1988 Los Angeles	Notre Dame (10–0) vs. USC (10–0)	Tony Rice, qb Rodney Peete, qb	27–10, N.D.
Jan. 2, 1989 Fiesta Bowl	Notre Dame (11–0) vs. West Virginia (11–0)	Tony Rice, qb Major Harris, qb	32–21, N.D.

Of these 200 games, by my math, Notre Dame turns up in the most—big surprise. The Irish appear in 29, winning 18, losing seven, tying four.

Southern Cal was in 22 of the big games, winning 14, losing five, tying three.

What this means is that Notre Dame and USC are pretty good bets in Poll Bowls.

Another mathematical exercise tells me that I saw 26 of these 200 games in person, 44 of them on TV, and parts or all of 51 others on game film in coaching offices—and got paid to do it.

GOLF

What Is It?

GOLF IS A LONG WALK SPOILED — AND ALL THOSE JOKES. GOLF IS A way for a man to get away from his wife. Golf is what a salesman does when he's supposed to be selling big ones and little ones.

Some people have said that golf is not a sport because you don't sweat enough.

I say golf is the hardest sport in the world to play well consistently. Think about it. There are 14 clubs, all of them different. There are 18 holes, all of them different. There's sand, water, trees, wind, high grass, fences, and a very small cup for a very small ball.

Golf may have driven more grownups crazy than whiskey, lawyers, or children.

As for tournament golf, there used to be a lot of big stars out there winning trophies all the time. They had names like Hogan, Nelson, and Snead, or Nicklaus, Palmer, and Trevino, and they almost never went to Bible study group.

The best description of golf I ever heard came from a friend who once turned up at The Masters in Augusta, Georgia, one spring. He was a sports information director at the time who worked for a college in the Midwest, dealing mostly with black athletes who played basketball.

He had never been to a golf tournament before, much less something like The Masters.

So the first thing I did was take him on a tour of the beautiful course.

As we strolled down the second fairway, I pointed out Jack Nicklaus and Tom Weiskopf, two super stars, who were paired together for that day's round.

My friend studied the scene.

"Golf," he said. "I get it. A couple of blond Nazis walking through the woods with two spades carrying their shit."

The Greatest Golfer

THE ARGUMENT IS AS OLD AS THE DANDRUFF ON HARRY VARDON'S shoulders, as old as Hell Bunker, as Mary Queen of Shanks. Older than heather and gorse. Certainly older than the loop in Bobby Jones's backswing or Ben Hogan's car wreck.

Who was the greatest golfer that ever lived?

I began asking the question about 40 years ago, shortly after I learned how to improve my lie with the toe of a Foot-Joy, and I've kept asking it through the years of learned individuals who were said to know more about the game than I do, which was hardly possible.

Harry Vardon, they said first.

Won six British Opens when the British Open was the only championship worth winning, the only major. Also invented the grip.

A picture told me Vardon swung in a coat. Could rarely keep his eye on the ball because of the pipe in his mouth. Never cleaned the ball. Never had a shag bag. Played in the rain and mud, but kept winning and inventing the grip.

I say, okay, Vardon was the greatest golfer who ever lived that swung in a coat with a pipe in his mouth and sometimes had to hit a muddy ball the size of a pound cake.

Next, they said Bobby Jones.

His good friends called him Bob. Won more major championships (13) than anyone until Jack Nicklaus came along. Won them in a shorter span of time. Played for fun. An amateur. Didn't even have a wedge because nobody had thought of it yet.

Big stat: Walter Hagen never won a major championship that Bobby Jones played in.

They say Jones had a temper. They say he brooded. They say he did it all with a hickory shaft. They say he enjoyed a cocktail—or six, or eight. But he dominated the game and won the Grand Slam in 1930 and enjoyed two tickertape parades in New York and even got a couple of degrees in college.

Okay, I say Jones was the greatest golfer who never turned pro until Hollywood came after him.

Meanwhile, they said Walter Hagen. Same era.

Walter Hagen was the greatest golfer who ever traveled the globe by boat. They give him 11 major championships, but I give him 16—he won five Western Opens and the Western was a major in Walter's day, before The Masters.

He did all this while he was also winning in Calcutta and Cairo, and frequently wearing a tux. A showman.

Hagen didn't have a wedge either, but he made remarkable recovery shots, was almost unbeatable at match play, and said, "You ought to stop along the way and smell the flowers."

Fine. Hagen's the greatest golfer who ever stopped to smell the flowers.

Now they said Ben Hogan.

Hogan won four or five U.S. Opens, depending of whether you want to count a wartime Open in 1942 for which Ben has a gold medal that looks just like his other four. He won The Masters twice, the PGA twice, and the British Open the only time he ever played in it, in 1953.

That was the year he won the Triple Crown, becoming the only golfer ever to win three major professional championships in the same year.

In 14 consecutive U.S. Opens, he was never out of the top 10— and rarely out of the fairway.

After the Triple Crown, they gave him the first ticker-tape parade in New York since Jones, and no golfer has had one since.

He had a car wreck, which inspired a movie, and he wrote an instruction book that golfers still read because they can't figure out what "pronate" means.

It's obvious that Ben Hogan was the greatest golfer who never missed a fairway or green and should have won 14 U.S. Opens and had a car wreck.

Some said Byron Nelson.

Byron won five majors and retired before Hogan really got started, although they were from the same town and had caddied together in Fort Worth.

In 1945, Byron won everything but Gene Sarazen's knickers. He won 19 tournaments, including 11 in a row. He retired at the age of 34, the earliest retirement since Jones at 28.

Nelson was the fastest of the great players, probably the worst putter, and the greatest golfer who ever wanted to own a chicken ranch.

Some have said Sam Snead.

Sam won more tournaments than anybody. He started winning in 1937 with his "picture swing," and he won again in 1965 on the Tour, at the age of 52. At the age of 62, he finished third in the PGA Championship. That was in 1974.

Along came the Senior Tour, and Sam kept on winning. He became the only golfer ever to win tournaments in six different decades.

It's clear that Sam Snead is the greatest golfer who never died.

And now they said Arnold Palmer.

Arnold took golf to the masses. He sweated and chain-smoked and drove the ball through tree trunks. He won majors when it was impossible, eight in all, and he lost majors when it was impossible. He gave Gary Player a Masters and he gave Billy Casper a U.S. Open.

Arnold was just as nice to his fans. He signed everybody's autograph.

He also invented golf on television, which enabled the purses to increase. Golf on TV has given us a lot of players you've never heard of, but I don't think you ought to hold this against Arnold Palmer.

Finally, they said Jack Nicklaus.

Jack Nicklaus has won more major championships than anybody, with two National Amateurs, four U.S. Opens, five PGAs, six Masters Tournaments, and three British Opens, a grand total of 20, but at the same time, he's been second more times than anybody, and third more times than anybody, and so on.

Jack Nicklaus lost weight and fluff-dried his hair and got popular after he murdered Arnold Palmer. He started his own tournament and became one of the best course designers.

There's no question that Jack Nicklaus is the greatest winner who ever played golf, and there's no telling what he might have accomplished if he hadn't been color blind, hadn't used the interlocking grip, and had known how to hit a wedge or play bunker shots.

There are two other candidates that people overlook. One is Jimmy Demaret. Demaret saved golf after Bobby Jones killed it in 1930. He wore pink shoes and beltless slacks and told jokes and hung out with movie stars and loved the press and became "colorful Jimmy Demaret, golf's goodwill ambassador."

The other is Lee Trevino. Trevino saved golf after Jack Nicklaus killed it. He did it in much the same way as Demaret had, by being a "character" and winner at the same time.

Lee Trevino is the greatest golfer who ever putted with a burrito and called his gallery "Lee's Fleas" and sent them off to war against "Arnie's Army."

Most historians agree that the three most dominant golfers were Bobby Jones, Ben Hogan, and Jack Nicklaus, and therefore, they were the greatest players.

No argument from me. I would add, however, that they were all so good, they almost put the game to death, and that's why Walter Hagen, Jimmy Demaret, and Lee Trevino may have done almost as much for the sport.

They saved it with "color."

Bobby Ray Furnace

I CAUGHT UP WITH BOBBY RAY FURNACE, THE NEWEST STAR ON THE PGA Tour, as he stood in front of a clubhouse in Nabisco, Florida, complaining about the color of his courtesy car.

It was a white Seville, not the blue one he had asked for. "And look at this trunk," he said. "It's too small. How am I supposed to get $537,000 in here? These jerk-off sponsors better get on the ball if they expect me to come back to *this* cesspool next year."

Bobby Ray had just won the $537,000 by finishing in a tie for 19th place in the Chrysler/Shearson/Nissan Sausage-'n'-Biscuit K mart Klassic at L'Arbitrage Country Club. He had asked for the prize money in small unmarked bills, a habit he had developed in a prior profession.

And now, to save air fare, he was hoping to drive to the next stop on the tour, the Isuzu/Kemper/Providential Independent Chili Cook and Bank of Dollars Classic in Nabisco, Georgia, where, as is the custom of some touring pros, he planned to leave the courtesy car in a ditch.

Bobby Ray zoomed into stardom in professional golf in the first half of 1988 by setting two spectacular records. In the Epson statistics, he became the first player on the tour to leave 12 consecutive courtesy cars in ditches. He also became the first golfer to earn more than $3,000,000 without winning a tournament.

"On the all-exempt tour, winning is for nobodies," Bobby Ray said. "Show me a tournament winner and I'll show you a guy you've never heard of, or a guy you'll never hear of again. But I'm there every week, man. Look at the names who finish between nineteenth and thirty-second. That's where you'll find Bobby Ray Furnace. I wouldn't be on so many magazine covers right now if it weren't for the streak I had from Nabisco Springs to here—seven straight weeks in twenty-second place! Try that on, pal."

Bobby Ray said there was no question that some of the new rules on the tour had helped him become a star, specifically, the rules governing distribution of prize money. The difference between first and 19th place is now only $7.16.

"We still have a way to go," said Bobby Ray. "There's no reason why a guy who doesn't enter a tournament shouldn't get a check too. We're all out here trying to make a living for our families. This is something the press, the sponsors, and the spectators don't seem to understand."

Bobby Ray is only 5'4" and weighs only 130 pounds, and yet he is one of the longest and straightest hitters in golf, which is part of his charm. Apparently, he is a true believer in the new technology. I talked with Furnace about his career and his sport.

"I understand you're a true believer in the new technology, Bobby Ray."

"The what?"

"Your equipment. The clubs you use. The balls you play."

"That's kind of personal."

"It's common knowledge that your grooves are going to be illegal someday."

"That's really a crock of shit too. I'm talking to my lawyer about it."

I asked, "Is it true that Greg Norman's teeth put the grooves in your irons?"

"Yeah, so what? Greg's a friend of mine."

"How did he do this?"

"I asked him to chew on 'em for an hour and he did it. Show me a rule that says Greg Norman can't chew on your club face. I don't see why everybody's down on my ass because I thought of it first."

I said, "Where did you get the idea for the plutonium shaft?"

"Simple. I saw this TV show about the H-bomb."

"The clubhead is pure granite?"

"Actually, it's granite around the core of a week-old grilled cheese sandwich. One degree loft."

"Hardly any loft at all, as far as I can tell. Did you get this idea from studying Ben Hogan?"

"Who's Ben Hogan?"

"Let's talk about the grip. I understand you've signed a contract to endorse the condom grip."

"Hell of a product, man. It's a combination of unborn lamb and Krazy Glue. Your hands never slip."

"When it comes to greater distance, how much difference does the new golf ball make?"

"It depends on where you get your specimen."

"I don't understand."

"Hey, it's no secret we all carry a hypodermic needle. One day I took a sample out of Tom Watson's ball and put it in my own. Talk about a hot ball. Holy shit!"

"What would be your idea of a Grand Slam today?"

"A what?"

"That thing Bobby Jones won."

"Who's Bobby Jones?"

"I'll put it a different way. Which four tournaments would you like to win, all in one year?"

He thought it over, then:

"I guess I'd go for the Nabisco Insurance Agent, the Nabisco Shopping Mall, the Nabisco Safety Deposit Vault, and the Nabisco Head Job."

"Last question. Has God helped you as much as He seems to have helped so many other players on the tour?"

"God? You mean like . . . up there?"

"Right."

"Yeah, uh, God's helped me. He got me through all six weeks of college, and then through the qualifying school, but I don't think he helps me so much anymore. Like on the first hole today, after my tee shot. I'd like to see God try to hit a three-iron out of the fucking divot *I* was in."

The Host Club

As one who had been unable to decide between the investment firms of Arnold Palmer and Tom Watson on television, I was naturally excited when a PGA Tour event came to my country club. I dashed right out there, not only to pick up some portfolio advice, but to see all of the famous pros in their own flesh and blood and checkered cottons.

The first shock came when I was forced to park on a school playground five miles away, ride a shuttle bus, and then buy a badge just to get into my own country club. The badge cost $5,000, but the money was for charity, somebody said.

The club sure looked different. A lot of big trucks and mobile homes were sitting around, circus tents had been put up, and a good many wives of members I knew were wearing the same bonnets, blouses, and polka-dot skirts, and were hastily jumping in and out of white Pontiacs.

"Hi, Mildred," I said to one of the wives. "Where's Fred?"

"I can't talk now," she said, panting. "Mark Wiebe needs to go to the dentist and Don Pooley has to find a discount store."

She sped away in a courtesy car.

My next shock came when I entered the clubhouse and a security guard refused to admit me to my own locker room.

"I wish you wouldn't push me in the chest," I said, trying to smile.

"Players and officials only," he said, gruffly.

"I'm a member," I said.

"Move along, please. Can't you see how crowded this hallway is?"

"I want to use the bathroom," I explained.

The security guard spoke into a walkie-talkie.

"Ralph, we've got a code three in the locker area. Want to send some help down here to get the asshole out? Over."

I got the point and went downstairs to the Men's Grill to grab a bite to eat. There was another security guard on the door.

"Wrong badge," he said, stopping me.

"This is supposed to be good for the clubhouse," I said, fondling the badge pinned to my shirt.

"You're not a Patron."

"A what?"

"Patrons only. Sorry."

"How do you get to be a Patron?" I asked.

"You buy a Patron's badge for ten thousand dollars."

I thought I might find a snack in the Mixed Foursome Room, but, alas, I ran into another security guard.

He shoved me backward.

"My wife and I play bridge in this room," I said.

"You're not a Saint."

"A what?"

"This room is for Saints only."

"What does it cost to be a Saint?"

"I think it's twenty thousand dollars, but you get a seat on the eighteenth fairway along with it."

The next place I looked for food was the teenage recreation parlor, which our club calls the Peppermint Lounge.

Yet another security guard was on the door.

I peeked around him and noticed several men and women with cocktails in their hands, while others were loading up their plates at a sumptuous buffet.

"Press only," the security guard said.

"The tournament's outside," I argued.

"They bring the leaders in here to be interviewed," he informed me. "Clear the doorway, please. Greg Twiggs is on his way here."

It turned out that the only place where a clubhouse badge holder could find food was in the lobby, along with 4,000 other people. I stood in line for two hours and finally got a fat roast-beef sandwich and a warm Coke.

"I'll just sign for this," I said when I reached the cashier.

"You need scrip," the lady said.

"I need what?"

"Members can't sign this week. You have to buy scrip. I have a twenty-dollar book for a hundred dollars or a forty-dollar book for five hundred dollars."

Giving up on food, I went outside to watch the tournament. At the ninth green, I squeezed into a throng of 10,000 people and caught a glimpse of three golfers down on their hands and knees, evidently staring at insects.

"Which one's Nicklaus?" I asked a fellow spectator.

"Nicklaus doesn't play in this tournament," he said.

Moments later, another group of golfers came to the ninth hole. Mostly, they walked around in circles and held their putters out in front of them, vertically, and squinted.

"Is this Watson?" I inquired.

"Watson never plays here," I was told.

"He doesn't?"

"Naw. Neither does Trevino, or Crenshaw, or Norman, or Zoeller. Palmer plays here, though."

"Great," I said. "When's Arnie coming up?"

"He's not here this year."

I asked which of the famous players *were* here.

The man said, "Well, that's David Ogrin in the bunker. Bob Lohr's the guy behind the tree trunk. Wayne Grady's waiting on a ruling about the water."

The player I most wanted to watch was Seve Ballesteros, the greatest golfer in the world. A woman told me she thought Ballesteros was on the back nine.

I walked out to the 14th hole, the farthest point from the clubhouse. There were maybe a dozen fans watching three players who were identified to me as Tim Simpson, Ronnie Black, and Steve Elkington.

"I guess Seve will be coming up pretty soon, huh?" I said to a man sitting under a tree.

"Not this year," the man said. "Ballesteros can't play in the United States, except in four or five tournaments. Our pros voted on it."

"That's ridiculous," I said, exhausted, hungry, thirsty. "Why am I at this golf tournament if there are no players I've ever heard of?"

"Beats me," the man said. "I'm just sitting here till the goddamn thing's over. The committee closed the street in front of my house and I don't have the right badge to get back home."

Designers and Developers

EXCUSE ME, I DIDN'T MEAN TO YAWN, BUT I WAS JUST SITTING HERE trying to remember the last time I ran into an old friend who wasn't designing a new golf course somewhere and participating in the real estate development around it.

My old friend Jim is a good example. I bumped into Jim in an airport lobby the other day.

"How's it going, Jim?" I said.

"Great! I'm designing a new golf course and I've got a piece of the real estate deal."

"What happened to the brokerage business?"

"You ought to see the land we've got," Jim said. "Our money people say it's the best parcel they've ever acquired."

"Where is it?"

"Tristan de Cunha."

"Mexico?"

"No, it's south of the Equator. An island."

"I get it," I said. "Go to Rio de Janeiro and take a left."

"You could. It's probably easier if you go to Cape Town and take a right. You won't believe what our money people have planned for this place. Hotels, condos, villas, three-acre lots. The landing strip will be ready next year."

"Sounds like paradise," I said. "How do you get there now? Shipwreck?"

"Hovercraft. There are two a week from Queen Maude."

"Queen Maude in Antarctica?"

"Yeah, on a clear day, you can see Antarctica."

"I guess we're talking about a second-home development, huh?"

"Third home," he said. "Our money people say it's all over for the second-home market. You can't get a tee time anywhere."

I asked Jim what he was going to name the course.

"St. Andrews at Tristan de Cunha," he said, rushing off to hug an Arab.

I went to a pay phone, which is where I bumped into my old friend Tom. I asked Tom what was up.

"Everything!" he beamed. "I'm designing a new golf course and I've got a piece of the real estate deal."

"What happened to the fast-food business?"

"You ought to see the land we've got," Tom said. "Our money people say it's the most fantastic acreage they've ever leased. Half of it's in Wyoming, the other half's in Montana. Our money people are talking about three luxury hotels, five hundred townhouses, two hundred club villas, and a marina. No homesites. It's all over for primary residences. People want no worries, they want recreation. A marina's the key."

"If a marina's the key, what are you doing in Wyoming and Montana?"

"Hey, pal, do I look stupid?" said Tom. "Wait till you see the lake we're gonna build!"

"What are you calling the place?"

"St. Andrews at Little Bighorn," he said, dashing away to hug two Japanese gentlemen.

The car rental counter is where I bumped into my old friend Ken.

"Hi, Ken, how you doing?"

"Couldn't be better," he said. "I'm designing a new golf course and I've got a piece of the real estate deal."

"What happened to the roofing business?"

"You ought to see this piece of property we've got. Our money people say it has more potential than anything they've ever looked at. You know Toledo, Ohio, right?"

"Not intimately."

"You know where the interstate curves around after it passes the jeep plant? Stay to the right. Don't go downtown. Exit at the Sheraton. Go to the shopping strip on your right. Behind the K mart? That's the first fairway. Par five."

"It is?"

"Second hole is a blind par three. You hit over the discount drug. I'm pretty excited."

"I can see why. Where are the condos and villas?"

"All underground."

"I'm sorry," I said. "I thought for a minute you said they were underground."

"Every unit," he said. "Our money people say it's all over for inconvenience. You walk out of your living room, go up an escalator, you're on the first tee. Come off of eighteen, you buy wicker furniture, eat Chinese, go to Adult Video, take the escalator home. People want to golf where they shop."

"Does the club have a name?"

"St. Andrews at Spark Plug Mall! We broke concrete this week."

I wished Ken luck and told him in all sincerity that I'd like to meet his money people someday.

"You'll love 'em," he said. "Two guys from Dallas. They used to be in the savings and loan business."

Tips From the Shelf

IT IS A KNOWN FACT THAT THE BEST TIPS ON HOW TO IMPROVE your golf game come from instruction books, so here's some advice from my own rare collection of volumes, beginning with that old, out-of-print favorite, *How to Play Your Best Golf with Corporate Assholes:*

The grip: Get a firm grip on your credit cards; otherwise, you will have to buy all of the drinks and lunch. Rich guys never pay for shit.

The stance: Never stand next to one of the dickheads at a cocktail party. He will tell you this golf joke he heard in Bermuda.

The clubs: Check out the social functions at any club before you apply for membership. If you see a lot of pink and green blazers, fuck it.

The bag: That's what you put over the head of the corporate asshole's wife, to keep her from telling you her plans to redecorate their farmhouse in Connecticut.

The pro: She will be with one of the corporate assholes at the club's spring dance. The wives will say she's disgusting because she's got these tits, but trust your first impression.

From *Better Golf Occasionally Instead of When You Least Expect It:*

Tee shots: Your tee shot should always wind up in the fairway (mowed surface), ideally 280 yards from where you swung at it. Make sure the ball is in the fairway before taking your next swing. This may entail throwing the ball into the fairway from out of the rough (high grass), from behind a tree, from out of sand, or even out of water, but it is essential. You may incur a penalty stroke by doing this but by and large you will make a lower score on the hole if you do not try to hit the ball out of weeds, trees, sand, or, it should go without saying, water.

Long irons: Break all of them in half immediately. Throw them into the nearest river, lake, ocean, creek, or sewer, depending on the type of layout your club has. If you insist on trying to hit a long iron, be sure to whistle a merry tune as you swing the club.

Short irons: These clubs are used for chipping and pitching, and it is the 7-iron that throws best when angry and aiming at a tree trunk. Also, the 9-iron can be relied upon to take nasty, vicious divots out of fairways when a shot goes astray.

Sand wedge: You do not need this club since you are always going to throw your ball out of bunkers, but keep it handy. The sand wedge can make memorable dents in the hood of your car after a frustrating round.

Putter: No golfer can own too many putters. The average country club golfer has between 50 and 75 putters at his disposal. Rotate putters regularly, never allowing one of them to con you into thinking it is the most reliable.

From *Piss on Par (What Par Doesn't Know Don't Hurt It):*

Just because par is three, four, or five on a hole should not affect your game. If you take the attitude that par should be six on a hole, what is par going to do about it—call the police? The fact is, par should be six on any par-3 hole that has water around it, five on any par-3 hole that has sand around it, and four on any par-3 hole that has undulating greens.

Do not be intimidated by what par claims to be. Stand up to par!

Keeping score: There is a tendency among most golfers to let their scores bother them. No golfer has ever shot a score that he thought was as low as it should have been.

Never keep score. This applies especially to the recreational golfer. As we know, the touring pro is asked to keep score accurately, and sometimes does. But the only time the recreational golfer may wish to keep score is on that day when he has a very real chance to break 90 for the first time, having taken so many mulligans off the tees and conceded himself so many six-foot putts.

Always bear in mind that clothing, footwear, and equipment are more important than keeping score.

Know your swing: Most golfers do not know what they look like when they swing the club. They think they look like Jack Nicklaus but in reality they look like somebody having a spasm.

Addressing the ball properly is the key to looking good when swinging the club.

Stand erect but not too erect. Your feet should be slightly wider than your shoulders but not too wide. Bend over from the waist but only slightly. Flex your knees but only a bit. When you feel you are in the proper erect-bent position, have somebody hand you the club.

Now, with the club in your hands, go over some routine checkpoints. Are you too crouched? Are you too erect? Are your knees too stiff? How is your balance? How is your weight distribution? Is your weight primarily on the balls of your feet? Can you lift your heels without too much effort?

Remember, it is better to err forward when swinging the club. If you err forward, you at least may hit the ball. By erring backward, you may risk serious injury and not hit the ball at all.

When you are finally in the proper erect-bent position and feel reasonably comfortable, there is one last thing to check before actually swinging the club. Are you pointed toward the golf course or the clubhouse?

Oh, and you'd probably better let all those groups behind you play through.

Drives and Whispers

TALK ABOUT YOUR PRESSURE SHOTS IN GOLF! ONLY MOMENTS AGO on videotape, this was Severiano Ballesteros—ankle-deep in quicksand, the green more than 260 yards away, the wind dead against him as it howls in off the ocean here at the rugged but scenic Realtor's Swamp Country Club. Not a very hopeful situation for the two-time winner of The Masters, but watch what happens, golf fans! The determined Spaniard takes a lusty swing with his 3-wood and—splat! The shot rises above the tall, protruding palms. It clears the hotel and spa. It clears the teeming hordes of hotpants and halter tops in the gallery. Good bounce across the cart path—and on the green! And *now*, as the drama continues to unfold, Seve Ballesteros has this birdie putt of about 27½ feet to go eight under through nine holes and grab the lead in today's fourth and final round of the Franchot Tone National Pro–Comedian, Singer, Car Dealer, Estate Planner, and Bank of Kowloon Knitwear Classic!

Good afternoon, ladies and gentlemen, I'm Don Void, and what a feast we have for you here on the beautiful northeast coast of Florida. The oil slick has disappeared, the red tide has receded, most of the condominiums have been refinanced, and it's all winding down to a climax in the third annual F.T.N.P.C.S.C.D.E.P.B.K.K.C., one of the truly great events on the PGA Tour and, I might mention, a tournament that's contributed more than $6 million to local charities, less expenses, advertising costs, promotional fees, and what have you.

I'm Don Void, as I said earlier, and working with me today on the 18th hole is my friend and cohort, Wristy Stark, the former PGA champion, probably the greatest chipper the game has ever known, and a guy who knows how to provide the lighter touch. We'll be looking forward to his comments throughout the telecast.

Right now, as Seve lines up his putt—there's a nice shot from our Goodyear blimp, Albatross, piloted today by Captain Stormy Werther of Lakehurst, New Jersey—let's catch you up on the action that took place on Thursday, Friday, and Saturday at this clambake-classic.

Arnold Palmer and Jack Nicklaus, magical names of course, stole the thunder on Thursday. Making a couple of those patented charges of theirs, they blazed in with 77s and shared the early lead. Talk about thrills! Before the day was over, however, the lead belonged to Howell Rowell Jr. and five other second-year pros, all tied with 10-under 62s. Among the group was Ed Fusilli. Here we see Ed's pretty wife, Rachel, asking him to examine a W-2 form.

Friday was the day young Brad Method made a move. The Houston rookie put a sizzling 61 on the scoreboard and leaped into a tie with Howell Rowell. Brad's pink polyesters flap in the breeze as he pulls the trigger on a 1-iron. There's Brad's wife, Debbie, showing us two reasons she once held the title of Miss Sioux Falls.

The wind kicked up on Saturday—there goes the press tent, as you can see—but the subpar rounds continued. Howell Rowell and Brad Method were still leading at the end of the day, but Ballesteros was close, and who could overlook Arnie and Big Jack, only 22 shots off the pace?

Fine camerawork there on Mrs. Brad Method, being helped with her troublesome halter top by tournament officials.

So we're up to date on all the scoring. Now let's go out on the course and meet the expert commentators who'll be helping me bring you all the live action. First to the 13th hole and Steve Gunch.

"Hello, I'm Steve Gunch. I'll be reporting from the two-hundred-twenty-seven-yard, par-three thirteenth hole, a severe test of the golfers' nerves. The green is bordered on three sides by waterfalls, but the biggest problem for the players, as I see it, is the reptile farm that comes right up to the front edge of the putting surface. I look for most of the fellows to go at it with a driver—try to bounce one off the synagogue behind the green. It's the percentage shot. And now to the fourteenth and our colleague from overseas, Peter Brace-Asher."

"Jolly good fun to be here, I must say. And my, what marvelous stuff we're seeing from all the lads as they nestle their wedges around this rather intoxicating marshland. As for the fourteenth, well, what a diabolical thing it is! One bloody slip, to my way of thinking, and you're consigned to a watery grave. On to the fifteenth, then."

"Hi, I'm Vern Utterance. I'll be describing the action here at the fifteenth, a six-hundred-three-yard par-five that—no, wait a minute, that's the sixteenth. Sorry. The fifteenth is a four-hundred-twenty-three-yard par-four that appears to have a good bit of grass in the fairway. From my vantage point, in fact, I can see grass all the way back to the tee. Over to sixteen."

"This is Frank Murk at the crowd-pleasing sixteenth hole, where we've seen thirty-eight pars, two hundred thirty-seven birdies, and forty-nine bogeys posted by golfers ranging in height from five feet five inches to six feet two inches with an average weight of one hundred sixty-five pounds. In addition, most of the touring pros from California and Texas were born there. That's the story from sixteen. Now over to seventeen and the colorful J. L. Starnes, who's just completed his round and agreed to join our announce crew today. Welcome aboard, J.L."

"Uh, this is J. L. Starnes. I'll tell you one thing. They can take this seventeenth hole and give it back to the goats. The summitch cost me about three grand a while ago. I drove it perfect, right down the left side, but I must have hit a sprinkler head or something. I wound up in the shit. Got on the green after I chipped out and cold-jumped a four wood, but the green's slicker'n Sam Snead's head, so I three-putt the cocksucker. Maybe I got what I deserved. Play the fucker like Mother Goose, you're gonna make six."

Right you are, J.L.! I'm Don Void back at the 18th where I've been informed by the studio that the basketball game is about to get under way. We'll be returning to the Franchot Tone for all the golf action after today's all-important contest between the Mavericks and the Suns. So for Steve Gunch, Peter Brace-Asher, Vern Utterance, Frank Murk, J. L. Starnes, and Wristy Stark, this is Don Void, saying so long from Realtor's Swamp!

The Masters Its Ownself

SOMETHING MYSTICAL HAPPENS TO EVERY WRITER WHO GOES TO the Masters for the first time, some sort of emotional experience that results in a search party having to be sent out to recover his typewriter from a clump of azaleas. The writer first becomes hypnotized by the "cathedral of pines," down around the 10th fairway normally, then he genuflects at the Sarazen Bridge on the 15th, and eventually takes up a position on the Augusta National veranda, there to wait for an aging wisteria vine to crawl up his sleeve and caress his priceless clubhouse badge. It is a peculiar state of mind, a sort of sporting heaven in which the writer feels that if Bobby Jones could only waggle a hickory shaft once more, it would instantly turn him into F. Scott Damon "Ring" Hemingway. My own problem is that I still feel this way after 39 consecutive years of being on — or around — the Masters veranda.

Where has the time gone? Yesterday it was 1951. I'm a college sophomore but a working journalist following Ben Hogan every step of the way to report on the color of Ben's slacks and the contents of Valerie's thermos to the readers of the now-deceased *Fort Worth Press.* Now it's all these years later but I'm still a fixture in my favorite area, the upstairs grill and balcony, wondering how much fun it would have been to have stood around there with Granny Rice and Bob Jones.

As it is, I make do with an assortment of rogues: golfers, ex-pro football players, TV folks, poets, and other privileged souls who turn up in the clubhouse every year. I'm accused of having done a record amount of time in the upstairs grill and on that balcony overlooking the veranda. It's true that I've spent a lot of hours up there, but I can tell you that eggs, country ham, biscuits, red-eye gravy, a pot of coffee, a morning paper, a table by the window, and the idle chitchat of competitors, authors, wits, and philosophers hasn't exactly been a bad way to start off each day at the Masters all these years.

That room, the upstairs men's grill, was once the interview area, so designated by those writers who wished to include quotes in their stories. Strangely enough, not every writer wanted quotes in his story 30 years ago. Many believed that their own observations were all their readers deserved. I was always a quote guy, trained by Blackie Sherrod, my mentor, a Texas sportswriting legend, to pick up the good quote, not just any old quote. So trained were a few other writers, such as my old friend Bob Drum, now with CBS, then with the *Pittsburgh Press.*

In those early 1950s, we would ordinarily have the daily leaders all to ourselves upstairs at the completion of their rounds. Then more quote guys began coming out of the dogwood as the press corps of The Masters started to double, triple, and upward. And suddenly one year, Hogan and Snead found themselves being smothered on separate sofas while journalists stood, knelt, and shouted, "What'd you hit to the sixth?" . . . "How long was the putt on twelve?" . . . "Where was the pin on fifteen?" They practically swung from chandeliers.

This was the first time I heard Ben use a line he would rely on again in the future. He said, "One of these days a deaf mute is going to win a golf tournament, and you guys won't be able to write a story."

Cliff Roberts, The Masters chairman, observed this scene one day, saw things were getting out of hand, and ordered an interview room installed in the press building, which used to be a tent and then a Quonset hut before it became a structure to accommodate the largest number of journalists who attend any of the four majors. The problem these days with the interview area is that the interviews themselves have become so orchestrated by Masters edict that the interview area is quite possibly the worst place in Augusta, Ga., to look for news. Locker rooms and grill rooms are still the best places to find out things you don't know — at The Masters or any other golf tournament.

I probably remember the 1954 Masters more vividly than any of the others. No doubt this has something to do with the fact that Hogan and Snead were involved, but it was only my fourth year there. I was still as awed as a teenager around a swimming pool of shapely adorables.

I'm not willing to argue that the '54 event was the most thrilling of them all. The competition is too stiff. There was 1960, for example, the tournament where Arnold Palmer stabbed Ken Venturi in the heart with closing birdies at the 71st and 72nd holes.

There was 1962 when Palmer birdied two of the last three holes to tie Gary Player and Dow Finsterwald, and then dusted them off in an 18-hole play-off during which the scoreboard operators showed no favoritism whatsoever when they posted "GO ARNIE" signs all over the golf course. And I couldn't overlook 1975, the year a trim, now-beloved Jack Nicklaus waged a Sunday birdie war—and won—over Tom Weiskopf and Johnny Miller.

But 1954 was extra special. It was important, too, because Hogan and Snead, the two great players of the era, were in it all the way and wound up in a tie that forced a play-off. And the tournament proper was all the more exciting because of Billy Joe Patton, an obscure amateur from North Carolina. He very nearly won, and would have if he'd known how to play safe at the 13th and 15th holes in the final round.

The last round began with Hogan in the lead by three strokes over Snead. Keep in mind that this was a Ben Hogan who had merely scored a Triple Crown the year before by capturing The Masters, the U.S. Open, and the British Open, and this was a Sam Snead who had merely won The Masters twice and the PGA twice in the four previous years. We're talking legends here.

Meanwhile, there was Billy Joe Patton, who had never won anything. Which I largely attributed to his fast backswing. Nevertheless, Billy Joe had stolen the hearts of the huge crowds, not to forget the press, by taking every conceivable risk on the course and babbling about it with everybody in the gallery. Billy Joe had surprisingly led through 18 and 36, but now he trailed by five—only not for long that Sunday.

My friend Bob Drum and I, being quote guys, went out early with Billy Joe. Ben and Sam—and the tournament—would come along later. At the sixth hole, a par 3 that then had an enormous hump in the green (a mound that was once known as "the hill where they buried the elephant"), it will be to my everlasting embarrassment that I left Drum in the crowd behind the green and went to a nearby concession stand only seconds before Billy Joe struck his tee shot. The roar was deafening, similar to the kind we would hear for Palmer in later years, only this one trailed off in irregular Rebel whoops. Billy Joe had made a hole-in-one.

"What did it look like?" I said, having rushed back to Drum.

"It looked like a hole-in-one, whaddaya think it looked like?"

Drum, a large man who was even larger then, has a guttural, Irish voice that has often been compared with the percussion section of the Ohio State band.

"Did it go in on the fly, bounce in, roll in, or what?" I wondered.

"It looked like a one!" said Drum, a man not known for his patience, a writer who cared little for detail in those days. "Here's the cup and here's the ball. The ball did this. That's a one!"

He scribbled something on a pairing sheet.

"Here, this is what a two looks like," he said. "That's not as good as a one. Okay? Let's go before Mush Mouth's gallery tramples us."

Mush Mouth was every golfer or writer Drum ever knew who came from the Old South.

I suppose I should interject that Drum and I became friends in the first place when we had been accidentally seated next to each other in the press emporium at my first Masters. Who could resist striking up a friendship with a man who would lean back and laugh so raucously, so often, at his own copy? I confess that he would catch me doing the same thing on occasion. We were to joke in future years that if Arnold Palmer had ever actually spoken the lines we dolled up for him, he could have had his own lounge act in Vegas.

But back to '54 and Billy Joe. The amateur reclaimed The Masters lead that Sunday after he birdied the eighth and ninth holes, and by the time he reached the par-5 13th, The Masters was his to win or lose.

We were standing within a few feet of Billy Joe at the 13th after his drive had come to rest in an awkward lie in the upper-right-hand rough. He pulled a spoon out of the bag, and Drum and I looked at each other. A wooden club from a bad lie in the rough to a green guarded by water? When you're leading The Masters? On Sunday? When maybe you can be the last amateur ever to win a major? When you've probably got Hogan and Snead beaten—and we've got Pulitzers riding on it?

Billy Joe only grinned at us, and the crowd, and said, "I didn't get where I am by playin' safe!"

"Great!" Drum said to me. "Where does this guy want his body shipped?"

Billy Joe didn't hear my pal, not that it would have mattered. All week long, Billy Joe had heard nothing but his own muse. And he was too far away to hear his shot when it splashed in the creek. He made a seven. Minutes later, at the 15th he did it again—went for the green on his second. He found the water again, made a six. History books record that Billy Joe Patton played those two holes in three over par that Sunday, holes he could easily have parred by laying up, and he only missed tying Hogan and Snead by one stroke. With those pars, he would have won The Masters by two.

Even touring pros are sometimes aware of historic importance. Many in the field stayed over on Monday to watch the Hogan-Snead playoff. Bob Jones and Cliff Roberts rode along in a golf cart. From tee to green, it was a clinic, but neither player could make a putt on those old scratchy but lightning rye greens. They used to say you could actually hear the ball rolling across the barren rye. Snead won with a two-under 70 to Hogan's 71, and the difference was a 30-foot chip shot that Sam holed from just off the 10th green.

I lost $100 to Drum on the playoff, a $100 that neither of us had. Knowing he admired Hogan's game as much as I did, I later asked him why he had wanted to bet on Snead.

"It ain't the Open," he had said, having outsmarted me again.

While it's true that I missed seeing Billy Joe's ace, I wasn't always in the wrong place at Augusta. On the night before Art Wall Jr. birdied five of the last six holes to win the 1959 Masters, I ran into him in the lobby of the ancient Bon Air Hotel, once the only place to stay before it became a retirement home. The Bon Air was headquarters for everyone, just as the old Town Tavern in downtown Augusta used to be the only place to stand in line and try to bribe your way in for dinner.

Art and I were making small talk that evening when he was recognized by one of your typical Augusta fans, a red-faced, over-beveraged Southerner in an ill-fitting blazer.

"Hey!" the man said. "Ain't you Art Wall?"

Art smiled, nodded.

"Ain't you the fellow who's supposed to make all them hole-in-ones?"

"That's him," I said.

"Thirty or forty of them suckers? Something like that?"

"It's up to thirty-four now," said Art, politely.

"*Thirty-four?*" the man frowned. "Boy, who you tryin' to kid? Bobby didn't make but *three!*"

At a more recent Masters, I was lolling around on the veranda with Mike Lupica, a columnist for the New York *Daily News*. He's considerably younger than I — this was maybe his second Masters — and I guess I momentarily forgot that Mike is noted for his mouth. He was thumbing through the Green Book, the press guide, looking for lore items, when he said, "Your first year was fifty-one?"

"Yeah."

He started to count something.

Then he said, "Do you realize your first year was only the fifteenth Masters they'd ever played?"

I'd never thought of it that way.

"I'll be damned," I said.

And he said, "So how 'bout it, old-timer? Were the greens really that fast in those days?"

I almost made the mistake of seriously answering him. Happily, a wisteria vine grabbed me around the neck and prevented it.

Back to Baltus Oak

THE OPEN CHAMPIONSHIP OF THE UNITED STATES GOLF ASSOCIATION—our National Open—is a tournament with its own flavor, personality, look, attitude, atmosphere, continuity, history, mystique, and charm. It is the most important championship a golfer can win, which is why it is more often lost by a number of competitors than won by a single individual. As Cary Middlecoff once said, "Nobody wins the Open—it wins you."

What it is like is, well, it is sort of like . . .

OPEN FIELD MAY REVOLT

OYSTER BISQUE, N.Y.—A glittering field on the eve of the National Open golf championship agreed today that there is so much exotic plant life bordering the narrow fairways of historic old Baltus Oak Country Club that only an anorexic fashion model wearing leotards could walk down the middle of them without snagging a garment.

During today's final warmup round, two foursomes actually got lost in the foliage on the back nine holes and wound up at a Southampton lawn party.

Deane Beman, commissioner of the PGA Tour, said he was

encouraging as many touring pros as he could to withdraw from the championship.

Beman said, "As talented as our players are, they've never learned how to hit long irons out of waist-high asparagus."

M. Traxton Hudspeth, president of the USGA, defended Baltus Oak, saying it belonged in the same category with Oakland Hills, Oakmont, Oak Hill, Oak Tree, and Olympic, "which sounds like oak, when you think about it."

UNKNOWN LEADS OPEN

OYSTER BISQUE, N.Y. — Jesse Ray Rives, an unheralded driving range pro from Hoot, Utah, grabbed the opening round lead in the National Open here today with a sizzling even-par 70 on historic old Baltus Oak, the course where Bobby Jones first wore knickers.

Rives, who wore coveralls and a straw hat with a band on it that said "Root for Hoot," birdied the first nine holes and blew out all of the computers in the press tent. Although he came back in 44, his score held up against an array of glamorous challengers.

Incredibly, Rives took only six putts for the round, tying a record set by Bob Rosburg. He tied another record held by Bob Tway when he holed out eight sand wedges.

Rives, 25, said he would feel better about his chances if he weren't so lonely so far away from home. "I wisht my uncle Clyde and my pet bobcat was here," he said.

OPEN JOLTED BY SECOND MYSTERY MAN

OYSTER BISQUE, N.Y. — R. J. "Bo" Mackey, an obscure pro at a putt-putt course in Clump, Calif., seized the halfway lead in the National Open here tonight when he added a 65 to his first-round 81 for a 36-hole total of 146, only six over par on historic old Baltus Oak, the course where Walter Hagen had his first hangover.

Having teed off at 5:14 A.M., Mackey was one of the day's early finishers at 4 o'clock in the afternoon as the field of 150 moved along briskly despite the 101-degree heat. Sweating out his lead in Baltus Oak's non-air-conditioned clubhouse, Mackey had some anxious moments until shortly before midnight when defending champion Jack Nicklaus came in.

Nicklaus had threatened to overtake Mackey until the 17th hole. Jack finished with a horrendous 13 and then a 15 on the last green when several real estate developers seemed to be clawing at him on his backswing.

Nicklaus failed to make the 36-hole cut, but did not act disappointed.

"The fact is, I'm tired of golf," said Jack. "All I really want to do is design courses now, provided there's ample beachfront property."

First-round leader Jesse Ray Rives also failed to make the cut, largely because a lurking animal—believed by some to be a bobcat—swallowed his ball on the 10th fairway.

Mackey, who wore khakis and a tool dresser's helmet, confessed that he had received a lot of help in molding his game. He said he owed a lot to the crew on the B. W. Roberts No. 2 oil rig in Clump. They had encouraged him to leave town, he said. He also specifically singled out two men who had pieced together his compact swing: Ralph Tibitt, his ex-warden, and Roy Sangry, his parole officer.

UNKNOWN LOG JAM IN OPEN

OYSTER BISQUE, N.Y.—Billy Tom Riddle, an assistant pro from Harper Valley, Tenn., playing in his first professional golf tournament, tied for the 54-hole lead in the National Open here today with four amateurs, all from the powerful University of Houston. Their score was 223, only 13 over par on historic old Baltus Oak, the course where Harry Vardon tripped on a dining room carpet.

Best known of the Houston collegians was Rex Zark, who has been the Western, Trans-Miss, Southern, North-South, Broadmoor, British, and Idaho State amateur champion every year since the age of 9. The other talented members of the Texas team are Kermit Blank from Albany, N.Y., Babe Stimmett from Seattle, Wash., and Joel Wuthergrind from Worcester, Mass.

None of the leaders could rest easily, it appeared, for only 16 strokes off the pace, poised to make one of his patented stretch runs, was Arnold Palmer.

The championship was struck with an indelicate misfortune during Saturday's third round when R. J. "Bo" Mackey, the putt-putt pro, was disqualified on the first nine holes of his round. A USGA spokesman said Mackey had been warned repeatedly since Thursday to refrain from making obscene gestures and comments to women in his gallery but that he had refused to heed the warning. "We had no other course of action to take," said T. Phillip Carter duPont Lawrence, a USGA vice-president. "This, after all, is the

Open championship. We're trying to identify the best golfer, not the crudest."

HOGAN WINS UNPRECEDENTED NINTH OPEN

OYSTER BISQUE, N.Y.—With the coveted National Open championship all but sewed up, Arnold Palmer caught his backswing in a flowering banyan today on historic old Baltus Oak, the course where Tommy Armour once bought lunch, and Ben Hogan, looking tanned and fit despite his 76 years, flashed past Palmer to capture his ninth Open title.

Palmer caught his swing in the tree at Baltus Oak's 17th hole and had to be rescued by a demolition team from the Corps of Engineers. Palmer was unable to complete the round and the tournament, and thus he will have to endure sectional qualifying again next year.

"It's pretty disheartening to know you can finish 10-10 and win, and then not even be able to play," said Palmer.

Hogan shot a flaming 67 in the final round for a 72-hole total of 301, only 21 over par. Hogan's round was the lowest since architect Robert Trent Jones had revamped Baltus Oak, placing a number of bunkers in the center of some tees and forcing carries of 280 yards or more over water.

There was a moment of pure drama at the final green after Hogan finished, flashing his familiar outgoing, quick-smiling expression. Hogan went over to Jones and shook his hand until the architect knelt down, uttering a bit of a whimper.

"I brought the monster to its knees," said Hogan.

Sam Snead, who mailed in his scores, again finished second.

None of the third-round leaders managed to finish. Billy Tom Riddle, tormented by the sight of his first gallery, picked up at the third hole after striking his ball 21 times in a bunker. The entire University of Houston team, including Rex Zark, quit after nine and mysteriously departed for West Lafayette, Ind., the site of next week's NCAA championships.

Palmer was one of several blowups as the Open pressure mounted late in the day.

Steve Jones needed only to play even bogey over the last nine holes to tie Hogan, but he lost the Bible out of his golf bag and shot an incoming 46. A man of great inner peace, however, Jones only smiled and said, "Boy, it looks like God got up on the wrong side of the bed today."

Curtis Strange had a good chance but couldn't control his temper.

Needing a par at the 72nd for a tie, he aimed his 5-iron at a marble statue instead of the green and hit it 240 yards, and out of bounds. The statue was that of T. Phillip Carter-Hughes Bentley duPont Lawrence Sr., the man who built Baltus Oak.

As Hogan accepted the unprecedented ninth Open trophy in a moving ceremony at the putting green and in turn presented the USGA with his full set of clubs and his white cap for the Golf House museum, some 30 players were still out on the course, completing the last nine holes in the dark. Word circulated that one of them, Frank Clack, a driving range operator from Davenport, Iowa, could tie Hogan with two birdies over the last four holes, but officials dismissed the news as a wild, malicious rumor.

In its only other action of the day, the USGA announced that next year's Open had been awarded to the Upper Course at historic old Baltus Oak, the club where Deane Beman ate his first Nabisco product.

The Glory Game at Goat Hills

Goat Hills is gone now. It was swallowed up by the bulldozers of progress, and in the end it was nice to know that something could take a divot out of those fairways. But all of the regulars had left long before. I suppose it will be all right to talk about it now, about the place and the people and the times we had. Maybe it will explain why I don't play golf so much anymore. It's swell to get invited to play Winged Dip and Burning Foot and all those fancy

*clubs where they have real flagsticks instead of broom handles, but
I usually beg off. Frankly, I'm still overgolfed from all those years at
Goat Hills in Texas. You would be too if . . . well, let me tell you
some of it. I'll try to be truthful and not too sentimental, but where
shall I begin? With Cecil? Why not? He was sort of a symbol in
those days, and . . .*

WE CALLED HIM CECIL THE PARACHUTE BECAUSE HE FELL DOWN A
lot. He would attack the golf ball with a whining, leaping move—
more of a calisthenic than a swing—and occasionally, in his spectacular struggles for extra distance, he would soar right off the end
of elevated tees.

He was a slim, bony, red-faced little man who wore crepe-soled
shoes and a heavily starched shirt that crackled when he marked
his ball, always inching it forward as much as possible. When he
was earthbound, Cecil drove a truck for Grandma's Cookies, and he
always parked it behind a tall hedge near the clubhouse, out of
sight of passing cars, one of which might have Grandma in it.

Anyhow, when the truck was there, you could be pretty sure
that not only was Cecil out on the course but so, most likely, were
Tiny, Easy, Magoo, and Foot the Free, Ernie, Matty, Rush and Grease
Repellent, Little Joe, Weldon the Oath, Jerry, John the Band-Aid,
and Moron Tom—and me. I was known as Dump, basically because
of what so many partners thought I did to them for money.

There would be an excellent chance that all of us would be in
one hollering, protesting, arguing, club-slinging gangsome, betting
huge sums of money we didn't have. In other words, when Cecil's
truck was hidden behind the hedge, you knew the game was on.

The game was not the kind the United States Golf Association
would have approved of, but it was the kind we played for about 15
years at a windy, dusty, seldom mowed, stone-hard, practically
treeless, residentially surrounded public course named Worth
Hills in Fort Worth, Tex.

Goat Hills we called it, not too originally.

It was a gambling game that went on in some form or other,
involving anywhere from three to 22 players, almost every day of
every year when a lot of us were younger and bored silly. The game
not only survived my own shaft-breaking, divot-stomping, club-
slinging presence, it outlasted rain, snow, heat, wars, tornadoes,
jobs, studies, illnesses, divorces, births, deaths, romances, and
pinball machines.

Nearly all of the days at the Hills began the same way. Some of us would be slouched in wicker chairs on the small front porch of the wooden clubhouse, smoking, drinking coffee or Cokes, complaining about worldly things, such as why none of the movie houses in town had changed features in five or six weeks, and why most of the girls we knew only wanted to hump rich guys—didn't they care anything about debonair?

Say it was August. We would be looking across the putting green and into the heat. In Texas in the summer, you can see the heat. It looks like germs. In fact, say it was the day of The Great Cart Wreck.

There on the porch, Matty, who had a crewcut and wore glasses, was playing tunes on his upper front teeth with his finger nails. He had learned how to do this in study hall in high school, and for money he could play almost any tune, including *Sixty-Minute Man* and *Sabre Dance,* and you could actually recognize it.

I was reading a book of some kind as usual. Something light by a Russian or a German.

Tiny, a heavyset railroad conductor, came out of the clubhouse in his flaming red shirt and red slacks, and said, "Dump, what you gonna do with all that book crap in your head?"

"None of it stays there," I said.

Foot the Free, which was short for Big Foot the Freeloader, was practice-putting at a chipped-out crevice in the concrete, a spot that marked the finish of the greatest single hole I've ever seen played—but more about that later.

Little Joe was out on the putting green, trying to perfect a stroke behind his back, a trick shot, in the hope that somebody would one day suggest a behind-the-back putting contest.

Magoo was sitting next to me on the porch.

"Anything about God in that book?" he asked.

"Some."

"Anything in there about what God did to me on the back nine yesterday?"

Around the corner came John the Band-Aid, cleats on, clubs over his shoulder, handkerchief around his neck, impatient as always.

"You, you, you, and you, and you too," he said. "All of you two, two, two, automatic one-down presses, get-evens on nine and eighteen. Whipsaw everybody seventy or better for five."

We began tying our golf shoes.

John the Band-Aid removed three clubs from his bag, dropped

the bag on the gravel, and started swinging the clubs in a violent limbering-up exercise.

"Me and Little Joe got all teams for five match and five medal— dollar cats and double on birdies," he said.

Little Joe, who played without a shirt and had a blond ducktail, said, "Damn, John, I'd sure like to pick my own partner someday. You gonna play good or scrape it around like yesterday?"

John the Band-Aid said, "Well, you can have some of *me*, if it'll keep your interest up."

"I try five," said Little Joe in his high-pitched voice. "Five and a R-ra C."

Little Joe and I took a cart. So did John and Magoo. We had won money the day before so we could afford to ride. The others walked, carrying their own clubs. We were an eightsome, but others would no doubt join us along the way. It wasn't unusual for other players to drive their cars around the course, find the game, hop out, and get it on.

It was Matty one afternoon who drove his red Olds right up to the edge of the third green, jumped out with his golf shoes and glove already on, and said, "Do I have a duck in the car?" He had driven straight to the game from the University of Oklahoma, a distance of some 200 miles, and he had the duck in the car in case somebody wanted to bet him he couldn't hit a duck hook with a putter.

We played the first eight holes and then came the long inter-lude of bookkeeping on the ninth tee.

John the Band-Aid had earned his nickname by bleeding a lot, such as he did this day because he had shot even par but was losing to everybody. Which was why he had teed up his ball first—the game worked in reverse etiquette.

"All right, Magoo," he said, "you got me out, out, even, even, one down, and one down. I press your young ass for ten. Foot, you got me out, out, out, and one down. You're pushed for eight. Win-dow closed?"

And so it went.

The ninth tee at Goat Hills was on a bluff, above a steep dropoff into a cluster of hackberry trees, a creek, rocks, and weeds. It was a par 4. The drive had to carry the ravine and if you could hit it far enough, you had about a 7-iron to the green, going back toward the clubhouse.

John the Band-Aid tightened his straw hat and dug in for the tee shot.

"I'm gonna hit this summitch to Dallas," he said.

"Outhit you for five," Magoo said.

"You're on. Anybody else?"

"I try five," Little Joe said.

"You're on."

John the Band-Aid then curved a wondrous slice into the right rough, and coming off his follow-through, he slung his driver in the general direction of Eagle Mountain Lake, which was 30 miles behind us.

He just missed hitting Little Joe, who was nimble enough to dance out of the way.

Little Joe said, "Man, they ought to put you in a box and take you to the World's Fair."

John's arms were folded and he was staring off in an aimless direction, burning inside. Suddenly, then, he dashed over to his bag, jerked out his 2-iron, and slung it against the water fountain, snapping the shaft in half.

"That goddamn club cost me a shot on the fourth," he explained.

I wasn't all that happy myself. One under and no money ahead. Maybe that's why I pointed the three-wheel electric cart straight down the hill, full speed ahead, a getaway cart.

Over the rocks and ditches we went darting, and that's when the front wheel struck a large stone in the creek bed. All I recall hearing was Little Joe's voice.

"Son of a young . . . !"

We both went over the front end, head first, the bags and clubs flying out over and behind us.

I guess I was out for 10 seconds. When I came to, the cart was pinning down my left leg, battery acid was eating away at my shirt, and broken clubs were everywhere.

Little Joe was sitting down in the rocks examining his skinned elbows, and giggling.

The others were standing around, looking down at us, considering whether to lift the cart off my leg, or leave me there to lose all bets.

Magoo glanced at Little Joe's white canvas bag, which was already being eaten into by battery acid.

"Two dollars says Joe don't have a bag by the fourteenth," Magoo said.

My ankle was swollen. I had to take off my shoe and play the rest of the round in one shoe.

It is a remarkable footnote in golfing history that I birdied that ninth hole, to which Matty said, "I done been beat by everything now. Dead man comes out of the creek and makes a birdie."

Little Joe's bag lasted exactly until the 14th hole. After holing out a putt, he went to pick it up but there was nothing left but the two metal rings and a shoulder strap.

And most of his left trouser leg was going fast.

"Two says Joe is stark naked by the seventeenth," Magoo said.

That day, Little Joe and I both managed birdies on the 18th, winning all presses and get-evens, and Magoo and John the Band-Aid talked for weeks about the time they got beat by a cripple and a guy who was on fire.

On other days at the Hills, purely out of boredom, we played the course backward, or to every other hole, or every third hole, or entirely out of bounds except for the greens, which meant you had to stay in the roads and lawns. We also played the course with only one club, or just two clubs, and sometimes at night.

One game we invented was the Thousand Yard Dash.

This was a one-hole marathon that started on the farthest point on the course from the clubhouse—beside the 12th green—and ended at the chipped-out crevice in the concrete on the clubhouse porch.

I'm not quite sure, but I think this game was the brainchild of either Foot the Free, Matty, or me. We had once played through six blocks of downtown Fort Worth, from Seventh Street to the court-house, mostly on Commerce Street, without getting arrested.

On the day of the first Thousand Yard Dash, some of us went to the left of the rock outhouse perched atop the highest point on the course, and some played to the right of it. I followed Foot the Free because he could never afford to lose—he carried the same $5 bill in his pocket for about eight years.

We hooked a driver, hooked another driver, hooked a third driver, then hooked a spoon—you had to hook the ball to get distance at Goat Hills—and this got us within a pitching wedge of the porch.

Most of the other 12 were out of it by now, lost in creeks or the flowerbeds of apartment houses bordering the first fairway.

My approach shot carried the porch, slammed against a wall of the clapboard clubhouse, chased Wells Howard, the pro, inside the front door, and brought a scream from Lola, his wife and book-keeper. The ball came to rest about 20 feet from the crevice and was puttable, if I moved a chair.

Foot played a bounce shot at the porch. He lofted a high wedge, let it bounce off the gravel. It hopped up over the curb, skidded against a wall, and stopped about 10 feet from the crevice.

We borrowed a broom from Lola and swept dirt particles out of our putting lines.

The other players gathered around to make side bets.

Two rent-club players came out of the clubhouse and stepped in our lines.

"Hey!" I said to them. "This is business!"

"Smart-ass punks," one of them mumbled.

I gave my putt too good a rap. It went past the crevice and wound up in a row of pull carts at the end of the porch.

"Unnatural hazard," I said. "Free drop."

An instantly formed rules committee consisting of Magoo, Matty, and Grease Repellent, who worked at a Texaco station, basically decided that my request was bullshit.

I had to play it out of the pull carts, which was why I 18-putted for a 23.

Against anyone else, I might have still had a chance, but Foot was one of the great putters in history, on any kind of surface. If anything, the concrete looked like bent to Foot compared to the texture of the gnarled Bermuda greens out on the course.

He calmly tapped his 10-footer and it wobbled slowly, slowly, slowly over the concrete, wavered, and went in!

That was one of the two greatest holes I ever saw played. The other was when my friend Bud Shrake made a 517 on a five-block hole that stretched from Goat Hills's first tee to a brown leather loafer in another friend's apartment.

The longest hole we ever played was from the first tee at Goat Hills to the third green at Colonial Country Club, roughly 15 blocks away.

The first time we played it, Rush's dad, a retired oilman, caddied for him in a black Lincoln, and Cecil got bit by a cocker spaniel.

Playing through neighborhoods required a unique shot, we discovered. A blade putter was an ideal club to keep the ball low so it would get extra roll on the pavement.

Some of us went down Stadium Drive, past the TCU football stadium, then left on Park Hill and over the houses. Others went the back way, down Alton Road.

I happened to have sliced a blade putter into a bed of irises on

Alton Road and was looking for it when I saw Cecil down the driveway.

He was contemplating a shot that would have to rise quickly to clear a cyclone fence, then duck sharply under an oak, then hook severely to get around a tile roof, and then slice to land in the street.

As Cecil studied the shot, a dog was barking at his ankles.

Cecil leaped at the ball in his customary manner and drove the ball straight into the fence, about eight feet in front of him, and his follow-through carried him forward and into the ground on his elbows and stomach. He slid into the fence, and the spaniel chased after him as if it were retrieving a sock.

Cecil scrambled to his feet and tiptoed back down the driveway, and withdrew from the competition.

"Hurried the shot," he said. "That sucker was growlin' at me and just when I started to swing, I seen a lady cussin' me through the kitchen window."

Tiny quit at a fishpond. Grease Repellent lost his ball when he struck a sundial. Easy Reid met a fellow and stopped to sell him some insurance. John the Band-Aid broke his blade putter when he sailed it into a chimney. Foot and Magoo were the only two who finished, and they had to play out fast after they climbed over the Colonial fence because some members sent a caddy back to the clubhouse to get the club manager, who would, in turn, call the police.

There was an argument about who won, and a playoff was decided upon. Magoo wanted to play back to Goat Hills, to the cold drink box in the lunchroom. Foot wanted to play to Herb Massey's Cafe, about three miles away, to the third leg of the shuffle-bowl machine. Herb's was where Matty once showed up one day with his shirt and pants on backward, and his glasses on the back of his head, and posted a score of 280 on the shuffle bowl, sliding the puck backward.

Foot and Magoo wound up splitting the money, and we all went back to Goat Hills and got in a putting game that lasted until midnight.

Why we did such things was because we lived in Fort Worth, the town that gave you Ben Hogan and Byron Nelson, and offered little else to do.

Besides, it was Texas.

Golf had always received lavish attention in the newspapers, and it was at a very early age that you knew about Hogan and Nelson and others: Jimmy Demaret, Lloyd Mangrum, Ralph Guldahl, Harry Cooper, Gus Moreland, Harry Todd—all Texans.

There was also a vast amateur circuit you could travel, if you wanted to take your game out of town. All summer long, you could go play in invitation tournaments in towns like Ranger, Midland, Abilene, Wichita Falls, Waxahachie, Longview, Corpus Christi, everywhere.

In these tournaments, you could win shotguns, radios, silverware, lawn tools, and quite a bit of money in Calcutta pools.

It was this amateur circuit that gave us Hogan, Nelson, and Demaret from the old days, and then Jackie Burke Jr., Tommy Bolt, Billy Maxwell, Don Cherry, Don January, Earl Stewart, Dave Marr, Bill Rogers, Charley Coody, Bobby Nichols, Miller Barber, Howie Johnson, Ernie Vossler, Homero Blancas, Fred Marti, Jacky Cupit, and then in later years your Ben Crenshaws, Tom Kites, and John Mahaffeys.

Ernie Vossler, who is now richer than pigshit in Palm Springs, came right out of our game at the Hills.

Even then, he was a relentless competitor who never understood why anybody but him ever made a putt.

Sometimes, when Weldon the Oath, a postman, made a putt, Ernie would walk off the course, fuming.

Ernie was never as proficient as myself or John the Band-Aid at breaking clubs. I once broke the shaft on my 8-iron nine days in a row at the 17th because I couldn't make the ball hold that green, a par 3. But Ernie had his moments. He bladed a 6-iron one day in the sixth fairway and almost killed everybody. He hurled the club into the brick fairway, and the shaft snapped, and both parts of the club went into the air, and one jagged end sprang back and hit Ernie in the palm, causing five stitches, and another jagged end caught me in the leg. As the shafts sparkled in the sun, it was as if we were being threatened by lightning bolts for a moment.

And this was the man who knew nothing of golf before I had once recruited him for the golf team at Paschal High. He went on to win the Fort Worth city championship, which was something that Hogan, Nelson, and I could never do—we all finished second in our best effort—and Ernie won the State Amateur, and then some tournaments on the PGA Tour, and then he got into real estate and bought Oklahoma City and Palm Springs. Ernie Vossler became our honor graduate.

But our funniest graduate was Weldon the Oath.

Weldon had talking fits—talking to the ball.

He would take oaths. He would rush out to the game so quickly, he would play golf in his postman's cap and without golf shoes, which could have had something to do with his chronic slice.

"All right, this is your last chance," Weldon would say to the ball as he waggled his driver. "You lousy little crud, if you slice on me one more time I'm gonna bite you in half and chew your rubber guts up. You're goin' straight this time, you hear me? You *hear* me tellin' you this? All right, then. Geeeeooood, daaaammmmmm, aaaaiii, ga!"

And Weldon would hit another slice.

It would cross two fairways to his right, a marvelous half-moon of a shot.

The ball would scarcely leave the clubface before Weldon would start to spin around in circles, pawing at the air, slugging at imaginary evils. Frequently, he would dash over to the tee marker and start beating the driver on it. He would stomp on the club.

Then just as quickly, he would calm down and say, "Let me hit one more, I got to figure out what I'm doin' wrong."

And he would slice again.

That's when he would break the shaft over his knee. "Geeeaaa, rrrreeeaaa, aaaddd," he would snarl. "This is my last time on a golf course, you can book it! Gaaddd raaaap son of a baddered bat rop ditch bastard." When Weldon was hot, the words didn't come out right. "You picks have guyed me damn stick—this rotten, stinking, miserable, low-life spicky dop whore bubbin' game—feck it, babber sam!"

Weldon would hike to the clubhouse, but of course he would be back the next day.

It was in the last couple of years at Goat Hills, shortly before the city sold those 106 acres to TCU so the school could build more cream-brick buildings, that the games grew too big, too expensive, for working men and college students.

Some of the guys got to where they couldn't pay when they lost, and others didn't want to collect it, and some of us were developing other interests—snooker, 8-ball, newspapers, divorces.

Moron Tom had something to do with the games disappearing, going the way of other endangered species.

He was a muscular, likable West Texan who had come to Fort Worth on a football scholarship at TCU, but had quit football when he found out you had to work out every day in the fall. He hit a long ball and he loved to bet, on anything. He could hold his breath longer than anybody, for money, or inhale a can of beer in four seconds, for money, and he rarely spoke English.

Everything was quadruple unreal to Moron Tom, or, "Hit it fine, pork-e-pine," and many of the words he uttered were something else spelled backward.

"Cod Ee-rack Fockle-dim," for instance, was Dr. Cary Middlecoff spelled backward.

The day of one of the last big games, Moron Tom walked onto the porch and said, "I'll take toops and threeps from Youngfut, Youngjun, and Youngdump."

This meant Moron Tom wanted two up and three up from young Foot, young John, and young me.

"Ten and ten with Grease's men," he added, "and two and two with Joe-Magoo."

Everyone drifted out to the first tee.

Wagers were made, partners chosen, practice swings taken.

Moron Tom brought a big hook in from over the apartment houses and found the fairway.

"Think I can't, Cary Grant?" he said.

Magoo and I wound up as partners against all other combinations, and this was not altogether good—neither of us knew how to play safe, and Magoo was also unlucky. Once in the Glen Garden Invitation in Fort Worth—that's the course where Hogan and Nelson caddied as kids—Magoo hit a 285-yard tee shot but found his ball in a man's mouth, being cleaned.

We were in good form today, however. Teamed well for a blaze of birdies and had everybody bleeding to death by the time we got to the 18th.

I would hit a good drive and Moron Tom would say, "Cod Ee-rack Fockle-dim," and Magoo would hit a good drive, and Moron Tom would say, "Wod Daw-ret-sniff," meaning Dow Finsterwald spelled backward.

When either of us holed a putt, Moron Tom would say, "Take a nap, Einra Remlap," which was Arnie Palmer spelled backward.

By the time we came off the 17th green, Magoo and I had somehow birdied six holes in a row, and we calculated that if we only parred the 18th, we would win so much money we wouldn't be able to haul it home in Cecil's cookie truck.

Everybody pressed to get even, of course, on the 18th tee.

John the Band-Aid summed it up for most of the players, who must have numbered 12 in all, when he said, "I'm out, out, out, out,

out, and out, and one down, one down, one down, one down, one down, and even. Want me to bend over?"

The 18th at Goat Hills was slightly uphill. You drove from a windy knoll with the south wind usually helping and aimed across a tiny creek and a couple of sycamore trees. A big drive would leave you only 30 or 40 yards short of the green, a flip and a putt from a birdie or a flip and two putts from an easy par.

Not to birdie the 18th often resulted in a wedge being broken, and not to par the 18th was unthinkable.

The only conceivable trouble was far, far to the right, across the 10th fairway, where Stadium Drive was out of bounds. But nobody had ever sliced that badly, not even Weldon the Oath, until Magoo did.

At the height of Magoo's backswing, when he was coming out of his shoes to try to drive the green and make us richer, Moron Tom quietly said, "Tissim, Oogam." Which was "Miss it, Magoo" backward.

Needles were commonplace in the game. Coughing, sneezing, dropping a full bag of clubs, yelling, burping, all such things could be heard on backswings at times—you took it for granted and dealt with it.

But Magoo came apart with laughter at Moron Tom's remark and almost fell down like Cecil when he swung at the ball.

Even Magoo had to laugh again when Moron Tom said, "Oogam dewolb the Nepo," which translated into "Magoo blowed the Open."

To say this put extra pressure on me, with Magoo out of the hole, would be to say that the meatloaf in the lunchroom at Goat Hills contained grease.

Right here, I should explain that on the other side of the creek at the 18th, set upright into an embankment, was a storm drain about three feet in circumference. We often pitched at it with old balls from the ladies' tee, but it was a remarkable thing if anybody ever got one in there.

And from up on the men's tee, 100 yards or so back, it was an incredibly small target. In fact, I didn't even think about it as I got set to drive the green and make another birdie, or know the reason why. All I wanted to know was where everybody wanted their bodies shipped.

But at the top of my swing, Moron Tom whispered something else.

"Clutch, Mother Zilch," he said.

The clubhead hit about two inches behind the ball, and the drive snaphooked into the ground just in front of the ladies' tee, took a big hop to the right off of some rocks, and—I swear to you— went straight into the storm drain.

It remains the only hole-in-one I ever made, and it was, you might say, the shot which semi-retired me from golf forever.

Interview Area

THE PROS ALWAYS ASK DUMB QUESTIONS, THE SAME OLD ONES, BUT you try to cooperate to avoid somebody like Deane Beman, who was the commissioner of golf before he became pope, spreading the rumor that you don't have any charisma.

"Why don't you just go through the story and hit some of the high points?" Jack Nicklaus suggested as I settled down in a chair behind a microphone in the interview area.

I lit a cigarette and glanced down at a Xerox copy of the story I had filed. Tom Place gave me the copy. Tom is the public information officer for the PGA Tour. He provides statistics for the pros on various members of the press. He supplies them with anecdotes on how many times we throw up in the middle of a paragraph, who owes the most car rental bills, who makes the most wisecracks about the Bible study group. Things like that.

"Well," I said, "I got off to a pretty good start. Only six strike-overs on the first page."

Curtis Strange said, "Are you still going with a manual typewriter?"

"Yes, but over the years I've rewrapped several keys," I said.

It was Tom Watson who said, "You hit your opening sentence fairly long, I noticed. Do you think you're longer now than you used to be?"

"It was a long sentence," I confessed. "It must have rambled on for fifty or sixty words. It was definitely one of the longest sentences I've hit this year, at least in the English language."

Ben Crenshaw had dropped into the interview area between Nabisco outings. He wasn't playing in the tournament. He was confining his schedule to outings now.

"What's your favorite letter?" he asked.

"The q," I said quickly. "It's the toughest letter to find in the bag. That's why you get so much satisfaction when you type 'quadruple bogey.'"

Seve Ballesteros asked a question I couldn't really understand, but I tried to answer it the best way I knew how.

"Seeks eyed-yurn," I said. "Picking weg, two putts."

Seve asked another question.

"Fife eyed-yurn," I said. "Picking weg, one putt."

Jack Nicklaus spoke up again, rather impatiently. He said he was on deadline and he wanted to get the details of the piece out of the way before everyone got into the "feature-type" questions.

I said, "Well, let's see. On the second page, I recovered from a tasteless joke about corporate sponsors with a reference to the increases in prize money. I think I may have misquoted Gary Player on page three. I thought he was talking about God, but he was referring to himself. On page four, I almost never got out of a paragraph about how much Deane Beman had done to uplift the game with Oreo cookies."

While everybody took notes, I lit another cigarette. I always like to have two going in case the questions get indelicate.

Tom Place said, "You've often complained that none of these fellows outside of Lee Trevino or Mac O'Grady or Peter Jacobson ever give you a good quote. What's your idea of a good quote?"

I thought a moment.

"Well," I said, "a player named John Schlee once said that watching Sam Snead hit practice balls was like watching a fish practice swimming."

The pros only stared at me.

I tried again.

"Bob Hope once said he'd give up the game if he didn't have so many sweaters."

No reaction.

Before he rushed out of the room, Jack Nicklaus seized the opportunity to announce that he was designing a new golf course and building condominiums on top of the World Trade Center in New York.

Arnold Palmer stood up in the back of the room and seized the opportunity to announce that he was building 57 new golf courses that week and expected them to be finished by Saturday.

Gary Player seized the opportunity to announce that after he won the Peruvian Four-Ball next week, he would have a total of 217 lifetime victories on eight different continents, including two he was not at liberty to name.

"G'day, mate," came a voice from out of the crowd.

I recognized it immediately as belonging to Greg Norman. I have an ear for that kind of thing.

Greg wanted to take me to task for changing his nickname.

He said he much preferred The Great White Shark to Crocodile Tee Ball.

I reminded him that he couldn't win with the press unless he captured a few more major championships. If he won a couple more majors, I said, we would probably start calling him Greg Norman.

A question was asked by Dave Eichelberger.

He wanted to know who I thought had made the most contributions to the game of golf.

Without hesitation, I said, "In the old days, it was Joe Bob Greater. More tournaments were named for Mr. Greater than any other man. He was responsible for the Greater Milwaukee, the Greater Hartford, the Greater Jacksonville, the Greater New Orleans, and the Greater Greensboro."

"What about today?" said Dave. "What about Mark Calcavecchia?"

"He's certainly got the most vowels in his name," I said, "and he's the Typhoid Mary of square grooves, as we know, but I think he still has a few things to prove."

I thanked the pros for their attention, wished their corporate logos well, and walked up to the office supply shop by the clubhouse to see if they had any old fast-action, Tommy Armour typewriters around.

The Best Things in Golf

TELL ME ABOUT PLUMBING, FINE. HOW IF THIS FITTING DOESN'T GO into that pipe, my kitchen looks like the Danube. Tell me about carpentry. Terrace gardening. The timer on VCRs. Go ahead and explain cellophane—and why I can't get a package of crackers open without a chain saw. Tell me about all of these things, but don't try to tell me about golf, okay? Golf, I know.

For one thing, I'm older than beltless slacks. For another, I've been around golf since touring pros knew how to hit fades and draws instead of 200-yard 7-irons.

Here sits a guy who's been to The Masters for almost 40 years, who's hung out at almost as many U.S. Opens, who's slept through almost as many PGAs, who's been eating sausage rolls at the British Open since 1962.

And God forbid I should overlook the 500 Crosbys, Dorals, Akrons, Colonials, Hopes, and L.A.s to which I've been sentenced over the same period of time.

All in all, that's more armbands than the Nazis wore.

Watched golf? I've seen more golf than Irving Berlin's seen piano keys.

Listened to golf? I've heard more golf stories in locker rooms than a Bolshoi dancer's heard *Swan Lake.*

Played golf? I've played every great course from Goat Hills to the Augusta National, from Pine Valley to St. Andrews, and I've still got the looping hook to prove it. I've played rounds with Jack Nicklaus, Arnold Palmer, and Ben Hogan, just to drop three names at random. I used to play at scratch from the blues, and gamble for my *own* money, so don't tell me about pressure.

All of which introduces me as the only person arrogant enough to pick the Best Things in Golf, which I now present:

BEST FIRST TEE

Merion. Out on the Philadelphia Main Line, this elegant patch of shaded ground is impossible to gaze upon without thinking that this was where Bobby Jones teed it up on the morning of the Amateur final in 1930 when he was going to complete the Grand Slam.

BEST PUTTING GREEN

Reeking with history and atmosphere, Oakmont is located in a suburb of Pittsburgh, and its putting green is actually a suburb of its par-5 ninth green. The upper half of it, in fact. The confusion that this can sometimes cause among golfers playing the course and golfers merely practicing is worth it for the unique charm of it all.

BEST VERANDA

The Augusta National, which also has the Best Driveway (Magnolia), the Best Creek (Rae's), and the Best Balcony overlooking the Best Veranda.

BEST TREE

The huge elm hanging over the 10th green on Winged Foot East, right by the sprawling Gothic clubhouse. The tree would be more famous if the '29 U.S. Open, because of pretournament rains, hadn't been moved from Winged Foot East to Winged Foot West. This resulted in the Opens of '59, '74, and '84 also being played on Winged Foot West, and Winged Foot East, a more scenic and interesting layout, rarely being heard of again.

BEST BRIDGE

The Swinging Bridge at Bel-Air Country Club in Los Angeles. It gets you over a canyon from the 10th tee to the 10th green. There are other nice bridges, the Sarazen at Augusta, for example, or the one that crosses the Pennsylvania Turnpike at Oakmont (eighth green to the ninth tee), but Bel-Air's bridge has held the cleats of the most movie stars.

BEST BROOK

Baffling, on the 11th hole at Merion. It guards the front of this par-4 green and curls around to the golfer's right. The Baffling Brook does not suffer any by the fact that on the green side of its ripples was where Bobby Jones dusted off Eugene Homans 8 and 7 and completed the Slam, or "the impregnable quadrilateral," as some sportswriter called it, which was the Best Thing Anybody Ever Called the Grand Slam.

BEST PAR-3 HOLE
The 12th at Augusta. Only a short iron over water but the site of countless tragicomedies during The Masters.

BEST PAR-4 HOLE
No. 17, the Road Hole, on the Old Course at St. Andrews. Drive and a long iron, dogleg right, with a pot bunker to the left of the green and the road itself, which is in bounds, brushing up against the green on the right—and the ancient spires of the town all around you.

BEST PAR-5 HOLE
The 13th at Augusta. Sharp dogleg left around a forest of tall pines, Rae's Creek beckoning and guarding the green, a bank of azaleas for set decoration, and Do-I-Go-for-It-or-Don't-I? always built into the second shot.

BEST TWO HOLES IN A ROW
The 12th and 13th at Augusta.

BEST THREE HOLES IN A ROW
The 11th, 12th, and 13th at Augusta, or Amen Corner, which is the Best Corner. At times, the whole Masters.

BEST THREE HOLES IN A ROW THAT AREN'T AT AUGUSTA
The eighth, ninth, and 10th at Pebble Beach, which is the Best Abalone Corner.

BEST THREE HOLES IN A ROW THAT AREN'T AT AUGUSTA OR PEBBLE BEACH
The 16th, 17th, and 18th at Merion, the quarry holes, as in Best Quarry.

BEST BACK-TO-BACK PAR 3S
The short 15th and long 16th at Cypress Point.

BEST BACK-TO-BACK PAR 5S
The 17th and 18th on the Lower Course at Baltusrol.

BEST LUNATIC NINE HOLES

The back side at Glen Garden Country Club in Fort Worth, where Hogan and Nelson caddied as kids. It features back-to-back par 5s once and back-to-back par 3s *twice*. It plays to a par of 4-4-5-5-3-3-4-3-3—34. When Glen Garden's peculiarities were pointed out to Byron recently, he said, "That *is* crazy. I wonder why we always thought it was normal?"

BEST ASSORTMENT OF BLIND SHOTS ON ONE GOLF COURSE

Prestwick, Scotland, site of the first 11 British Opens. It largely consists of heather and sky.

BEST 18 HOLES

Pine Valley by a landslide. Amid raw beauty in Clementon, N.J., every hole is distinctive, haunting, and memorable.

BEST GOLF COURSE AT A COUNTRY CLUB THAT WON'T ALLOW MOVIE STARS TO JOIN AND HAS NEVER HELD A U.S. OPEN

North Course, Los Angeles Country Club.

BEST CITY IN WHICH TO STUDY GOLF COURSE ARCHITECTURE

Columbus, Ohio, which only has courses designed by Jack Nicklaus (Muirfield Village), Donald Ross (Scioto), Alister Mackenzie (Ohio State Scarlet), and Pete Dye (The Golf Club).

BEST SHOTMAKER

Ben Hogan, it almost goes without saying.

BEST SWING

Sam Snead.

BEST GOLFER I NEVER SAW PLAY

Bobby Jones.

BEST DRIVER

Hogan. But not on the highway, necessarily.

BEST LONG-IRON PLAYER

Jack Nicklaus. He was the first to get them up, to keep them up and turn them either way, and to keep them on the greens when they came down.

BEST SHORT IRONS

Byron Nelson. Between 1937 and 1946, Byron would have birdied every short hole he ever played if he hadn't used a dumb blade putter, or if he'd known how to putt. He almost had to shank an iron to wind up outside of 10 feet.

BEST BUNKER PLAYER

Seve Ballesteros. A true magician who can do more from sand with a 5-iron than most golfers can with a sand wedge.

BEST WIND PLAYER

Lee Trevino, who learned to play in the Texas gales for his own money.

BEST PLAYER FOR HIS OWN MONEY

Lanny Wadkins, by one emergency press over Raymond Floyd and Lee Trevino.

BEST GOLFER WHO NEVER PRACTICED

Jimmy Demaret. It cut into his party time. Besides, he didn't know what practicing was until he saw Ben Hogan hitting a bag of balls one day.

BEST STROKER OF YOUR NORMAL, EVERYDAY PUTT

Ben Crenshaw, who's also the Best Golfer That Never Hit a Fairway.

BEST GOLFER WHO NEVER WORE PANTS

Gene Sarazen.

BEST GOLFER WHO USED TO SMOKE, SWEAT, AND LET HIS SHIRTTAIL COME OUT

Arnold Palmer.

BEST GOLFER WHO NEVER DIED

Sam Snead. Name another pro who's won tournaments in six decades.

BEST WOMAN GOLFER

Babe Zaharias—in a play-off over Mickey Wright.

BEST GOLFER WHO EVER ACTUALLY GRADUATED FROM OHIO STATE

Ed Sneed.

BEST GOLFER WHO EVER ACTUALLY GRADUATED FROM THE UNIVERSITY OF HOUSTON; IN FACT, THE BEST GOLFER WHO EVER PLAYED FOR THE UNIVERSITY OF HOUSTON

John Mahaffey.

BEST FOREIGN GOLFER WHO ALMOST SPOKE ENGLISH

Roberto De Vicenzo.

BEST AMERICAN GOLFER WHO ALMOST SPOKE ENGLISH

Andy Bean.

BEST COLOR-BLIND GOLFER WITH INTERLOCKING GRIP

Jack Nicklaus.

BEST CHIPPER

Not even close. Over his full career, Bob Rosburg hit more froghair in regulation than anybody.

BEST (OR ONLY) TOUR PRO WHO EVER PICKED UP DINNER CHECKS

Dave Marr.

BEST MAKER OF PUTTS HE HAD TO HAVE OVER AN ASTONISHING PERIOD OF 25 YEARS

J. W. Nicklaus.

BEST GOLFER IN THE U.S. OPEN

Hogan, of course. From 1940 through 1960, in 16 consecutive Opens (he missed '49 and '57 because of injuries), he never finished worse than 10th, seldom worse than sixth, and he won five of them. This counts the wartime Open of '42 at Chicago's Ridgemoor, which the USGA says was unofficial but which I count, seeing as how Ben was given a gold medal for it that looks just like the ones he received for winning in '48, '50, '51, and '53.

BEST GOLFER IN THE MASTERS

Nicklaus, who holds a greater distinction than being the only six-time winner. He won three of them fat and three of them thin.

BEST GOLFER IN THE BRITISH OPEN

Harry Vardon—in a play-off over Old Tom Morris and Young Tom Watson.

BEST GOLFER IN THE PGA CHAMPIONSHIP
Walter Hagen, who won it five times, in a close call over Byron Nelson, who won it twice but should have won it five times.

BEST GOLF WIFE (WITH KIDS)
Barbara Nicklaus.

BEST GOLF WIFE (WITHOUT KIDS)
Valerie Hogan.

BEST BAR
Downstairs in the Pebble Beach Lodge (the old Del Monte Lodge) there is a place called Club 19 where you can drink or dine, or both. It's small, dark, cozy, convivial, and some think expensive, but so what? No Crosby tournament would be complete without it, and not to play Club 19 one evening is not to play Pebble Beach at all.

BEST HAND-LETTERED SIGN EVER HELD UP TO A WINDOW FROM INSIDE THE COLONIAL CLUBHOUSE AND MEANT FOR A CLUSTER OF SHOW-STOPPING HALTER TOPS OUTDOORS
"Tell the one in blue to turn around."
> —anonymous member

BEST RULING
All those times that Joe Dey, when he was executive director of the USGA, looked down at a competitor's ball sitting in an impossible lie and said, "Hit it."

BEST PLACE TO LOOK AT SUNTANS AND JEWELRY
Palm Springs, Calif.

BEST TROPHY ROOM
Ben Hogan's alcove. Just inside the main entrance at Colonial Country Club in Fort Worth, the Hogan trophy room is three walls of display cases filled with treasures.

BEST PUTTER
An old Tommy Armour—in a play-off over an old George Low, which was patterned after an old Tommy Armour.

BEST RULE OF GOLF
That thing about the burrowing animal, whatever it means.

BEST FREE DROP
They gave it to Arnold Palmer on the 12th hole at Augusta in the final round of the '58 Masters. Having hit over the green, he played out to a double-bogey 5, but then he played an alternate ball, invoking the imbedded-ball rule. With this ball, he made a 3, a par. The green coats gave him the 3 and with it, he went on to win his first Masters.

BEST TOMMY BOLT STORY
One day Tommy attacked Tom Lobaugh of the *Tulsa World* for writing that he was 49 years old when he was only 39 at the time. Lobaugh explained that he knew better, that it had only been a typographical error. "The hell it was," said Bolt. "It was a perfect 4 and a perfect 9!"

That story barely edges out the one where Bolt backed away from a putt because a fan had inadvertently cast his shadow across Tommy's line. Whereupon Bolt, chin jutted out, muttered to his playing companions, "Well, I never could read *Poa annua* in the *dark!*"

BEST LAST ROUND EVER SHOT IN A MAJOR
Hogan's 67 to win the '51 Open at unplayable, incorrigible—"The Monster"—Oakland Hills.

BEST THING ANY GOLFER EVER SAID ABOUT THE PRESS
"Whatever amount of fame I have achieved from the relatively unimportant pursuit of hitting a golf ball, I owe to O. B. Keeler and his gifted typewriter."
                                                        —Bobby Jones

MAJORS

What Are They?

A MAJOR IS ONE OF THE BIG FOUR TOURNAMENTS IN GOLF, AS IN major championship. As in U.S. Open, Masters, British Open, and National PGA.

Each year, The Masters comes first, in April, and always at the Augusta National Golf Club in Augusta, Ga. The U.S. Open is played in June, the British Open in July, and the PGA in August.

Three of the majors got to be majors because they were the championship of something. The U.S. Open is the championship of the United States Golf Association, the ruling body of golf in America. The British Open is the championship of the Royal & Ancient Golfing Society, the ruling body of golf in Great Britain and Europe. The PGA is the championship of the Professional Golfers Association, those guys who give you lessons at the country club. The Masters became a major because it was the creation of Bobby Jones and because it was the first—and is still the best—of the exclusive invitational tournaments.

All this was decided by the press, which knows a major when it sees one.

There are about 40 other tournaments on the PGA Tour each year, and while some of them used to be distinctive for one reason or another, none of them are today. They have all been taken over by corporate sponsors, which use them for their own marketing purposes.

And this has only enhanced the status of the Big Four.

A player can earn big money in the other tournaments, but so what? Until he wins a major, he's a second-class citizen.

Every major is important, no matter who wins it, but some have become epic and lived on in history, epicly.

To Kill a Monster

IT WAS THE KIND OF COURSE WHERE YOU COULD LOSE YOUR FEET IN the rough. Yeah, your feet, Foot-Joys and all. When you walked across the fairway of a par 4, you only took about 19 steps—and you were back in the rough again, looking for your feet, which might be standing on somebody's ball. And on those frequent occasions when the competitor would find himself on the "wrong side" of a green, there was usually something between him and the cup, either the Sahara Desert, played by an intruding bunker, or the Himalayas, played by the undulations of the putting surfaces.

This was Oakland Hills back in 1951, a layout doctored so severely that only Ben Hogan could have won the U.S. Open championship, which, of course, he did. Hogan won it over the final 18 holes with a 3-under-par 67, the greatest single round he, or anyone else, ever shot. And it was after that round that Ben supposedly made a remark for the ages: "I finally brought the monster to its knees." Nice editing on the part of the sportswriters. Some of us don't remember Hogan using the word "monster" on that sweltering Saturday of June 16, 1951, on the outskirts of Detroit. It sounded more like he said, "I finally brought the !#$%&@)! to its knees."

Actually, he may have said, "I got mad at this course, and I went out to bring the #$&%! monster to its knees."

Or maybe it was a writer in the Oakland Hills locker room who said, "By golly, Ben, you brought this stupid !$#&% course to its silly #$%&! knees, didn't you?" and Ben smiled in agreement.

What I *do* remember is how tough the course was and why.

Before the '51 Open, both the U.S. Golf Association and the Oakland Hills members had been afraid of what the pros might do to the old Donald Ross layout. Fourteen years earlier at the 1937 Open, Ralph Guldahl had set the 72-hole record of 281 at Oakland Hills, and for 11 years, or until the mark was bettered by Hogan at Riviera in '48, Oakland Hills had lived with the shame of being the club that surrendered the record. If the pros could shoot 281 in '37, what might they shoot in '51 unless changes were made? Enter now three men chosen by destiny to "protect" Oakland Hills in order for the club to stage a "proper" championship: Joseph C. Dey Jr., then the executive secretary of the USGA; Robert Trent Jones, the architect hired to "modernize" Donald Ross; and perhaps most important, John Oswald, chairman of the greens committee at Oakland Hills. An engineer at the Ford Motor Company, Oswald pushed harder than anyone for a rugged, if not impossible, golf course. "The Open is the greatest title there is," Oswald said to Dey and Jones. "The course should be so hard, nobody can win it."

Henceforth, Trent Jones removed 80 Ross bunkers that were no longer in play and added 60 new ones that *were* in play for the modern pro. He placed pot bunkers in the very center of some fairways, forcing the golfer to drive to the left or right of the bunker, to a narrow slit in the fairway, where it would usually take a bounce and wind up in the snarling "Open rough." On most long holes, Trent's fairways were only 19 paces wide at the landing area. Further, Jones reshaped all of the greens, creating a definite "wrong side." Par was trimmed from 72 to 70, a final psychological taunt for the competitor.

From the moment they arrived in town, the pros howled and complained, unlike they have at any Open since.

Cary Middlecoff said, "The only way to walk down these fairways is single file!"

Hogan said, "If I had to play this course for a living every week, I'd get into another business."

To fully appreciate Hogan's epic 67, you have to know where he came from. Sam Snead's 71 led the first day. Ben shot a 76, which left him five strokes and 31 players behind. "I made six mistakes," he said, "and paid for all of them." Hogan shot a 73 on Friday ("Three mistakes") as Bobby Locke, the South African, seized the lead at 144 for 36 holes. Ben was still five back.

"A couple of sixty-nines might take it tomorrow," a friend said to him that evening. "I'm afraid it's out of reach," he replied.

In those days, they played 36 the last day— "Open Saturday," as it was known. Hogan almost whipped the course in the morning round. He was 3 under going to the 14th, but he finished with a double bogey and two bogeys for a 71. He was hot, to say the least, both at himself and the course, but he was creeping up on the leaders. Locke and Jimmy Demaret were tied at 218 at noon. Hogan was at 220, now only two strokes behind.

Ben went out in 35, even par, in the afternoon, playing flawlessly, hitting "the slits." At the long 10th, he hit a driver and a "career" 2-iron to within five feet of the cup. Birdie. At the 13th, he birdied again with a 6-iron shot and a 14-footer. He took three from the edge for a bogey at the 14th. At the 15th, where he made a double bogey in the morning, Hogan drove with a 4-wood and then hit a 6-iron to within five feet of the hole and made it for a birdie. And he birdied the 18th with a driver and another 6-iron and a 15-foot putt for his 67 and winning total of 287. Clayton Heafner's 69 and 289 brought him second place. Hogan and Heafner were the only players to break 70 in the tournament, the only players to break 290. Locke finished third at 291. Poor Demaret collapsed with a 78, tied for 14th.

Ben Hogan shot many scores lower than 67, so why was this the greatest 18 ever played? Well, the average score of the field that afternoon at Oakland Hills was 75, give or take a fraction. In that sense, you can say that Hogan's 67 was actually 8 under par on the "monster"—and it *was* the last round of the Open, right? Case closed.

Whoo-ha, Arnie!

THEY WERE THE MOST ASTONISHING FOUR HOURS IN GOLF SINCE Mary, Queen of Scots found out what dormie meant and invented the back nine, and now, given all these years of reflection, they still seem as significant as the day Arnold Palmer first hitched up his trousers, or the moment Jack Nicklaus decided to trim down and fluff-dry his hair, or that interlude in the pro shop when Ben Hogan bought his first white cap.

Small wonder that no sportswriter was capable of outlining it against a bright blue summer sky and letting the four adjectives ride again: It was too big, too wildly exciting, too crazily suspenseful, too suffocatingly dramatic. What exactly happened? Oh, not much. Just a routine collision of three decades at one historical intersection.

On that afternoon, in the span of just 18 holes, we witnessed the arrival of Nicklaus, the coronation of Palmer, and the end of Hogan. Nicklaus was a 20-year-old amateur who would own the 1970s. Palmer was a 30-year-old pro who would dominate the 1960s. Hogan was a 47-year-old immortal who had overwhelmed the 1950s. While they had a fine supporting cast, it was primarily these three men who waged war for the U.S. Open championship on that Saturday of June 18, 1960. The battle was continuous, under a steaming Colorado sun at Cherry Hills Country Club in Denver.

Things happened *to* them, *around* them.

Things happened in front of them, behind them.

Nobody knew where to go next, to see who had the lead, who was close, who had faltered.

Leader boards changed faster than stoplights.

And for a great while they were bleeding with red numbers.

In those days there was something known as Open Saturday. It is no longer part of golf—thanks to TV, no thanks, actually. But it was a day like no other; a day when the best golfers in the world were required to play 36 holes because it had always seemed to the USGA that a prolonged test of physical and mental stamina should go into the earning of the game's most important championship. Thus, Open Saturday lent itself to wondrous comebacks and funny collapses, and it provided a full day's ration of every emotion familiar to the athlete competing under pressure.

Open Saturday had been an institution with the USGA since its fourth championship in 1898, and there had been many a thriller before 1960, Saturdays that had tested the nerves and skill of the Bobby Joneses, the Gene Sarazens, the Walter Hagens, the Harry Vardons, the Byron Nelsons, the Sam Sneads, and, of course, the Ben Hogans.

But any serious scholar of the sport, or anyone fortunate enough to have been there at Cherry Hills, is aware that the Open Saturday of Arnold, Jack, and Ben was extra special—a National Open that in meaning for the game continues to dwarf all of the others.

It was the Open in which Arnold Palmer shot a 65 in the last round and became the real Arnold Palmer. Threw his visor in the air, smoked a bunch of cigarettes, chipped in, drove a ball through forest and onto a green, tucked in his shirttail, and lived happily ever after in the history books.

And that is pretty much what happened. But there is a constant truth about tournament golf: Other men have to lose a championship before one man can win it. And never has the final 18 of an Open produced as many losers as Cherry Hills did in 1960. When it was over, there were as many stretcher cases as there were shouts of "Whoo-ha, go get 'em, Arnie." And that stood to reason after you considered that in those insane four hours Palmer came from seven strokes off the lead and from 15th place to grab a championship he had never even been in contention for.

Naturally, Palmer had arrived in Denver as the favorite. Two months earlier he had taken his second Masters with what was beginning to be known to the wire services as a "charge." He had almost been confirmed as the Player of the New Era, though not quite. But as late as noon on Open Saturday, after three rounds of competition, you would hardly have heard his name mentioned in Denver. A list of the leaders through 54 holes shows how hopeless his position seemed.

The scoreboard read:

Mike Souchak 68-67-73—208
Julius Boros 73-69-68—210
Dow Finsterwald 71-69-70—210
Jerry Barber 69-71-70—210
Ben Hogan 75-67-69—211
Jack Nicklaus 71-71-69—211
Jack Fleck 70-70-72—212
Johnny Pott 75-68-69—212
Don Cherry 70-71-71—212
Gary Player 70-72-71—213
Sam Snead 72-69-73—214
Billy Casper 71-70-73—214
Dutch Harrison 74-70-70—214
Bob Shave 72-71-71—214
Arnold Palmer 72-71-72—215

Through Thursday's opening round, Friday's second round, and right up until the last hole of the first 18 on Saturday, this Open had belonged exclusively to Mike Souchak, a long-hitting, highly popular pro who seldom allowed his career to get in the way of a social engagement. His blazing total of 135 after 36 holes was an Open record. And as he stood on the 18th tee of Saturday's morning round, he needed only a par 4 for a 71 and a four-stroke lead on the field.

Then came an incident that gave everyone a foreboding about the afternoon. On Souchak's backswing, a camera clicked loudly. Souchak's drive soared out of bounds, and he took a double-bogey 6 for a 73. He never really recovered from the jolt. While the lead would remain his well into the afternoon, you could see Mike painfully allowing the tournament to slip away from him. He was headed for the slow death of a finishing 75 and another near-miss, like the one he had suffered the previous year in the Open at Winged Foot up in Westchester County.

Much has been written about Arnold in the locker room at Cherry Hills between rounds on Open Saturday. It has become a part of golfing lore. However, there could hardly be a more appropriate occasion for the retelling of it than now. As it happened, I was there, one of four people with Arnold. Two of the others were golfers—Ken Venturi and Bob Rosburg, who were even farther out of the tournament than Palmer—and the fourth was Bob Drum, a writer then with the *Pittsburgh Press*. It was a position that allowed Drum to enjoy the same close relationship with Palmer that *The Atlanta Journal*'s O. B. Keeler once had with Bobby Jones.

Everybody had cheeseburgers and iced tea. We bathed our faces and arms with cold towels. It was too hot to believe that you could actually see snowcaps on the Rockies on the skyline.

As Palmer, Venturi, and Rosburg sat on the locker room benches, there was no talk at all of who might win, only of how short and inviting the course was playing, of how Mike Souchak, with the start he had, would probably shoot 269 if the tournament were a Pensacola Classic instead of the Open.

Arnold was cursing the first hole at Cherry Hills, a 346-yard par 4 with an elevated tee. Three times he had just missed driving the green. As he left the group to join Paul Harney for their 1:42 starting time on the final 18, the thing on his mind was trying to drive that first green. It would be his one Cherry Hills accomplishment.

"If I drive the green and get a birdie or an eagle, I might shoot sixty-five," Palmer said. "What'll that do?"

Drum said, "Nothing. You're too far back."

"It would give me two eighty," Palmer said. "Doesn't two eighty always win the Open?"

"Yeah, when Hogan shoots it," I said, laughing heartily at my own wit.

Arnold lingered at the doorway, looking at us as if he were waiting for a better exit line.

"Go on, boy," Drum said. "Get out of here. Go make your seven or eight birdies but shoot seventy-three. I'll see you later."

Bob Drum had been writing Palmer stories since Palmer was the West Pennsylvania amateur champion. On a Fort Worth newspaper, I had been writing Ben Hogan stories for 10 years, but I had also become a friend of Palmer's because I was a friend of Drum's.

Palmer left the room but we didn't, for the simple reason that Mike Souchak, the leader, would not be starting his last round for another 15 or 20 minutes. But the fun began before that. It started for us when word drifted back to the locker room that Palmer had indeed driven the first green and two-putted for a birdie. He had not carried the ball 346 yards in the air, but he had nailed it good enough for it to burn a path through the high weeds the USGA had nurtured in front of the green to prevent just such a thing from happening. Palmer had in fact barely missed his eagle putt from 20 feet.

Frankly, we thought nothing of it. Nor did we think much of the news that Arnold had chipped in from 35 feet for a birdie at the second. What *did* get Bob Drum's attention was the distant thunder which signaled that Arnold had birdied the third hole. He had wedged to within a foot of the cup.

We were standing near the putting green by the clubhouse, and we had just decided to meander out toward Souchak when Drum said:

"Care to join me at the fourth hole?"

I said, "He's still not in the golf tournament."

"He will be," Drum said.

And rather instinctively we broke into a downhill canter.

As we arrived at the green, Palmer was in the process of drilling an 18-foot birdie putt into the cup. He was now four under through four, two under for the championship, only three strokes behind Souchak, and there were a lot of holes left to play.

We stooped under the ropes at the fifth tee, as our armbands entitled us to, and awaited Arnold's entrance. He came in hitching up the pants and gazed down the fairway. Spotting us, he strolled over.

"Fancy seeing you here," he said with a touch of slyness.

Then he drank the rest of my Coke, smoked one of my cigarettes, and failed to birdie the hole, a par 5. On the other hand, he more than made up for it by sinking a curving 25-footer for a birdie at the par-3 sixth. At the seventh, he hit another splendid wedge to within six feet of the flag. He made the putt. And the cheers that followed told everybody on the golf course that Arnold Palmer had birdied six of the first seven holes.

It was history book stuff. And yet for all of those heroics it was absolutely unreal to look up at a scoreboard out on the course and learn that Arnold Palmer still wasn't leading the Open. Some kid named Jack Nicklaus was. That beefy guy from Columbus paired with Hogan, playing two groups ahead of Palmer. The amateur. Out in 32. Five under now for the tournament.

Bob Drum sized up the scoreboard for everyone around him.

"The fat kid's five under and the whole world's four under," he said.

That was true one minute and not true the next. By the whole world, Drum meant Palmer, Hogan, Souchak, Boros, Fleck, Finsterwald, Barber, Cherry, etc. It was roughly 3:30 then, and for the next half hour it was impossible to know who was actually leading, coming on, falling back, or what. Palmer further complicated things by taking a bogey at the eighth. He parred the ninth and was out in a stinging 30, five under on the round. But in harsh truth, as I suggested to Bob Drum at the time, he was still only three under for the tournament and two strokes off the pace of Nicklaus or Boros or Souchak—possibly all three. And God knows, I said, what Hogan, Fleck, and Cherry—not to mention Dutch Harrison, or even Ted Kroll—were doing while we were standing there talking.

Dutch Harrison, for example, had gone out very early and was working on a 69 and 283. And way back behind even Palmer was Ted Kroll, who had begun the round at 216, one stroke worse off than Palmer. Kroll and Jack Fleck had put almost the same kind of torch to Cherry Hills' front nine holes that Palmer had. Kroll had birdied five of the first seven holes, with one bogey included. Fleck had birdied five of the first six, also with a bogey included. Kroll was going to wind up firing the second-best round of the day, a 67, which would pull him into what later would look like a 200-way tie for third place at the popular figure of 283. One last footnote: Don Cherry, the other amateur in contention, was the last man on the course with a chance. There was this moment in the press tent when everyone was talking about Palmer's victory, and somebody calculated that Don Cherry could shoot 33 on the back nine and win. Cherry was due to finish shortly after dark. He quickly made a couple of bogeys, however, and that was that. But, meanwhile, we were out on the course thinking about Palmer's chances in all of this when Drum made his big pronouncement of the day.

"My man's knocked 'em all out," he said. "They just haven't felt the shock waves yet."

History has settled for Bob Drum's analysis, and perhaps that is the truth of the matter after all. The story of the 1960 Open has been compressed into one sentence: Arnold Palmer birdied six of the first seven holes and won.

But condensations kill. What is missing is everything that happened after 4 o'clock. The part about Mike Souchak losing the lead for the first time only after he bogied the ninth hole. The part about Nicklaus blowing the lead he held all by himself when he took three ghastly putts from only 10 feet at the 13th. This was the first real indication that they were all coming back to Palmer now, for Nicklaus' bogey dropped him into a four-way tie with Palmer, Boros, and Fleck.

But so much more is still missing from the condensation. Nicklaus' woeful inexperience as a young amateur cost him another three-putt bogey at the 14th hole, and so, as suddenly as he had grabbed the lead, he was out of it. Then it was around 4:45 and Palmer was sharing the lead with Hogan and Fleck, each of them four under. But like Nicklaus, Fleck would leave it on the greens. Boros had started leaving it on the greens and in the bunkers somewhat earlier. He was trapped at the 14th and 18th, for instance, and in between he blew a three-footer. In the midst of all this, Palmer was playing a steady back side of one birdie and eight pars on the way to completing his 65. And until the last two holes of the championship, the only man who had performed more steadily than Palmer, or seemed to be enduring the Open stress with as much steel as he, was—no surprise—Ben Hogan.

It was getting close to 5:30 when Hogan and Palmer were alone at four under par in the championship, and the two of them, along with everybody else—literally everyone on the golf course—had somehow wound up on the 17th hole, the 71st of the tournament.

The 17th at Cherry Hills is still a long, straightaway par 5, 548 yards, with a green fronted by an evil pond. In 1960 it was a drive, a layup, and a pitch. And there they all were. Hogan and Nicklaus contemplating their pitch shots as the twosome of Boros and Player waited to hit their second shots, while the twosome of Palmer and Paul Harney stood back on the tee.

Hogan was faced with a delicate shot of about 50 yards to a pin sitting altogether too close to the water, on the front of the green, to try anything risky. Ben had hit 34 straight greens in regulation that Saturday. He needed only to finish with two pars for a 69 and a total of 280—and nobody understood better than Hogan what it meant to reach the clubhouse first with a good score in a major.

Armed with all this knowledge, I knelt in the rough and watched Hogan address the shot and said brilliantly to Drum:

"He probably thinks he needs a birdie with Arnold behind him, but I'll guarantee you one thing—he'll be over the water."

At which point Hogan hit the ball in the water.

It was an inch shy of perfect, but it hit the bank and spun back in.

He made a bogey 6. And in trying to erase that blunder on the 18th with a huge drive, which might conceivably produce a birdie, he hooked his tee shot into the lake and suffered a triple-bogey 7. Sadly, only 30 minutes after he had been a co-leader with just two holes to go, Hogan finished in a tie for ninth place, four strokes away.

Second place then was left to the 20-year-old with the crew cut, and Nicklaus' score of 282 remains the lowest total ever posted by an amateur in the Open.

All in all, these were tremendous performances by an aging Hogan and a young Nicklaus. The two of them had come the closest to surviving Palmer's shock waves.

It was later on, back in the locker room, long after Palmer had slung his visor in the air for the photographers, that Ben Hogan said the truest thing of all about the day. Ben would know best.

He said, "I guess they'll say I lost it. Well, one more foot and the wedge on seventeen would have been perfect. But I'll tell you something. I played thirty-six holes today with a kid who should have won this Open by ten shots."

Jack Nicklaus would start winning major titles soon enough as a pro, of course. But wasn't it nice to have Arnold around first?

Into the Valley of Sin

AMID THE GLOOMY AND YET INTOXICATING OLD RUINS OF A TOWN called St. Andrews and on the golf course that held the first cleat, history and tradition were caned and flogged throughout a July week in 1970 in a musty thing called the British Open. It was done by a modern cast of legends and hustlers, as if the whimpy and whipsy had come to the Royal and Ancient, along with black-eyed peas and corn bread: as if, for a while, the oldest course were only a stroll through Knightsbridge. While Tony Jacklin shot the heather off the land, Lee Trevino shot down a prime minister. And then while Jack Nicklaus played himself into the immortality of the record books, the lord of night life, Sir Douglas Sanders, played himself back from nowhere and into the hearts of those who savor the three-piece, phone-booth golf swing.

It was one of the most thrilling major championships that had been staged in years, one that suffocated in all kinds of atmosphere. It had overtones of America against the world, elements of the best and worst of shotmaking, ghastly pressure, enormous crowds, a buffet of seaside weather, the purity of British humor, the suspense of overtime—all of these things—until it was mercifully concluded by Jack Nicklaus' rendezvous with history.

The fact that the 99th British Open was being held at St. Andrews, the birthplace of golf, had been largely responsible for luring the strongest field of Americans in the history of the event. Aside from the three who finally settled it—Nicklaus, Sanders, and Trevino—there were Arnold Palmer, of course, and Bert Yancey, Dave Marr, Miller Barber, Raymond Floyd, Dale Douglass, Orville Moody, Billy Casper, Tommy Aaron, Gay Brewer, Tommy Shaw, Tom Weiskopf, and Steve Melynk, the amateur champion. Why even more Americans didn't make it was a bit mystifying. It would seem to be part of a professional's education—to see the Old Course once, at least, to investigate the wind and whins and heather, to drive over the Beardies, to relish all of this history.

All week long the Americans who did come were enthralled by the Scots' sophistication in golf. When they weren't glancing around pointing out famous hazards to each other, they were listening for marvelous lines. Dave Marr, plunging into the lore of the place, waggled an 8-iron and asked his caddie one day if the shot was a hard 8 or a soft 8 to the green.

"Just the true value of the club, sir," the caddie said.

When Tony Jacklin had completed the grandest 10 holes in the history of major championships—in other words, when he was eight under par through 10 holes on Wednesday—a couple of weathery old Scots, a man and woman sitting in the stands behind the 11th green, were not so dazzled. Jacklin's tee shot there ate up the flag, but it soared 30 feet beyond the cup.

"A bit long," said the lady.

"Right on the stick, though," the man said.

"Well," the lady said, "that's *half* the game, isn't it?"

In terms of crusty sophistication, it was almost unbelievable the way the British Open began at St. Andrews. In contrast to the U.S. Open, which has at least a touch of ceremony to it, the British Open begins more like a starter sending off the first twosome of any weekday. Everybody stands around quietly, an old gentleman moves the tee markers back about three feet, an aging steward empties out the trash in the tee box, somebody coughs. Finally, the starter looks at one of the two unknowns and says, "Your honor, I believe." And the game is on.

The first day the field caught the Old Course in a calm, with the greens slowed down by constant watering, and turned it into a shambles. It was a giddy day for Great Britain as all sorts of British subjects wrecked par. Neil Coles, for example, shot a record seven-under 65, largely due to the holing out of some enormous putts, plus a 9-iron for an eagle. But all day the big throngs had been waiting for their hero, Tony Jacklin, who had won the U.S. Open a month earlier and had won the British Open a year earlier. The wait was worth it. Tony promptly launched into a memorable afternoon of golf. He birdied the first three holes with wedge shots that hugged the flags. He two-putted for a bird at the fifth. He ran an 8-iron around the lip of a bunker at the eighth to within six feet of the cup and made that, and then he holed out a 100-yard wedge shot for a birdie at the ninth. He was eight under par, out in 29!

But he didn't stop. He wedged to six feet at the 10th, and sank another putt. He calmed down with pars through the 13th, and that was where the elements took over, as if the elements saw what was happening to St. Andrews and came to the rescue.

A sudden rainstorm swept over the course. Actual rivers washed across the greens. After a hurried conference, officials halted play.

As it turned out, Tony would have been better off playing through the lightning and rivers. For one thing, he had to worry for 12 hours over an unplayable lie in the rough at the 14th. He had hit a wild slice from the tee, and that was where play was stopped.

There was a lot of joking of how on Thursday morning at the 14th there wouldn't be a rough there, and how some British writer would have a front-page story: I GUARDED TONY'S DROP AREA THROUGH THE NIGHT.

History would note that Jacklin marked the lie under the bush with two tees, and put the ball, a Dunlop 1, in his golf bag and went home. The ball slept well, if Jacklin didn't.

He arrived at 7:15 the next morning, promptly announced that he would take a penalty for an unplayable lie, dropped the ball about 25 yards behind the bushes and played a nice shot onto the green some 12 feet from the hole. When that putt failed to drop, his luck was gone, and he wound up losing the title by the three strokes he had slept on.

Then, for a while, the lead had belonged to Lee Trevino. The second day had seen him move ahead with his second 68, a stroke in front of Jacklin and Nicklaus. Trevino was the only player besides Jacklin the crowd seemed to warm to. He loved it and they loved it. His big moment actually came during Friday's third round. On the first tee Lee was introduced to Prime Minister Edward Heath. Trevino grinned and said, "Ever shake hands with a Mexican?" The R&A building, along with the prime minister, gently swayed with laughter.

Lee probably beat himself on Saturday with a colossal boner, or at least he went a long way toward it. At the fifth hole he laced an iron at the wrong flag on the huge double green, leaving himself about 80 feet from the right one, and he three-putted for a bogey at a time when Nicklaus and Sanders were moving away. The moment he hit the approach shot, he slapped himself in the forehead, like one of the Three Stooges, and said, "I done hit to the wrong stick." Then he said, "And I'm just dumb enough to have done it too."

From then on the championship alternately belonged to Nicklaus or Sanders. Nicklaus played splendidly enough on Saturday to have won two British Opens and a Pensacola thrown in. It was a day when the wind blew up to 50 mph. As somebody said, they must have sent to Carnoustie for the wind machine. In any case, the Old Course was a violent place, and 73 was like four under.

Nicklaus was striking the ball about as well as anyone ever saw him do it, but he left it on the greens with five three-putts, missing several times from inside eight feet. One of these came on the 18th, where he rolled his drive through the Valley of Sin as if he were going for old Tom Morris' grave across town and then missed a putt coming back.

It all came down to Sanders then, and whether he could par the last two holes. With one of the great bunker shots of our time, he survived 17, the Road Hole. But with one of the worst wedges of our time, he got a hitch in the heart at 18 and put himself on the back of the green. Then he jerked up on a 28-inch putt that would have won it.

"Good God," Arnold Palmer said to Doug later. "Pitch and run is *your* game. What were you doing out there?"

"I just don't know," said Sanders.

It may long be said that Nicklaus made the finest putt of his life Sunday on the final hole of the play-off, where he slammed a howling monster of a shot that carried over Granny Clark's Wynd, the little road that crosses the course, and blazed up to the high grass behind the green, merely 370 yards.

Sanders had crept up from four strokes behind in the last four holes and now was within one sinister stroke. No one could ever know how he had done it. He was just a nervy veteran hanging on with some kind of instinct. Sanders took out a 4-iron and hit a run-up shot through the Valley of Sin that he should have hit on Saturday, within four feet of the cup. And so it was up to Jack. He came out of the tough, high grass with about as gutsy a wedge shot as one will ever see and left himself an eight-footer for the whole thing. With the patience only Nicklaus can display, with the confidence of a man who felt the championship truly belonged to him, he jammed it in. Two nights before, Gay Brewer had said, "Jack's in the mood to win. You can tell by the way he swings that he's ready. And when he's ready, it's all over." It was all over now.

The British were happy in the end, one felt. Considering the exciting prospects of the four big challengers going at it in the fourth round—Nicklaus, Jacklin, Trevino, and Sanders—one old Scot had said, "Quite a show coming up, it appears, but whatever happens, we want a proper champion, don't we?"

Would Jack Nicklaus do?

Slammed Down

HE STOOD AGAINST ONE OF THOSE SAND HILLS, ONE FOOT HALFWAY up the rise, a gloved hand braced on his knee and his head hung downward in monumental despair. He lingered in this pose, with what seemed like all of Scotland surrounding him, with the North Sea gleaming in the background and with the quiet broken only by the awkward, silly, faraway sound of bagpipes rehearsing for the victory ceremony. This was Jack Nicklaus on the next to last hole of the 1972 British Open after another putt had refused to fall. It was Nicklaus in the moment he knew, after a furious comeback, that he had finally lost the championship and what might have been the grandest slam in golf. One more putt of any size on any of these last seven holes and Nicklaus would have completed what could seriously have been termed the most brilliant rally the game had ever known.

But one more putt did not drop for Nicklaus, and on the same hole minutes later one more chip shot *did* curl implausibly into the cup for the implausible Lee Trevino. Finally, then, after all of the shattering heroics at Muirfield on the east coast of Scotland on that July day, the golfing world had a right to feel oversuspensed.

Nicklaus had won the Masters and the U.S. Open earlier in the season, but now he had lost the British Open in the final hour—his quest for a Grand Slam was over—and Trevino had captured the British Open for the second year in a row.

Trevino tossed out all the usual lines about God being Mexican or else Nicklaus would still be alive for the Grand Slam; about switching back and forth from the small British ball to the larger American ball and how the American ball always looked like a melon; about the castle he had rented for the week ("They got to have some kind of princess locked up in there someplace"); and about the lukewarm drinks the Scots are accustomed to ("No wonder everybody over here's so wrinkled up"). That was Trevino all week.

It probably can be said that Nicklaus waited too long to attack Muirfield, that he perished with his own conservative game plan on a course that played easier than he expected because of some unanticipated glory-be weather. When Jack finally turned aggressive for Saturday's closing 18, when he was six shots down and the lids came off his driver and 3-wood, he shot a 66 to tie the course record and, at one point, miraculously lead the tournament by one stroke. Jack will think long about the holes he let get away during the earlier rounds and he will dwell, too, on the six late putts that refused to disappear into the cups—a 12-footer for a birdie at the 12th, a 15-footer for a birdie at the 13th, an 18-footer for another birdie at the 14th, a four-footer for yet another birdie at the 15th, a three-footer for a saving par at the 16th, and, the last gasp, the 20-foot birdie putt at the 17th.

Saturday began with only four potential winners of this Open. Trevino held a one-stroke lead by virtue of a flood of Friday birdies. They came five in a row from the 14th through the 18th, including an astonishing hole-out of a sand shot at 16—which even Lee admitted should have been a double bogey—and the sinking of a 30-foot chip on the last green. Next was Tony Jacklin, who was up three despite a triple bogey during the second round; and then Doug Sanders, who was only four back despite a triple bogey of his own along the way. And finally Jack Nicklaus—if he could muster an Arnold Palmer type of thing.

Jack did exactly that. Through 11 holes, as he was being cheered madly by a rousing British crowd of 20,000, he seemed to be playing, at last, the definitive round of golf. He was perfect with every club, and he had pushed to six under par. "Look at this," Trevino said to Jacklin as they went to the ninth tee. "Nicklaus has gone crazy. We're out here beating each other to death, and that son of a gun's done caught us and passed us."

Two little dramas of high order were going on at this point. Up ahead, the crowds were yelling for the Nicklaus Slam as he strode the length of the 11th fairway toward another short birdie putt. Back at the ninth, Trevino had told his caddie, "We're behind, son. Gimme that driver, we got to make something happen." Trevino absolutely killed his drive at the skinny ninth fairway. He then put a 5-iron within 18 feet of the hole and made the putt for an eagle. Suddenly he was back to even par for the day, and back to six under for the tournament. And Jacklin, too, eagled the ninth, to stay within one shot of Trevino.

Nicklaus, meanwhile, tried to address the birdie putt on the

11th green that would put him in a tie with Trevino at six under. He heard the two roars for the eagles, backed away from his putt and smiled. Then he coldly made the birdie, and once more came an explosion of sound, this time from his own gallery. It was an eerie moment hearing those roars back to back to back. Trevino remembered later, "After our eagles at nine, I told Tony, 'That'll give Jack something to think about.' Then we heard his birdie roar and I said, 'I think the man just gave us something else to think about.'"

What could be said of Trevino and how he actually won? How could it be accounted for? Nicklaus worked for more than a week at Muirfield, while Trevino arrived late. Wearing a planter's hat and cracking jokes, he practiced only two days. "I brought this trophy back," he said upon arrival, "but I shouldn't have. It's just going back to El Paso."

The case certainly could be made that this was a lucky win for Trevino, unlike 1971 at Royal Birkdale when he destroyed the course with brilliant shotmaking. After all, he holed out four times—four—from off the greens during the course of 72 holes for his 278. And that is simply indecent.

On the second day, he chipped in for a birdie 3 at the second hole from 40 feet with an 8-iron. Then he holed his two ridiculous shots in the third round when he ran off from everyone but Jacklin. The first was from a terrible lie up against a bank in a bunker at the 16th. He had just dropped consecutive birdie putts of more than 20 feet at the 14th and 15th. Now he slammed his wedge into the sand. Out spurted the ball in a semi-line drive to take one harsh bounce and dive into the cup for a birdie 2. At the 18th, after two-putting for a normal birdie on the 17th, he chipped out of the weeds for a fifth straight birdie and a 66. "I think things like that happen to a man sometimes when he's trying," Lee said. "I was trying. I was aiming at the cup. I didn't come to Scotland to help Nicklaus win any Grand Slam. If I played golf with my wife, I'd try to beat the daylights out of her."

For all of this, it was one last chip shot that found its way into the hole that rescued Trevino from what looked, at the very end, like a certain victory for Tony Jacklin. Tony had won in 1969, and Tony could win again. Princess Margaret was there; wasn't this an omen?

Trevino had played the par-5 17th like a man choking on the trophy or a sausage roll or perhaps royalty. He drove into a bunker, poked it out, poked it again, and then ran a short pitch over the green. Jacklin, meanwhile, was just off the green in two. He chipped on, leaving himself a good birdie chance. He was about to go to 18 with a certain one-stroke lead. Perhaps two. Possibly three.

"I think I might have given up. I felt like I had," Trevino said. "My heart wasn't really in my chip shot." Something was. It went in for a saving 5. Jacklin, having watched all these crazy shots of Lee's go in for two rounds, now did what was human. He three-putted from 15 feet. And that was that. Trevino got a routine par on 18 for his second British Open.

"I feel sorry for Tony, who played really well. And I feel sorry for Jack. But Jack shouldn't have treated me like a butler when I had dinner with him the other night," said Trevino, still joking, still refreshingly Trevino.

In retrospect, one really had to wonder about Nicklaus' strategy, and Jack himself might well look back and question it. Maybe not, however. He is pretty stubborn about such things. He had a game plan for Muirfield and he stuck to it—at least until Saturday.

He arrived early to begin preparations for both the course and the smaller ball. There was nothing wrong with this—or else it could be said that he should not have arrived a week early at Pebble Beach for the U.S. Open. The argument that Jack was overprepared can be discarded. The final round proved as much.

There was tremendous pressure on him. The betting odds were an outlandish 2 to 1 before the championship even got under way and all of the Scottish newspapers were advertising the event as some sort of Nicklaus Extravaganza. *The Scotsman* (Edinburgh), for example, labeled its daily coverage, "The Grand Slam Open," with a portrait of Jack.

Muirfield has been called Scotland's best golf course by many authorities. This does not mean it is the toughest; that is probably Carnoustie in the wind. It means that Muirfield is the most elegant, the classiest, the most subtle, the best conditioned. It is not a long course; it has often been compared to our own Merion, given the right winds. There were one or two par 4s that Nicklaus could reach with a driver if he chose to try—and if he succeeded in hitting it straight enough. There were several others where he could reduce his second shot to a wedge if he hit with a big club off the tee. And there were par 5s he could surely reach in two blows.

Jack, having won at Muirfield in 1966 and sternly aware of the narrow fairways and numerous well-deep bunkers, had decided the only way to play the course was defensively, with caution and patience. He would 1-iron it and 3-iron it from the tees. On only five holes, depending on the wind, would his woods come out of the bag. "What happened, basically," he said afterward, "is that I didn't hit the other clubs straight."

It was only during Wednesday's first round that Muirfield played like a British Open course should—long, windy, and rainy. Nicklaus' 70 that day was a mad scramble as he missed seven fairways on the only day his game plan made sense. When the unusually glorious weather set in on Thursday, Jack woke up and said, "Ye gods, I'll have to shoot 65 just to stay in it. The course will be a piece of cake." Muirfield was bright with sun, windless—and short. But all Jack did was go on missing fairways. Still, the field did not run away from him. And he was due a good round, wasn't he? "I haven't wasted any of my good golf yet," Nicklaus said Thursday night.

He didn't waste any on Friday either. The weather was even more wonderful, and there really weren't that many contenders for him to worry about. The first-day leader, Peter Tupling—was a Tupling worth more than a shilling?—had slipped back the way Tuplings should. A few other British surprises were still around but they wouldn't last. It was only Nicklaus against Trevino, Jacklin, Sanders, and Johnny Miller, who had holed a 3-wood for a double eagle, and perhaps astonishing Dave Marr, back from nowhere.

Everyone felt that Friday would be the day Nicklaus would explode. Not so. Jack was still missing fairways and was well out of it, two over par going to the 16th hole at the very time Trevino and Jacklin were at their hottest. It was only through a miracle of his very own, a chip in at the 16th, another birdie at the 17th, and a struggling par at the 18th, that Nicklaus got home with a 71 and even par through 54 holes. Granted, in any other British Open that might have been fine. But Super Mex and Super Limey and the weather were seeing to it that this was no ordinary championship.

By attacking Muirfield, Tony Jacklin had met some tragedies, among them his triple bogey on the 13th hole the second day, but he had also stored up some birdies and eagles. Trevino had bounced between birdies and bogeys all along until nothing but birdies turned up late Friday in that mind-bending finish of his. And it seemed clear that Nicklaus had waited too long to change his strategy. But even after he had lost, Jack disagreed, contending, "I'll always believe I played the course the right way and just didn't play well. What can I do about a guy who holes it out of bunkers and across greens?"

A 1,000-to-1 Shot

FROM WHERE TOM WATSON WAS ON THE 71ST HOLE OF THE U.S. Open at Pebble Beach—in the garbage, on a downslope, looking at a green that was slicker than tile—you don't simply chip the ball into the cup for a birdie to beat Jack Nicklaus, not a Jack Nicklaus who's already in the scorer's tent with a total good enough to win the championship. First, you throw up.

Well, that was wrong, of course. This was 1982. And by then Tom Watson was accustomed to beating Jack Nicklaus on occasion. He had done it in The Masters, and he had done it before in the British Open. So he opened the blade of his trusty sand wedge and plopped the ball softly onto the putting surface and then watched the flagstick get in its way to keep the ball from racing all the way to his room in the Pebble Beach Lodge.

When the ball disappeared in the cup, Watson suddenly looked as if he were in a disco—on speed.

Nicklaus was watching Watson's progress on a TV monitor in back of the 18th green. Jack had completed his round, firing a three-under 69 and posting a 72-hole score of 284, a winning total in the estimation of most, especially since Nicklaus had shot it.

He had seen Watson's less-than-perfect tee shot at 17, a 2-iron. The ball had bounced and found the high grass on the upslope to the left of the green.

Certain bogey, Jack thought; this Open is mine. The two of them were dead-even at this point.

Nicklaus took his eyes off the monitor for a second, and the next thing he saw was Watson jumping up and down, and darting around, as a distant roar filled the air.

A few moments later, Watson was making a needless birdie at the 18th to win by two strokes, at 282, and Nicklaus was shaking Tom's hand, and saying, "You little son of a bitch, you're something else."

So ended a fantastic U.S. Open. In the end, it was another

Watson-Nicklaus saga. Watson-Nicklaus III, check your local listings.

No. 1 came at Augusta in 1977 when Tom outbattled Jack down the stretch, edging him out with a birdie putt at the 71st hole. No. 2 came later that same year at Turnberry in Scotland when Tom and Jack went head-to-head for the last 36 holes, and Watson prevailed 65-65 to Jack's 65-66.

Bill Rogers, who was playing with Watson in the final round at Pebble, said of the shot at the 17th, "You could hit that chip shot a hundred times and you couldn't get it close to the pin, much less in the hole."

"A thousand times," Nicklaus said.

Watson and Rogers, the 1981 British Open champion, had begun the last round in a tie for the lead with Nicklaus three strokes back. Other characters in the drama, such as Bruce Devlin, the 36-hole leader, had faded away. Watson's closing round of 70 included what Rogers described as "three knockout blows."

They were, in order of appearance, a 25-foot putt to save a par at the 10th hole, a 35-foot putt for a birdie at the 14th, and the chip-in.

Rogers said, "I saw Tom get a gleam of confidence after he got away with a par at the tenth, and on fourteen, well . . . humans three-putt from where he was."

The fact is, Watson had predicted he would hole out the chip shot.

When his caddie, Bruce Edwards, handed him the club, he said, "Get it close." Whereupon Tom said, "I'm going to chip it in."

He later explained, "I've practiced that shot for hours, days, months, and years. It's a shot you have to know if you're going to do well in the Open, where there's high grass around the greens."

Practice made perfect, but Watson may have won that Open in another way. There are two different golf courses built into Pebble Beach. There are the first seven holes, or the "easy holes," and then there's the real golf course, which starts on the eighth tee. Watson was four under par for the tournament on the real golf course, from the eighth to the Lodge, and that was about a thousand shots better than anyone else in the field.

Looking back on it, nobody could have summed up that Open finish better than Frank "Sandy" Tatum, an ex-president of the USGA, and a Stanford man, like Watson. The evening before the Watson-Nicklaus drama began, Tatum studied the leaders on the scoreboard in the press tent and turned to a friend.

"Look at that scoreboard," he said. "Tomorrow . . . wow."

Thus, Watson's chip-in later begged a question: What did Tatum know and when did he know it?

Fat Fang and Friend

IF YOU WANT TO PUT GOLF BACK ON THE FRONT PAGES AGAIN AND you don't have a Bobby Jones or a Francis Ouimet handy, here's what you do: You send an aging Jack Nicklaus out in the last round of The Masters and let him kill more foreigners than a general named Eisenhower.

Such was the story of the 1986 Masters.

On that final afternoon at the Augusta National Golf Club, Nicklaus' deeds were so unexpectedly heroic, dramatic, and historic, this winning of his sixth Masters had to go down as the biggest golf story since Jones won the Grand Slam in 1930.

That Sunday night, writers from all over the globe were last seen sitting limply at their machines, muttering, "It's too big for me."

What indeed could be said? That it was one for the ages? That Jack Nicklaus saved golf from the nobodies who populate the PGA Tour these days? That surely this was Jack's finest hour, this *20th major*? As much was said back in 1980 when he surprisingly won the U.S. Open and PGA. But here he comes again, six years later, now a creaking 46, hopelessly trailing a group of younger stars, most of them glamorous foreigners like Seve Ballesteros, Greg Norman, Bernhard Langer, Tommy Nakajima, Nick Price, and Sandy Lyle and what he does is suddenly catch fire over the last 10 holes of the tournament, shoot a seven-under 65 (with two bogeys), knock all of the invaders into a killer funk, and win a sixth Masters by filling the Augusta National's pine-shadowed corridors with roars unlike any before them.

And he does it at a time when it looked like you needed a visa to get on the leader board. He had to beat a league of nations.

The history book, please. Now that it's over and Jack has hugged his son, the caddie, and survived the cordon of policemen who hadn't surrounded a golfer in such numbers since Jones completed the Slam at Merion 56 years ago, or since Ouimet upset Vardon and Ray 73 years ago, what does it mean?

When he won his fourth U.S. Open at Baltusrol in 1980, it tied him with Ben Hogan, Bobby Jones, and Willie Anderson. When he won his fifth PGA at Oak Hill in 1980, it tied him with Walter Hagen. Now look, Nicklaus' sixth Masters victory gives him a tie with none other than Harry Vardon in an odd category. Vardon had been the only professional to win a specific major six times, having taken his half-dozenth British Open at Prestwick back in 1914.

In the case of Nicklaus, it wasn't so much *what* he did but *how* he did it. With 10 holes left in the final round, he was six shots off the pace being set by Seve Ballesteros, who simply looked as if he owned the tournament, and had been looking like the owner all week long. But let it be recorded that Jack played those last 10 holes in 33 strokes—with a birdie at the ninth, a birdie at the 10th, a birdie at the 11th, a bogey at the 12th, a birdie at the 13th, a par at the 14th, an eagle at the 15th, a birdie at the 16th, a birdie at the 17th, and a par at the 18th. Poor Jack. The guy almost didn't know how to make a par.

To be serious, it was this miraculous stretch of holes that tore the foreigners apart. None among them had a reason to take Nicklaus seriously until Jack hit the most gorgeous 4-iron you ever saw to the water-guarded 15th, and then rammed home a 12-foot putt for an eagle 3. That got their attention, and then when Jack put every pore of knowledge into a 5-iron and damned near aced the par-3 16th, it frankly scored a knockout over Ballesteros.

There stood Seve, back in the 15th fairway with a one-shot lead on the field. Here was a man who had already made two eagles in the round, one at the eighth with a 50-yard pitch and another at the 13th with a two-yard putt. Until this moment, Seve had looked indestructible. But the repetitious punches of Nicklaus finally got to the Spaniard, and he did the only thing he could have done to lose the tournament he wanted so badly to win. He jerked the worst-looking 4-iron shot imaginable into the pond with a one-handed finish and took a bogey that bruised his confidence beyond repair. Make no mistake: Jack knocked the club out of his hand.

Perhaps the next most amazing shot Nicklaus hit came then at the 17th, after his pulled drive left him on hardpan, 125 yards from the green. A shot like that is supposed to spin, but Jack just fluttered it up, hop, hop, and he had a 10-foot birdie putt that destiny would allow him to rap into the throat of the cup. Finally, he played to a masterful par at the closing hole for his winning total of 279.

Nicklaus has rarely won his stockpile of majors watching television—until this one. In the Jones cottage near the Augusta National clubhouse, Jack watched the failures of Tom Kite and Greg Norman.

Of these, Norman's was the most necessary, and perhaps the most deserving, given the fact that the way Greg struck the ball on Sunday, his 70 could well have been an 80. He bounced off of everything but a nearby shopping center, and kept getting saved by the crowds, whose numbers prevented his ball from finding even worse places to come to rest, or, in fact, be lost. It was Nicklaus' presence on the scoreboard that ultimately did in the Australian at the 18th hole when Greg needed a par to tie, just as it was Jack's presence on the course that had done in Seve and others. What do you do if you're Greg Norman in the 18th fairway of the Masters on Sunday and you're trying to get Jack Nicklaus into a play-off? You hit a half-shank, push-fade, semi-slice 4-iron that guarantees the proper result for the history books. When you stop to think about it, Norman probably didn't want to play the 10th hole again in sudden death; he already had double-bogeyed it twice that week, once four-putting. Oh well, Greg Norman always has looked like the guy you send out to kill James Bond, not Jack Nicklaus.

When it was all over, including the shouting, Nicklaus sat in front of 300 writers and explained the meaning of winning The Masters in "the December of my career." He said he never heard the crowds roar so loudly. "There were only three other times that compared," he said. "The 1972 British Open at Muirfield when I lost to Trevino, the 1978 British Open when I won at St. Andrews, and the 1980 U.S. Open I won at Baltusrol. It brought tears to my eyes.

"I'm not as good as I was ten or fifteen years ago," he went on to say. "I don't play as much competitive golf as I used to, but there are still some weeks when I'm as good as I ever was."

There was nothing to recommend Nicklaus going into the week. He hadn't won a major in five years. He hadn't won a minor in almost two years.

As usual, Jack gave credit to a short-game lesson he got from his son. This time it was Jackie who passed along a tip from Chi Chi

Rodriguez to "take the hands out of the swing, firm up the left side, and move more aggressively through the ball." (You may recall back in 1980, he was trying to put the hands into the swing, soften up the left side, and move more passively through the ball.)

But the credit really belonged to that outrageous putter he used to hole all those putts. Jack has putted with an old George Low flange in almost every major he has won. The last time he deviated and won was in the 1967 U.S. Open at Baltusrol, with a putter named "White Fang."

This time he used a putter he helped design at MacGregor, something on the order of an oversized Ping.

The press struggled for a name.

Pregnant Ping was dismissed.

Fat Fang was chosen.

Fat Fang wins Masters.

Fat Fang shoots 65.

Fat Fang takes Thin Jack to sixth green jacket.

Nicklaus' victory at the astonishing 1986 Masters underscored the fact that there's something about the second weekend in April that's quite impossible to change. The golfing year starts in Augusta, Ga. You feel it every year. They can play the Tournament of Champions in January, and they can claim all kinds of privileges for the Tournament Players Championship in Ponte Vedra, Fla., in March, but it's the second weekend in April when true excitement and elegance kick in; when the golfing establishment assaults the veranda, when the world media congregates, and when the players themselves know they're in the big time. At Augusta, there are no junk-food franchises sponsoring the marshals, no take-out restaurants catering the press, and the only logo to be seen on everything from a visor to a paper cup is that of the Augusta National.

The Masters is a sell-out annually, and even the scalpers mind their manners. Outside the club property, across the street from Magnolia Drive, a man was selling Masters hats this year. Someone had been told to go see him for a ticket. "I'm not selling tickets," the proprietor of the hat stand said. "I'm selling hats."

Strangely, the hats for sale had what looked like Masters tickets pinned to them.

"How much is a hat?" said an interested buyer to the man in the hat stand.

"Eight hundred and fifty dollars."

In the Augusta National golf shop, the articles with Masters logos virtually fly out of the room—the jackets, caps, towels, ash-trays, shirts, coasters, etc.

Very early in the week, a souvenir hunter wandered over to the jewelry and glassware counter, interested in pendants, money clips, paperweights.

"I'd like to have one of those Masters paperweights," he said to the lady behind the counter.

"Sir, I'm sorry," the lady said. "A Japanese gentleman was just here and bought the only sixty we ordered."

As most Masters junkies know, the Augusta National does not have a pro-am or a clinic, but it does have the Par-3 Tournament on Wednesday, a chance for everyone in the select field to gather some crystal they may not be able to collect during the tournament proper. The Par-3 is more like a picnic than a competition, but the crowds are enormous. No winner of the Par-3 has ever gone ahead to capture The Masters, and Gary Koch was no exception this time.

For most, the high point of this year's Par-3 was noticing a group of spectators in Bob Tway's gallery wearing shirts that said: "TWAY'S TWOOPS." The sighting of these people together with the fact that PGA Tour Commissioner Deane Beman was the only establishment person missing from the Augusta veranda said something, in a curious way, about where the sport has come in America since the days of "Arnie's Army," or even "Lee's Fleas." How could the commissioner not have been present at what is undeniably golf's foremost social occasion? And is "Tway's Twoops" the tenor of the humor we can expect from the future of the PGA Tour? What Beman missed, of course, was one of golf's most epic occasions.

The first round of the Masters on Thursday looked pretty much like every other tour event of the past two or three years. It was rather bland from the standpoint of thrills, and when the day was done, Ken (not Hubert) Green was tied with Bill Kratzert for the lead. They had shot 68s. Green had done it by holing an abominable number of long putts. Somebody said the only green he hit was Shelley, his sister, who caddies for him.

While Shelley is a cute thing, her presence nevertheless brought to mind that The Masters maybe shouldn't have given in to the touring pros and allowed them to bring their own caddies to the tournament—for their own good. Ken and Shelley Green's lack of knowledge caught up with Ken and he dropped out of sight. In the old days, such caddies as Ironman, Willie, and Stovepipe contrib-uted an awful lot to the reading of breaks and club selections because they knew the subtle contours of the course the way they knew the eyes on a pair of dice in the caddie pen. But, then, Jackie Nicklaus didn't do too badly, did he?

Weather-wise, Friday was just like Thursday, an old-fashioned, breezy, slightly cool day, the kind of day that reminded grizzled veterans of the '50s and early '60s. It was a day that was much to the accomplished player's liking, one that rewarded good shots and placed a premium on knowledge. And it more or less belonged to Ballesteros, whose four-under 68 was highlighted by an eagle 3 at the par-5 15th, the same hole that would do him in later. His eagle was the result of two stylish swings and a 20-foot putt. In his eyes, Seve had the look of eagles all the way around, having already said he was "ready to win." Of everyone involved, Ballesteros looked the most determined, the most dedicated, the player with the most motivation, having been banished from the American circuit for 1986 by the stubborn enforcement of a silly rule, or so growing numbers of fans, journalists, and competitors had come to think.

On this subject, Seve said in a press conference, "Deane Beman is a little man trying to be a big man."

After his Friday round, Ballesteros found himself in an exchange with *The Atlanta Journal's* gifted columnist, Furman Bisher, a conversation worth repeating.

Furman said, "Seve, you played like you were on a crusade today. Are you trying to prove something to the PGA Tour?"

Seve responded, "Did Deane Beman pay you to ask that question?"

Furman said, "No, it's a legitimate question. Are you on a crusade?"

"You talk too sophisticated for me," said Seve. "I don't understand."

"You ought to know what a crusade is," Furman said. "They started in Spain."

Seve didn't have a kicker line because, like most everybody else in the press building, he'd never learned that the Crusades had actually started in Rome.

Saturday was the day that the Augusta National course played easier than it ever had, or perhaps ever would again. The greens had been watered to begin with—reason unknown—and then the place got caught in a calm. Soft greens and no wind. The course was bound to take its bruises, and did. The average score of the field, those who had survived the 36-hole cut, was 70.98. Shots flew into greens and went splat instead of bounding into the dogwood. Tom

Watson said it was the "most defenseless" he had ever seen the course.

All sorts of competitors took advantage of the conditions to play themselves into contention, primarily because Ballesteros had one of those days when he played flawlessly from tee to green, at least for 16 holes, but never made a putt. He seemed always to be in just the wrong place on the undulating greens to get a "good read."

Nick Price was the player who committed the most brutal rape of the premises. There were several things astounding about Price's record 63. One, he bogeyed the first hole. Two, he had a "margarita" on the 18th, a birdie putt that rimmed the entire cup but stayed out. And three, he never hit a single par-5 hole in two and yet birdied all four of them. This was the same Nick Price who had begun the tournament with a woeful 79 on Thursday, mostly because of six three-putt greens. It was the same Nick Price who comes from Zimbabwe, or Rhodesia if you insist, but holds a British passport and is applying for U.S. citizenship.

What the pushover conditions on Saturday did was create the possibility of a swarm-off finish. There were 21 players only five strokes apart when Sunday's final round began. Norman was leading at six-under 210 after rounds of 70, 72, 68, and both Ballesteros and Langer said they "liked" their positions at 211. With five foreigners up there among the top eight contenders, it looked like America might be better off trying to take up cricket.

The situation was ripe, however, for someone to go out early, shoot a low number, and maybe steal the thing. That Jack Nicklaus, a 46-year-old golf course designer, would be the one to do it was the last thing in anybody's mind.

But Jack surprised us again, as he so often has, and none of us who saw it shall ever forget the sight of old Fat Fang bringing him up that 18th fairway.

Spain's Gift to Golf

ON A GOLF COURSE THAT HAS BECOME A GRAVEYARD FOR AMERICAN pros, it seemed more than appropriate that the greatest golfer in the game in the 1980s, Severiano Ballesteros, played one of the finest rounds of golf in the history of divots to win the 1988 British Open and strongly insinuate that he is the greatest thing to come out of Spain since a painting by Picasso that made sense.

Years ago, when Bobby Jones became the only American ever to win at Royal Lytham and St. Annes, they put a plaque next to a bunker at the 17th hole to commemorate the shot Jones hit on his way to that victory. But it wouldn't be possible to commemorate Seve's final-round 65 with plaques, for it would render the course unplayable.

When Ballesteros won his first British Open, at Lytham back in 1979, he was labeled the "car-park champion" because in those days his strength lay in his ability to find his wild tee shots and slash his way back to the greens and hole improbable putts for pars and birdies.

This time it was altogether different. In the rain-delayed final 18 of Monday, July 18, and although his round was stained by two bogeys, Seve's six-under-par 65 was distinguished by near-flawless shotmaking throughout. He missed only three fairways off the tee, and not too badly at that, and he missed only three greens. All in all, he was never in any of that deep gorse or caged among those bushes with which he has been so familiar.

And when it came right down to it, in the immense pressure that final rounds of majors always entail, Ballesteros was coolly, calmly, and amazingly up to the task of hitting three brilliant shots that actually clinched him the title over Zimbabwe's Nick Price. Price, in the final threesome with Seve and Nick Faldo, spent the afternoon dogging the Spaniard like a gumshoe, refusing to disappear, and ever threatening to capture the 117th British Open himself.

Seve's first test came at Lytham's par-5 seventh hole, where he trailed Price by one stroke, and yet watched Nick send a beautiful 2-iron second onto the green and within five feet of the cup for what would surely be an eagle 3. All Seve did was cover this shot with a gorgeous 5-iron of his own and sink the six-foot putt for his own eagle to stay within one of the leader.

They stayed as close as coins in a pocket through the next eight holes, and then came the telling 16th, a 357-yard par 4 with a blind tee shot, the very hole, in fact, where Seve had hit his famous "car-park" shot in '79, which catapulted him to the trophy. "I didn't find any cars this time," he said. Seve hit a 1-iron shot in the fairway, and his 9-iron to the green all but went into the cup. We're talking three inches here. It was his sixth birdie of the day, and don't forget he had an eagle too.

What a shot and what a time to pull it off!

Ballesteros' last bit of artistry came on the 18th, the 412-yard "home hole" that plays directly back to the old red-brick clubhouse and between the enormous grandstands that have become such a familiar part of the Open scenery in England and Scotland.

His drive was in the light rough and he needed a 4 to win, in all probability, but he didn't look or act the least bit worried about it. In fact, those near him even heard him make a joke.

"Let's hit this one before dinner," he said.

Earlier in the day, before he teed off, Seve stood in the locker room and looked out the window to the 18th green. "If I need a four on the last hole to win, I will play to the left," he told himself. As he stood over his approach to the last hole on Monday afternoon, he repeated the advice to himself.

Seve then hit it too far, about five yards over the green, but it was on the proper side. The ball was sitting "down" a bit. Not to worry. These are the shots Seve knows best, and with a sand wedge he damn near holed it from 60 feet.

Seve took us through the bag in that final round, is what he did, and consider for a moment those three crucial shots he hit on Monday—a long iron at seven, a short iron at 16, a chip at 18.

"I think I played about as well as this game can be played," Seve said after his 65.

"I felt confident," said Seve. "I felt relaxed. But I also felt pressure. Even Jack Nicklaus feels pressure."

The joy of watching an artist, Ballesteros, at the top of his game went a long way toward making up for what was, in many ways, a dreadful week, given the locale.

Royal Lytham and St. Annes is unique among British Open venues, largely because it is located about three penny arcades and two showbars from Blackpool on the Irish Sea, in Lancashire, where the unfathomable accents seem to be a blend of North Country and Glaswegian brogue, a Glaswegian being a Glasgow resident who each July drives four hours to Blackpool for fun and frolic. Blackpool, gaudy and vile, is what would happen in the U.S. if a tornado lifted up the worst parts of Disneyland and dropped them on Atlantic City.

Blackpool has what is called the Golden Mile, a promenade along the muddy beach that starts near the Blackpool Tower, a failed replica of the Eiffel Tower, and ends somewhere near a plaster statue of an unidentifiable nursery rhyme character, or an ice-cold mist, or both. In between are row upon row of little glass-fronted hotels, shooting galleries, pleasure piers, gift shops specializing in nothing for everybody, pubs catering to the shot-and-beer crowd, indoor swimming emporiums—the last person to swim outdoors in Blackpool was undoubtedly in a shipwreck—an array of kiddie rides, candle-carving exhibitions, bingo halls, and cabarets featuring such well-known acts from the showbiz world as "Mr. X, the Mystery Singing Star."

In addition, you can bet on pro wrestling in Blackpool, but no visiting American that anyone could track down had fancied Big Daddy and Kashmir of India in a tag team match at 3 to 1 over Cyanide Sid Cooper and Killer Karl Krammer. At night, when all Blackpool's neon is aflame— "Slots of Fun," and so on—it becomes a little bit of heaven for the vacationing lorry driver, and every American's worst nightmare.

However, if one has a fondness for red brick, the nearby villages of St. Annes and Lytham are rather quiet, respectable, and engaging. Friendly tearooms and shops and pubs abound, reeking with charm, hidden in nooks on narrow streets, all this surrounding the fabled golf course where Bobby Jones won that British Open of 1926. Royal Lytham is a patch of emerald polka-dotted with bunkers in a prison of red brick. You wouldn't know it was a links, actually, unless someone from the Royal and Ancient assured you of it, for the course is more than a mile from the sea. It is the only British Open course that is not within sight of any water, which leads to the theory that in Lytham's case, a links is any golf course built on land reclaimed from the penny arcades.

The layout itself is highly unusual in a couple of respects. It is the only known championship course used for a major, on either side of the Atlantic, that begins with a 206-yard, par-3 hole, hereafter to be known as Lanny Wadkins' hole inasmuch as he holed out his 5-iron for an ace at the start of the third round. Lytham is also the only layout that ends with six consecutive par 4s, all of them looking very much like the same hole to the non-architect. Some of the holes are longer than others, of course, and they are nearly always played into a prevailing wind that would knock down any human beings who weigh less than a sausage roll, so that on most given days at least two of these holes are unreachable in two shots and in reality become par 5s.

Officially, par at Royal Lytham is 35-36—71, but on a day like Thursday's opening round this year, when the gales reached 40 miles per hour and were cold enough to spread a pneumonia epidemic through the grandstands, par was more reasonably assessed to be in the neighborhood of 75. It was the most murderous day to try to play or watch golf in the memory of anyone who had been observing British Opens for two decades or more. Cold, damp, muddy, soggy, misty, rainy, windy. All this made Ballesteros' four-under 67 even more remarkable. It was closer, given the deplorable conditions, to eight under, and he even had two penalty strokes!

In this championship, Seve got off to the kind of start that golfers only dream about, by birdieing the first three holes. He was out in 30, five under, as he played downwind. It was on the inward half, as they say it in Britain, that he went wild on his 2-iron second at the 14th and on his drive at the 18th and found the bushes and had to declare unplayable lies and then still, miraculously, cut his losses with bogeys.

As Seve continues to master the English language, he struggles for more and more of what he would consider to be humor.

Of his two unplayables, he said, "Daniel Boone could not have recovered from there."

The press room roared with laughter at this, which did not speak well for many of its inhabitants.

Seve's round was all there was to talk about for three days, other than the horrendous weather, which guaranteed that this would be the longest British Open ever contested, not to end until Monday.

In past British Opens, there had been many days far worse than Saturday's constant drizzle, which caused the R&A to abandon play. For some curious reason, there were three greens at Lytham that wouldn't drain, nor did the R&A have any squeegees on hand, nor had the R&A taken the precaution to spot the pins in high places on the greens so that play could have continued despite the weather. Frankly, it all seemed like an ugly plot to keep everyone in Blackpool an extra day.

It was a swell week for the Americans, as Tony Jacklin had promised. Jacklin, the man who has captained two straight European Ryder Cup victories over the Yanks, said before it all got started at Lytham that the Americans had "no chance." This infuriated many Americans, pros and press alike, but Tony knew what he was talking about.

Even though the U.S. sent its strongest contingent ever, the best we could do was a tie for fourth by Fred Couples and Gary Koch, but eight shots back of Ballesteros.

And so Lytham remained a graveyard for American pros, a place where it's good to be a Spaniard, a South African, an Australian, a New Zealander, or a Brit to win. For the geographically uninitiated, past winners at Lytham include Seve twice, Bobby Locke and Gary Player, Peter Thomson, Bob Charles, Tony Jacklin. Maybe the solution for Americans lies in economics. Back in '26, Bobby Jones returned to his hotel for lunch between the two final rounds. He forgot his contestant's badge when he came back to the course, and rather than argue with the police on the gate, he bought a ticket to get back in.

When the British Open returns to Royal Lytham and St. Annes in five or six years, I heartily recommend that all American contestants pay the extra pounds they would normally spend on cashmere sweaters for a ticket. It could change their luck on that golf course.

BASEBALL

What Is It?

BASEBALL IS A GAME THAT USED TO BE PLAYED BY BABE RUTH AND Ty Cobb, and then by Joe DiMaggio and Ted Williams, and then by Mickey Mantle and Willie Mays.

Now it's a game that's played by a bunch of guys in leotards and helmets on wall-to-wall carpet, with Tommy Lasorda discussing pasta and cavorting with movie stars.

There used to be 16 teams in major league baseball and you could recognize all of the uniforms and most of the names, even on the Washington Senators.

Now there are 109 teams in major league baseball but you can only recognize the Yankees, Cardinals, Dodgers, Red Sox, and Tigers.

The rest of them look like they're in a softball tournament.

One of the things that saves baseball today is that the New York Yankees still have a logo that ranks up there with Nazi Germany's.

Baseball mainly attracts two demographic groups: boys under 14 and men over 60. Boys under 14 like it because their daddies made them play catch in the yard. Men over 60 like it because they have to piss a lot and they can do this while watching baseball on TV and not miss anything.

Occasionally, however, baseball gets exciting for everybody. That's when the World Series reaches the ninth inning of the seventh game and the score is tied.

For the next two and a half hours, even I am enthralled.

Ephemeral Meets Catharsis

CONSIDERING THAT MOST SPORTSWRITERS I KNOW ARE DRUNKS, speed freaks, adulterers, hopeless chain smokers, or bad harmonizers (often all five if it's somebody I really want to hang out with), I find it amusing every spring when many of them turn lyrical as they sit down at their typing machines. Baseball does it. Along comes baseball season and guys who later in the summer will be writing their normal hard-hitting, two-sentence paragraphs— "Fastballer Jesus Marquez likes to throw at white people. His father was a doorman"—suddenly begin to use words like ephemeral and catharsis. As it happens, ephemeral and catharsis were never a problem in the home where I grew up. My grandmother's mustard plaster usually cured them in no time at all.

But each spring I look forward to ephemeral (the streak) and catharsis (the slump) creeping into the literature of the press box. I also know I'll be reminded that the diamond is an emerald chessboard, that scrappy infielders are playing the game with a perspiring earnestness, that a slugger's timing can hinge on the imperceptible fractions of an instant, that the ball itself is an diabolical white speck, a handful of physics, a geometric force, and that the true charm of the so-called national pastime lies in the unwound tensions and eloquent silences that I'm supposed to behold as the sun shines down on the converging mathematics of an infield pop-up.

And yet the lyrical writers insist that something is happening down there on the chessboard to call back the tranquil, rustic tempo of an earlier time in our lives—all this about a sport in which, as far as I can tell, the athletes mostly like to stand around, chew things, and scratch their nuts.

There are, I think, two basic causes for these lyrical outbursts by my sportswriting brethren. In order of influence, I blame (1) daddies, and (2) book critics.

Chances are, unless he was an interior designer, Daddy was

probably the first person to hand us a ball and bat. He then took us out into the yard and hit fly balls to us in the early evening of a lazy summer. We all remember it as great fun, even when we back-pedaled into thornbushes, even when we dashed into the street, eyes upward, and almost got run over by a Ford roadster, even when the exercise extended into suppertime, which prompted our mother to do her famous impression of Joan Crawford on Benzedrine.

Some of us got over it and some didn't, and it occurs to me that those who didn't have forgotten something. Daddies taught us baseball *first* in those days because they were aware that we couldn't get our little hands around a football. These writers also disregard the fact that it was always Daddy who got to *hit* on those lazy summer evenings. How many daddies ever chased a fly ball into the street? None, that's how many—unless Daddy wanted to get a glimpse of Lisa Ann Tarlton, the divorcée, who might be watering the flower bed in her swimsuit and high heels.

My own daddy, by the way, rarely indulged in this activity— for two reasons. Either he could never quite get home from the golf course until dark or he would be on his way to California again, making another clean getaway from my mother's screaming mother.

Certain lyrical-bent sportswriters have argued that my daddy's selfish absence is the obvious reason that I've never preferred base-ball to, say, root canals. They're wrong, of course. There were granddaddies, uncles, and older cousins galore who hit fly balls to me and who regularly carted me off to a klieg-lighted stadium, where, in fact, I once saw the Fort Worth Cats, our class-AA team, defeat the New York Yankees in an exhibition game. It may be true that I would have embraced baseball more fondly if the Fort Worth Cats had ever been able to outscore the Beaumont Exporters. As it was, I found baseball only mildly interesting—for a sport in which nobody side-stepped tacklers or threw bullet passes.

Which brings up the influence of the book critic on many sportswriters. A lot of sportswriters yearn to write novels but keep reading book critics who say you can't write a good, "literary" sports novel unless you write about baseball, which happens to be the only sport the book critics think they understand. They're sure they understand it because, like girls, piano teachers, cellists, even *they* played baseball, in some form, at some point in their lives. Book critics like baseball because they relish the game's pauses. It gives them a chance to think about Milan Kundera. And book critics further like baseball because they can *see* baseball players, as opposed to football players, whose faces are hidden by helmets and wire cages and whose bodies are bundled up in baroque padding. Moreover, I suspect that there are scads of book critics who haven't forgiven football for the T formation. For them, the T formation not only eliminated the "Hup it to me" of their youth, it obscured the hand-off forever and introduced an obscene, almost pornographic element to the game, which is that moment when the quarterback hunches over the center's ass to receive the snap.

Maybe there's no sight on the emerald chessboard as unliterary as the quarterback's hunch, but there is something the more naïve book critics ought to understand about baseball: When the lyrical writer says a hitter is digging in, hoping to deflect the pitcher's tiny, onrushing dot, perhaps even to relaunch it in the opposite direction with an inexplicable response of eye and body, what the hitter's really saying to the pitcher is "Show me that slider again, you spick cocksucker, and it's comin' back at your cunt!"

But I have to confess that even I like baseball on those occasions when a hitter connects and sends a shot into an undense region of the outfield. This always gives me an opportunity to mutter some immortal words to myself: "Willie Mays's glove is where triples go to die."

Whoever said it—Fresco Thompson, Jim Murray; probably Jim Murray—that's baseball poetry at its best. And it don't even rhyme.

Improving the Game

THE BEST CURE FOR BASEBALL BOREDOM IS TO GO STRAIGHT FROM the excitement of opening week to the excitement of the play-offs and the World Series. What do we lose, a few stats?

Small payment, I say, for the valuable hours, days, weeks, months we'll save in not having to watch managers change pitchers every three minutes and 47 seconds.

Other cures are as follows:

Eliminate teams nobody has ever heard of.

The Seattle Mariners, for example. The San Diego Padres, for another. Maybe the Indianapolis Colts, or is that another sport?

If this causes an imbalance of some kind, we can bring back the Washington Senators, Philadelphia Athletics, and St. Louis Browns.

It is not a single unless the batter can whip the first baseman's ass.

This alone should get more physical contact into the game.

Get rid of one outfielder.

The result is bound to be more hits and fewer easy outs.

Right-handed pitchers must pitch left-handed and left-handed pitchers must pitch right-handed.

This will do away with the need for batting helmets. It should also create higher-scoring games.

It is not a stolen base unless:

The base runner actually loads the bag onto a golf cart or into a pickup truck and drives it to a pawn shop located near the bull pen.

The base runner must do this alone. It will be a contest between himself and one DBP (designated base protector).

No relief pitchers.

The man who starts the game must finish the game, unless his arm drops off or he is hit in the face with a line drive.

Foul balls count as runs scored.

Long foul balls count as four or six runs scored, as in cricket.

Three strikes are not out if:

The hitter is someone you've heard of, a hometown favorite, or a person with a chance to win the game, as long as he's not threatening to break a record belonging to Ty Cobb, Babe Ruth, or Joe DiMaggio.

The hitter is out only when he himself gets tired of swinging at the ball, says "Fuck it," and walks to the dugout.

Having declared himself out, he may, to add color or stir up a fascinating incident, give the finger to anyone he chooses.

Double plays are left to the discretion of the press box.

For instance, a double play may not count if it brings an abrupt end to a thrilling rally.

Home-run hitters get to bat again.

And a hitter may stay at the plate as long as he keeps hitting home runs.

An umpire's decision is not final if:

(A) The manager, hitter, or base runner can beat him up.

(B) A group of angry fans can beat him up.

(C) The television replay proves him to be an utter imbecile.

No more face masks.

The catcher is a person, too, and there will be no need for a face mask, since right-handers will throw left-handed and left-handers will throw right-handed.

No extra innings.

Nine innings are already five too many. In the event of a tie score after nine innings of play, the winner will be determined by the press box, which will decide what makes the best story for that day.

Go for extra bases at your own risk.

A pitcher will be allowed to try to tackle a runner going from first to second and the shortstop will be allowed to try to tackle the runner going from second to third.

Upgrading coaches.

A much keener interest will be shown in what, exactly, they do if the third-base and first-base coaches are entries from Miss U.S.A. pageants wearing their briefest bikinis.

A batter is out if he gets hit by a pitched ball, unless:

He can sling his bat and hit the pitcher anywhere between the neck and the knees.

No consultations.

A pitcher may not be spoken to by a manager, coach, catcher, or any infielder. It is much too time-consuming.

Organ music will not be permitted in any ball park.

This will, in turn, bring about Organ Night at the ball park, a night at which fans will be encouraged to bring an organ from home or office to be placed in a pile and set ablaze.

A player may not be busted for drugs if:

(A) He is involved in a tight pennant race.

(B) He is chasing any of Pete Rose's Astroturf records.

(C) He is in the on-deck circle.

No book writing during games.

Players working on exposés or confessionals in collaboration with a starving sportswriter must do so on their own time and never on the playing field.

"Kill the umpire!"

Umpires may be shot and killed by players or fans or any group thereof whenever there is a lull in the action or whenever they're unhappy with the strike zone.

Attention, all cup fondlers.

It is part of the game to scratch, claw, and caress your testicles, or rather, the encasement thereof. However, excessive fondling should be restricted to hitters, pitchers, first basemen, and promiscuous base runners.

All-out masturbation, as in the past, should continue to be frowned upon in most ball parks.

Time limits.

Only the seventh game of the World Series may be allowed to go into extra innings.

Scheduling.

All games of the regular season as well as the World Series must be completed before the first college football Saturday in September.

Actually, the ideal thing would be for baseball to be played during the winter. Then I could handle it the way I handle the NBA and ice hockey. I burn logs until a friend raps gently on the door and says, "You can come out now, they're gone."

Treatment Center

ALL OF MY PATIENTS ARE ENCOURAGED TO DROP BY THE OFFICE ANY time they wish, whether they have a session scheduled or not. Many of them do come just to sit around, drink coffee, read magazines, watch my secretary mail bills. Occasionally, some of them bring their deli sandwiches and sodas and have lunch in the waiting room. I would much prefer to have them here in the warmth and safety of my office rather than out on the street, where they might be tempted to go to another Red Sox game.

Basically, two kinds of patients come to me for help. There are those who are trying to fight their Red Sox addiction and those who have already been infected with the Red Sox virus and are struggling to cope with it, hoping to find some peace and happiness in the few months they have left.

Needless to say, I hear a lot of horror stories. Let me just play you a couple of tapes. First, here's part of a session I had last month with a Red Sox addict who now lives in New York:

"I never thought it could happen to me, Doc. I thought I could control it. At first, it was just bumper stickers. I didn't think anything about it. Everybody had a bumper sticker of some kind. Mine were harmless. They didn't say FUCK REAGAN or anything, they just said GO RED SOX.

"But then it gets a grip on you. Like, I went to this black-tie dinner and wore a Red Sox cap. I was getting seduced. Next I was taking showers in my Red Sox warm-up jacket. I couldn't take a shit without it.

"Pretty soon, you start calling in sick at work. All you want to do is stay home and watch the games you've taped. Somebody says you're about to lose your job, but so what? The Red Sox are the only thing that's important any more.

"Then come the lies. My wife said, 'What are you doing wearing that stupid cap and warm-up jacket around the house?' I said, 'What cap? What jacket?'

"She took away my cap and jacket, but I had others stashed away. I kept them locked up in drawers. I'd unlock a drawer, sneak a peek at the "B" on a cap or a jacket, then slam the drawer shut. Thirty-seven minutes later, I'd have to do it again. I'd have to see that logo.

"After a while, you get paranoid. You start to close the curtains before you unlock the drawer and look at the logo. And you stand for hours peering out of the window, keeping a lookout for all the Yankee fans who are out there wanting to give you a urine test.

"It's everywhere, Doc. It's on the school grounds; in corporate offices, restaurants, any bar you frequent, the discos, all over the streets. Why can't the cops do something? They know where most of it comes from. Boston! They know who's bringing it in. Perfectly respectable-looking people. Grown-up men and women.

"I guess I finally realized I needed therapy when I started sleeping with the photograph of Roger Clemens. And I knew the heartbreak I was in for. I knew I'd lose my wife, the kids, the job, my home, everything. I tried to tell myself it would be worth it if the Red Sox won the World Series; but somehow, I knew deep-down, it couldn't happen. They never win the World Series. Not with Ted Williams or Yaz or nobody. So how were they gonna win it with this bunch of creeps?

"That's the worst thing it does to you. It makes you feel brilliant, like you and the Red Sox are gonna win the World Series and you'll have these world-championship patches to put on your warm-up jacket and these world-championship bumper stickers to put on your car.

"You feel like nobody can outsmart you, but that's the Big Lie. All you're gonna do is wind up in the gutter.

"I know this is true, but I can feel it happening to me again. You got to help me, Doc. Make me a Met. Anything."

I'm happy to report that the patient is making some progress. I started him off on what I call the Texas Rangers program, and he's been clean for the past three weeks.

Of course, it's tougher to deal with someone who's been infected with the Red Sox virus. The tape you are about to hear is heartbreakingly typical of the person who's been stricken:

"My friends and I had always known how promiscuous the Red Sox are. We'd heard about all of these people who had been infected in '46 and others in '67 and still others in '75, but nothing serious happened to them, because penicillin took care of everything. Sure, a lot of them wound up in mental institutions, but nobody died, for God's sake.

"Now I don't know, Doc. I fear for the future. My life is over and I'm resigned to it, but what about the next generation?

"If we have a few more seasons like last year, there could be twenty million cases of Red Sox virus by 1992. I don't think the Red Sox are going to stop fucking people and that's mainly how you can catch it.

"It's so easy to get taken in. They flirt with you and fondle you, like they did last year, and you fall for it. You fall into the trap of making love with them in all the normal ways, and the next thing you know, they've stuck it up your ass.

"You know the risk you're taking, but somehow you can't resist. You get swept up in another world. The earth moves. You think, Here I am, just an ordinary person, but I'm making it with the Red Sox and we're going to win a World Series.

"Your eyes roll back in your head and you claw them on the shoulders, and you're on this roller-coaster ride you hope never ends. You forget the dangers. All that seems to matter is the moment.

"But then it happens. The unthinkable. The same old thing. Just as you're in the middle of the most wonderful dream you've ever had—you can even envision the ticker-tape parades—the ball rolls between this guy's legs, and suddenly you realize that love never had anything to do with it; you've only been fucked again.

"Forget me, Doc. I'm done for. But if we care about the future, there's only one answer. We've got to find a way to make the Red Sox wear condoms."

Big Boo

A MULTIMILLIONAIRE SPORTS HERO LIKE MYSELF, THE IDOL OF KIDS, needs an interest in something outside the game he plays, which is why I've gotten into two things that are somewhat connected: arbitration and wife-beating.

I got into both of them at about the same time. It was when I was married to my first wife, Yvonne, and she told me about this pitcher for the Cincinnati Reds who had become a free agent and was making $1,350,000 more money than I was.

Yvonne and I got into a "wrestling-type altercation," as the papers called it. What happened was, I knocked her through the screened-in porch on the back of our house in Boca.

Nothing came of it but the headlines. My lawyer, Barry Slumpkin, proved that I didn't hit her with my brass knucks or even with a "closed fist," like the papers first said.

My second wife, Cathy, encouraged me to keep up these hobbies.

One Saturday morning while I was sitting around wondering why a guy like me who had won 18 and only lost 17 and had a solid ERA of 5.06 wasn't making more money, she asked me to go to the grocery store.

I said I was busy. She said I was watching cartoons.

I slapped her around a few times and shoved her down the basement stairs.

They charged me with one misdemeanor count of "spousal

battery." The courts have some funny language, by the way. I told the judge I wouldn't drive a Spousal or any other foreign car.

Barry got me off with a $1,000 fine and that was the end of it.

Marilyn, my third wife, was always out for whatever she could get, I think, or she wouldn't have thrown Dwight Gooden up to me so often.

She provoked this argument one night and then screamed and ran across the street to a neighbor's house and called the police and told reporters I hit her with "open and closed fists," which ought to be worth a pretty penny to her after my arbitration hearing.

That was the year I settled on a salary increase of $2.3 million.

The scandal blew over after my lawyer issued a statement to the press that said, "Big Boo and Marilyn were in an argument that got out of hand, but neither party intended any harm to come to the other. Their marriage has been and continues to be strong."

Marilyn got $200,000 and four World Series tickets in the divorce.

My fourth wife, Nanette, used to try to get me ready for my next salary demand by pulling my hair and cutting off the electricity when it was 101 and humid outside.

I cured her of this when I got her into a neighborhood game and let her see my 95-mile-an-hour fastball.

I made sure I had witnesses that testified I wasn't throwing at her.

Amber, my fifth wife, wasn't anything but white trash, and I should have known it from the beginning. I mean, you just don't go around throwing a drink in the manager's face or the owner's face. That's what arbitration is for.

The manager suggested I break her jaw, and the owner suggested I just go on and kill her, but my lawyer cautioned me to be cool.

Barry said, "You might try an open fist sometime, but you have to remember you have several World Series rings at stake and they'll flush down a toilet real easy."

It got in the columns that my marriage to Amber was in trouble, primarily because Amber was going out in public with carpenters and plumbers.

This didn't bother me. I was already dating Nicole, who would be my sixth wife.

My marriage to Amber ended the day I came home from a salary negotiation and found her in bed with a deputy city attorney, who declined comment on the incident.

Amber left the house on crutches with her wig on lopsided, and Barry handled it with the reporters, saying, "Big Boo wants to put this behind him."

Nicole and I were a happy couple for a while. Oh, we'd have some "wrestling-type altercations" now and then, but it was nothing to get the gossip columnists stirred up.

I guess we'd still be fairly happy if she hadn't read in the paper about what the Dodgers gave Orel Hershiser. Frankly, I don't know how much longer I can take this shit.

A Man's Reputation at Stake

THE WORLD WAS CLOSING IN ON BOTH HANDS BENSON OF THE Swamp River Gerbils. The rumors, the allegations, the innuendo, the unsubstantiated reports in the papers, they were all affecting his decisions as a manager and causing trouble at home. Was he the kind of man who would actually bet his wife and kids on two bugs crawling up a wall? That's why he called the press conference.

"Nobody don't know nothin'," he said in his opening statement. "If somebody knew something, they'd know something, then there wouldn't be no more talk about it."

Over a period of months it had been reported that Both Hands Benson had a long history of gambling, of betting on sports events. Unidentified sources said he had not only bet on football and basketball games, and at the race tracks, but also on baseball games, including games in which he had played and managed.

If it was true that Both Hands had bet on baseball, he could be suspended for a year, and if it was true that he had bet on games involving his own team, he could be suspended for life.

"This is serious," he said to the press. "You don't take baseball away from a guy just because somebody says he does this and that. You could say somebody else did something, and what would that prove, except that somebody said it?"

He went on. "You got things that happen to you in your life but you say so what. You see these things in the paper and you wonder why anybody thinks it's news. I think news ought to be who won the game, not who did this or that in his personal life, which is gettin' infringed on and makes me wonder about the Constitution. Questions?"

A reporter stood up.

"Both Hands, a bookmaker told the district attorney that you lost forty-five thousand dollars to him on the Alaskan oil spill. Is that true?"

Both Hands looked sad.

"Yeah, I bet the Under," he said. "I had twenty-nine hundred square miles. What's that got to do with baseball? Next?"

Another reporter stood up.

"Both Hands, it's no secret that you go to the race track, right?"

"I go to the track occasionally. Everybody's got a hobby."

"Weren't you at the track last month when that horse dropped dead in the stretch? Collapsed and actually died?"

"I was there."

"Wasn't there a pretty good disturbance in the Jockey Club when that happened? I understand furniture got broken, people were punched out. Were you part of that?"

"I was in the room."

"Isn't it true that you had a sizable bet on that race?"

"I had the horse," Both Hands shrugged.

"The horse that died?"

"Yeah."

"How did you have him?"

"To live."

A question from the floor touched on Both Hands selling his autograph to crippled children in order to pay off his gambling debts.

"They ain't all crippled," he said. "Besides that, the cripples get a cut rate. A kid in a wheelchair don't pay more than three dollars. A kid who's got all his arms and legs, that's a different story."

Both Hands was asked if he thought it was right to sell his autograph at all. It seemed to be something that only baseball players among professional athletes would do.

"My name is my own," Both Hands explained. "If my name wasn't my own, other people would have it, and what kind of world would we live in if everybody had the same name? That's one way to look at it. Another way is to change the subject."

Both Hands pointed to the back of the room.

A reporter said, "What about your three World Series rings?"

"What about 'em?" said Both Hands.

"A man named Guido says he has your rings. He says you gave him the rings in place of the hundred thousand dollars you lost to him on a bet about highway death tolls."

"I forgot it was a holiday."

"What do you mean?"

Both Hands said, "No schools. I usually bet the Over on death tolls—one school bus can win it for you."

Both Hands was asked if he had ever sold any of his uniforms to pay off gambling debts.

"What's free private enterprise got to do with anything?"

A persistent reporter said, "The uniform you wore the day you broke Babe Ruth's record for pointing to centerfield fences has turned up in memorabilia collections in twenty-four different cities."

"I don't know nothin' about memorabilia," Both Hands said. "I been a healthy person all my life. I couldn't have played sixteen years in the show if I'd suffered from memorabilia. What a question."

"Are you saying you never sold your uniform to settle a gambling debt?"

"Who'd buy anything that stunk that much?"

The subject of a soccer bet came up.

Both Hands said, "You can't bet on a soccer game. It's guys outdoors in short pants."

A reporter said, "But we have proof that you made some sort of a bet on a soccer game in England last spring."

Both Hands shrugged again. "Not on the game itself," he said. "I took the wire fence and gave ninety-three. It was close."

Now he was asked if, as manager of the Swamp River Gerbils, he would be above putting a sore-armed pitcher on the mound and making a phone call to Guido.

"I wouldn't want to dignify that question with an answer," he said.

Fine, but why did it look as if his first-base coach and his third-base coach always seem to have their arms in the air, holding up base runners, even on doubles and triples?

"They're not holding up base runners," Both Hands said, looking indignant. "They're waving at their families. Where does it say in a free society like America that a guy can't wave at his wife and kids at a baseball game?"

Both Hands was joined at the press conference by his wife, Vera, and then by his mistress, Wanda, his mistress, Vivian, his mistress, Kathy, and his mistress, Maureen.

They all said they were there to stand behind him and give him a vote of confidence, although Vera did add that she was filing for divorce.

Both Hands was asked if he had anything to say about the divorce.

"Yeah," he said. "Five to one she gets child custody."

BASKETBALL

What Is It?

A BRITISH JOURNALIST ONCE ASKED ME THIS QUESTION: "EXACTLY which month of the year is it that Americans become preoccupied with tall black people?"

I told him that my own personal interest usually peaked in March, with the Final Four, but that many Americans followed pro basketball from November through June, for reasons that I found unexplainable, other than the fact that they were overly fascinated with soaring armpits.

Basketball is no longer for humans, of course. The shortest player on the court can leap over a three-story condominium.

Part of the charm of basketball lies in the fact that it's a simple game to understand. Players race up and down a fairly small area indoors and stuff the ball into a ring with Madonna's dress hanging on it.

Not every basketball player is black today. A white player was sighted in Fargo, N.D., in the winter of 1987, and there are reports circulating at this hour of a white kid playing high school basketball in Terre Haute, Ind.

Since most basketball games tend to come down to the final few seconds, I have often wondered why all basketball coaches don't have the life expectancy of a goldfish.

One of these days somebody will get to the bottom of it.

Super Scout

YOU HEAR A LOT ABOUT MAMBAS, HIPPOS, RHINOS, EVEN TERROR-ists and Commies, but I say Africa gets a bad rap. In basketball, you can't win without the big guy who can deal in the paint, work on top of the iron, fill it with baby hooks. When I can't find a good prospect in Africa, I look in Yugoslavia, Sweden, Germany, maybe Russia. The Dominican Republic comes up now and then. A scout never knows where he'll have to be. But I always start in Africa. They're taller. The kid in Belgrade who's 7'2" comes in at 7'6" in Ubangi. All I do is find 'em and place 'em. It's the coaches who have to teach 'em how to piss indoors.

You'll see me at the Final Four every year. I go to all the parties, hang out with the coaches, the SIDs, the media. The Final Four is where I write up my orders for the coming season. Everybody wants a big guy, an intimidator, an aircraft carrier. Today, the kid who can wham, jam, work the back door, that ain't enough.

Some coaches are hard to please. I was trying to peddle this Dominican last year. Good-looking kid, 7'2", covered the paint, which is what we call the keyhole now. I offered him to a coach in the ACC.

"Latins don't rebound," he said. "Get me one of them dissidents."

"A defector, you mean?"

"Yeah, one of them guys who parts his hair on the iron. A poet."

"What about an East German?" I asked. "He's six-ten, two hyphens."

"Not tall enough."

"Seven-foot spies are expensive," I explained.

He shrugged.

I sold him a Czech. Kid named Hrubia. He'll be okay as soon as he learns to walk.

Occasionally, I'm asked to find a short kid who can serve you ice cream. Teams need that one little guy, a waterbug, the player who can see the court, spread the floor, bury the J's—the jump shots.

I go to Italy for this kind of kid. That's where I found Gozzi, Tonani, Gambini, all those kids who could fill it in the Pac-10.

I got real lucky with Ugo Gozzi. I heard about this kid on the Adriatic coast and I happened to be close. I could get there in no time from the Nubian Desert. Ugo was 4.3 in the air with his flying layup, but of course he didn't develop his triple-pump, reverse, backdoor, letter-drop till he went hardship at USC and signed with the Rockets.

If you follow pro basketball, forget the all-America team this year. It's a pastry shop. I've five franchises ready to go in the first round of the NBA draft. Here are the kids who are gonna dominate the game in the future:

Ernst Helmut Dorfner, Indiana Institute of Liberal Arts & Grain:

He's 7'4" and a natural. I found him in a pickup game on an outdoor court in Dachau, a little town near Munich. His dad used to work in some kind of plant around there. His friends call him the Fourth Reich. I don't get it, but what do I know? All I see is an instinctive shot blocker. The other team fires one, his coach hollers, "*Sieg Heil!*"—something weird like that—and Helmut's right arm shoots straight up. The guy's murder on defense. I like this kid a lot.

Kust Thorfelt, Loyola of Wichita Falls:

Okay, the guy's 36 years old and he's had only one year of college ball, but he played on four Olympic teams for Finland and nobody laughs off a kid who's 7'5". His dad won the Nobel Prize for Thrift. They say he can't move. They say he talks to seals, walks like a penguin. So he can't move, no big deal. I say he's white and that makes up for it. He'll go high, don't worry.

Galooma Metbu Gwanda, Northern California Community College of Environmental Worship and Total Sharing (Mill Valley):

I disagreed bitterly with Notre Dame, Houston, UCLA, all the others. I say if a kid's 7'8", he can take his pet cow to school with him. Well, they blew it, so he wound up at a small college. Can you believe Houston passing on this guy? Now they know better. For 56 points a game, you let a guy play naked and eat raw dog. The Knicks say he'll grow out of it. He's young.

Mohammed Khadr Ahmed L. Mesba, Kentucky AM&T (Agricultural, Mobile Homes & Trucking):

I first knew him as Bobby Simpson. Just an awkward kid of 7′9″, but he could slam-dunk a concrete block into the rear end of a GMC pickup. Then he developed an arc, and I knew I had something. He comes from this rural town in Tennessee, one of them places where they brush their teeth with grits, and it was tough to communicate with him, take my word. Porsche, Jaguar—those were the only words he could chew. I've tried to tell him he'll get more money in the pros if he plays on both ends of the court. "Ain't no points down there" is all he says about it. Stubborn kid.

Chen "Slant Dunk" Hu-ching, Older Dominion:

I guess I don't need to tell anybody that Manchuria's no country club. How many fish heads can you eat? But I'd go back if I thought I'd find me another Chen Hu-ching. At 8′3″, she's the tallest player I ever recruited. And now that she's had the sex-change operation, she'll be the tallest player in the NBA. He, I mean. Want to talk match-ups? The thing I want to see is Mohammed Khadr Ahmed El Mesba try to deal in the paint against *her.* Him, I mean.

So that's it for now. I got a plane to catch. There's this kid in Tanganyika. He's 8′4″, has six fingers on each hand. You hear he's got a bone in his nose. So what? I say tell me you don't like him after he puts you in the NBA play-offs.

Jock Quiz

As CHANCELLOR OF THIS UNIVERSITY, I HAVE LONG BEEN IN FAVOR OF cleaning up the image of collegiate athletics, and I therefore wanted to be absolutely certain that we had nothing but student-athletes on our basketball squad before we sent the kids off to compete for the $800,000,000 that goes to the winner of the Final Four.

That was why I asked each member of our team to fill out a questionnaire. I wanted to be sure they were making satisfactory progress toward their degrees.

I'm happy to report to the NCAA that based on the results of my internal questionnaires, every single player at our institution seems more than interested in higher education. We have nothing to be ashamed of.

I hereby submit as evidence the questionnaire that was filled out by Tom "Trailer Hitch" Henry, our all-conference center and a 3.2 student in communications. Sure, you may find fault with some of the spelling and grammar, but Tom was in a hurry when he answered the questions. I know for a fact that he was late for a test in English lit.

Name: Same one I've always had, which is what people call me by, The Hitch.

Date of birth: I didn't have no time for dates when I was getting born.

Place of birth: In a hospital, like everybody else, unless you mean where my momma and daddy got it on. That could have been lots of places, just like nowadays when my daddy slips off to nail Irene and Claudette and my momma stays home to fuck Ed and Charley.

Mother's name: I never called my mother by no name, not ever, even though she was white trash.

Father's name: Dickhead.

High school: Which one? I can think of several in my town alone.

Junior high school: Junior went to the same school I did until the dumbass got hisself arrested for stealing a Winnebago.

Grade school: It's okay most of the time. The pizza joint ought to deliver quicker to the athletic dorm.

Favorite sport: Polo. What kind of a fucking question is this?

Hobbies: Drugs, whiskey, 924s.

Favorite food: Pussy.

Favorite team: Celtics, or anybody who comes up with enough gift wrap.

Why you chose this university: Mary Alice Johnson went here and I just followed them tits.

Favorite course: PE, but that thing where you look at maps is kind of fun.

Goals in life: I could score a lot more goals if the motherfuckers would pass me the ball.

Favorite book: I can't remember the name of it, or what guy with a beard wrote it, but it was real good.

Outstanding quality: I firmly believe in this and think everybody should have some.

Weakness (if any): Duke, Louisville, North Carolina.

Fondest childhood memory: The day I found old Billy Bob between my legs and saw that sumbitch stand up at attention!

Person who had greatest influence on your life: Coach T. in high school. He was a great man who taught me not to fart in mixed company.

Others who influence your life (list in order of importance): (A) Coach Big 'Un here at the university. He's responsible for my cars, my apartment, my $2,000 in aid per month, and making sure I pass everything. (B) Mr. Booter at the "M" Club, who outbid them other chickenshit schools in the first place. (C) Miz Baxter, my tutor, who writes real good term papers, because she knows old Billy Bob takes care of her. (D) Chancellor Tipper. He's a good ol' boy who likes to win. (E) "Bundle" Feinstein. An athlete can't have no finer agent. He's been with me since high school and I'd trust him with my best Porsche. (F) Mr. Furch, my jollogy teacher. He makes rocks and dirt and dinosaurs real interesting. (G) My wife, Sheila. She flys for a airline and stays gone a lot, but when she's home, she don't gimme no shit on days of a game. Billy Bob says it's a good thing or he'd cut her ass off.

In your opinion, who are the three greatest men in history? (A) Larry Bird. (B) Aberham Lincoln. (C) Clint Eastwood and Bruce Springstein (tie).

Is there anything you would change about your present curriculum? I have never used a curriculum. I say if the bitch gets pregnant, she can get the fucking thing fixed.

In what direction would you like to see your university go in the future? I just wish everybody would stay off our ass and let us play basketball.

How fair are the media? Them assholes don't know shit.

Should lady sportswriters be allowed in the locker room? Billy Bob don't complain.

What profession do you plan to pursue when your basketball career is over? This is really an unfair question to ask somebody who ain't even completed his education and don't know what opportunities has been stored up for him. I think I will probably work in free private enterprise, however, looking at it objectionally.

What is the most important thing you can say to a youngster taking up your sport? Get you a good outside shot and don't turn down no cock, it's bad luck.

Write a brief essay on what America means to you personally: America is a great country, because we have very few foreigners. America probably has fewer foreigners than any other country. When you look at television and see foreigners fucking around, it makes you glad to be an American. If we blew up more foreigners, we wouldn't have to put up with what we put up with, which is all that shit in the newspapers nobody reads. America is great because of sports, and I think it would be greater if people left sports alone and let athletes inspire little kids. Youth is important. If we don't watch out for youth, they will get fucked up and then what? We must keep youth from doing drugs until they are old enough to handle it. America should be against war, except when it happens, and then we shouldn't back off from no shitasses anywhere, because if we ever lost a war, there wouldn't be any sports per se, probably. I really believe what I think about America.

Scholar-Athletes

No sports event compares with the NCAA's Final Four in basketball, not if you want to watch the best scholar-athletes in our American universities do the things they do best. These astounding young men are not only taller than Nepal and capable of slam-dunking a handful of Sherpas, they can quote the great poets and philosophers, solve intricate mathematical problems, and even, in many cases, spell their own names.

I feel it my duty as a college president to attend the Final Four every year, even if our school isn't in it, and I must say, my heart swells with pride when I watch these typical, average students rise through the air like Hyatt Regency elevators, bump their heads on the coliseum rafters, and engage in prolonged discussions during hang time above the backboards.

The reason I feel warm and secure with these scholar-athletes on campuses is because they are nothing like those crass mercenaries who play football and embarrass us occasionally by taking illegal money from alumni in order to buy sinful cheeseburgers and Levi's.

Recently on my campus, when we were dealing with some nasty rumors about recruiting violations, I went straight to Shaver Dips, the basketball coach who molds our young men so admirably. Point-blank, I asked Coach Dips if we were conducting our affairs in a proper manner and well within the rules.

"What do you mean?" he said with a squint.

That was plenty good enough for me. I reported my findings to the NCAA's infractions committee immediately.

Of course, when the rumors in the trigger-happy media persisted, I thought I had better seek out our scholar-athletes themselves.

First, I met with Rondiel Jamesiason, our seven-foot center who carries a 3.2 grade average in stereo history. The unusual spelling of Rondiel's name dates back to the night of his birth at City-County Hospital in Atlanta when both his mother and a nurse were in a hurry to fill out a form, but that's beside the point.

"Rondiel," I said, entering his lake-front condo, "did you receive improper inducements to attend this university?"

"Co-itch say he gonna take my car if I don't play har-ud."

"Who said?"

"Co-itch say."

"Co-itch?"

"Co-itch Tibbs."

"Coach Dips?"

"Yeah, you know. The motherfucker who run the team. Same motherfucker who say no dope and no pussy on game day. You the president?"

I nodded.

"Yeah, well, you know, I be needin' a 'vance on my salaries. I got these family problems, you know. You tell Co-itch if I don't get no 'vance on my salaries, then I don't be gettin' no rebounds tonight. I'll be needin' to res' myself, you dig?"

The next condo I visited belonged to Wendiel Hamielton, our fine 6'10" forward, who carries a 3.4 in physical sciences, a successful program we patterned after the ones at Michigan, Penn State, Nebraska, North Carolina, Georgia Tech, Alabama, Kentucky, and UCLA.

"How's school, Wendiel?" I inquired.

"School be up on that hill?"

"Yes, those buildings near the bell tower."

"I was over there once, baby. They got some funny shit goin' on."

"It looks like you've pretty much made the adjustment from junior college, Wendiel."

"Yeah, well, you know, I'd be a lot happier if my check hadn't bounced last week."

"What check?"

"The check Co-itch gimme for my laundry money."

"Maybe I can take care of that right now. How much was it?"

"Thirty-eight thousand, four hundred and sixty dollars."

"Let me get back to you, Wendiel."

On the upstairs terrace of another condo, I found Dwoan McDonield, our other fine 6'10" forward, who carries a 3.6 in cassette rewind, a successful program we patterned after the ones at USC, Georgia, LSU, Oklahoma, Miami, Ohio State, and Arizona.

Dwoan was a rather touching human-interest story for us, a walk-on who earned a starting position purely on the basis of his height and police record. When we took Dwoan at our university, I had the pleasure of calling his mother with the good news.

"I'm giving Dwoan a chance to go to college," I told her on the phone.

"Who's Dwoan?"

"Your son."

"You mean Duane?"

"Uh . . . yes, I suppose it is Duane. It looked very much like Dwoan the way it was written on his enrollment card."

"Listen, mister, I don't know where the sorry shitass is, and I don't care. He's broke my heart for the last time."

When I interrupted Dwoan on his terrace to ask if he were receiving any improper inducements, he looked insulted, hurt, angry.

"What the fuck you doin' here, man?" he said. "Me and the bitch like to be alone when we shoot up."

I concluded my in-house investigation at this point. There was no need to question our other starters, Marshiel Everiett, our best defensive player, and Token White, our backcourt ace. I had all the information I needed to plead our case before the NCAA's infractions committee.

It was good to get to the bottom of things, to know that our university has made it to the Final Four with a clean program. And I think with these fine scholar-athletes and the Christian leadership of coach Shaver Dips, we have a very good chance to go all the way.

The Boring Brigade

LORD KNOWS, I'VE TRIED TO WATCH AN NBA GAME. IT WAS USUALLY one of those games where Michael Jordan scored 62 points and his team lost by eight.

I've even heard some of those movie stars who follow the Lakers say it's like going to the ballet.

Friends keep telling me that these are the greatest athletes in the world. So I have a question: Why am I so bored trying to watch pro basketball?

Is it because the athletes are *too* good?

Is it because the sport is too confined? Look, it's indoors, the courts are all the same length, the rims are all the same height, and everybody in the game can do a flying, hang-time, reverse, quadruple-pump, Phi Slamma Durkees, or whatever they call it.

It probably has something to do with the fact that the season is longer than a Russian winter. Everybody plays half a year and then everybody goes to the play-offs and the games last another three months.

I have another question: When does Jack Nicholson find time to make movies?

One thing I note about the NBA is that everybody wants the ball. It's a shooting gallery. Therefore, it's indistinct.

There is the story of an NBA coach once asking his team to play a zone defense. He was promptly dribbled, bounce-passed, and stuffed through the hoop.

I keep asking myself what I hate most about the NBA. It's not the movie stars that keep turning up on camera. It's not the sameness. It's not the fact that every guy with the ball gets to take five steps and carry it. It's the fact that I can go to a city like Dallas in October, in the middle of football season, and find nothing but the Mavericks on the sports pages.

There's something wrong with that but I guess it's newspapers that ought to be blamed instead of pro basketball.

My own careful study of the sport tells me that the best thing the NBA has going for it is the clock.

With only two seconds left in a game, I have personally seen six time-outs called and the lead change hands 12 times.

There was this game I was watching between a team named for automobile parts and a team named for solar systems.

I didn't turn the game on TV until there were only three seconds left because I knew I would still have an hour and a half of basketball to watch.

The Automobile Parts were leading the Solar Systems by eight.

Watching only casually, I did my income tax, baked a peach cobbler, washed the car, cleaned out a closet, and took a nap. By then, there were two seconds left and the score was tied.

I called a friend on the phone.

"Are you watching this?" I asked.

"Watching what?"

"The basketball game. The Solar Systems and the Automobile Parts are tied with two seconds to go."

"Two seconds left?" he said. "I'll turn it on after a while. I have to go to a dinner party first."

A player for the Automobile Parts went up for a soaring dunk. He stayed in the air throughout a full, two-minute commercial.

A time-out was called before he came down.

I'm not sure he came down at all.

Eventually, an announcer told me there was 1.5 seconds left to play. Plenty of time for the Automobile Parts to score two baskets and send the game into overtime, if they used the clock properly.

They scored one basket before the clock started.

The phone rang and it was my friend, who was back from his dinner party.

"What's the score now?" he asked.

I told him the Automobile Parts needed a basket to tie with 1.5 seconds left.

"Good," he said. "I'll make a pot of coffee and settle in to watch it."

There was half a second left when the Automobile Parts got the

DAN JENKINS   246

ball back. They called another time-out and made substitutions. They took out three black guys who were 7′6″ and put in three black guys who were 6′8″ and could dance like Fred Astaire, their back-court aces.

An announcer said this was a good move, the Automobile Parts needed to get the "water bugs" in the game.

The Automobile Parts could win the game with a three-point shot, I learned, provided the three-point shot was taken from just outside the suburb of a Midwestern city.

The buzzer started sounding as the Automobile Parts threw the ball in, but they quickly called another time-out.

Now it was tricky. Could the Automobile Parts fire a three-pointer before the buzzer stopped sounding after the time-out?

It was a pretty long buzzer because the Automobile Parts not only made the three-pointer, the Solar Systems were able to bring the ball back upcourt and get off two shots that missed before the game was over.

An announcer interviewed the Intimidator after the game. The Intimidator was 8′6″ with an arm-span of 44 feet. He had caused the last two shots to miss by swallowing the ball.

He said, "I figured if I hit 'em upside the head enough they'd lose their zealous."

Every team in the NBA has an Intimidator, but it's nice to know they can't intimidate all the people.

I know this lady sportswriter who has to go into pro basketball locker rooms all the time. The first time she had to do this a famous Intimidator saw her coming and took pleasure in standing before her, stark naked.

"Ever seen one of these before?" the Intimidator said, glancing down at himself.

To which the lady sportswriter said, "Why, it would look just like a penis if it weren't so small."

Sometimes the NBA's not so boring.

TENNIS

What Is It?

TENNIS WAS INVENTED BY A WOMAN NAMED SAMANTHA TENNIS IN 1839 in the village of Lobsworth, County of Kent, as a diversion for the wealthy and titled Englishmen of the region, who had nothing better to do at the time but drink, belch, and wear funny clothes.

Samantha was a chambermaid who worked in the stately home of Lord Wimbledon, a noted party-giver.

Even at an early age, she was known for her saucy manner and flirtatious ways.

In the game's earliest stages of development, no racquets or balls were used. Samantha would simply lure various gentlemen out onto the lawn, hike up her dress, and say, "Anyone for tennis?"

Another historical account says that Samantha would lure the gentlemen to her bedroom, hike up her dress, and say, "Tennis, anyone?"

In any case, it was Samantha's actions over this entire fun-filled summer that later inspired Charles Dickens to write *The Old Curiosity Sport.*

Yommick and Igor

DESPITE EFFORTS ON THE PART OF THE SOCIETY FOR THE PREVEN-
tion of Toenails in Pork Pies, they keep going ahead with Wimbledon every year, but that's all right. We need Wimbledon. The grass
courts. Strawberries and cream. Ivy-covered wing commanders
and squadron leaders, who have now become linesmen. Wimbledon is a reminder of what tennis was like before it died.

Of course, recreational tennis died a few years ago, after so
many middle-aged people started chasing lobs—and died.

It was spectator tennis that died at Wimbledon.

I was there that day, July 4, 1982.

It was the day John McEnroe and Bjorn Borg played this great
match that lasted 17 hours, and McEnroe won, thus preventing Borg
from winning his 14th Wimbledon in a row.

It also did away with the notion that the striped Fila shirt, Borg's
trademark, was a garment to be revered as much as the pin stripes of
the New York Yankees, who have very little to do with tennis.

What I remember best about the day was what went on before
the match, in the area of the hospitality tents, which are back
beyond the outdoor courts where teenage marvels pout while their
mothers scream and weep.

In Mark McCormack's hospitality tent, they were serving
champagne, smoked salmon, and caviar, and everybody was going
to root for Borg, inasmuch as McCormack was his agent/manager. I
was introduced to a tall man who was said to be the chairman of the
Nobel Prize committee.

I was then invited next door, to NBC's hospitality tent, where
they were serving hot dogs and brownies, this being the 4th of July,
a special day for Americans. I was introduced to Andy Williams,
who led everybody in a chorus of *God Bless America.*

I took this to mean that everybody in the NBC tent was going to
root for McEnroe.

My seat at centre court only cost $2,136.16, and the British lady next to me kept fidgeting throughout the match, saying, "Oh, dear, who's gang to win?"

"That's sort of what they're here to decide," I said.

"But who's gang to win?" she said, squirming about.

Tennis had almost died a number of years earlier when there was nobody around but introspective, left-handed Australians, but it rallied with the introduction of Open Tennis, a thing that said it was okay for amateurs to receive money above the table.

This only resulted in making billionaires out of rude children, producing an onslaught of moody defectors, and a lot of guys with hair that looked as if bats slept in it.

I say a contributor to the death of tennis is, also, the shirt.

Yeah, the shirt.

Show me a guy who wears one of those shirts with a skimpy, lay-down collar and scroochy little sleeves that tug at the armpit and I will either show you a tennis player or a yuppie bond trader on his day off in the Hamptons.

I can live with poor taste. Poor taste is the backbone of our economy.

But what about these repetitious results?

Every week, my eyes glaze over when I read about two guys named Yommick and Igor, in different parts of the world, winning $600,000 in some kind of non-event that sounds like a Spielberg movie: *Volvo and the Nabiscos.*

Where does this money come from, and why do people want to give it to a group of athletes who are largely arrogant, insulting, and uncommunicative?

It remains a mystery, but it is no mystery to me as to why tennis players are arrogant, insulting, and uncommunicative. You have a choice of three theories.

Theory One: The tennis player is arrogant because he believes he excels in a rich man's sport, but if he had a brain that extended beyond his next "exo fee," he would realize that yachting, Thoroughbred racing, buying countries, collapsing banks, and controlling politicians are the sports of the rich. Tennis is a middle-class game.

Theory Two: The tennis star is insulting because the pampered little shit has never had his ass kicked by a middle linebacker.

Theory Three: The tennis hero is uncommunicative because, basically—and I don't mean to generalize, but, well—he's stupid.

Finally, the death of tennis was clinched by the Tennis Interview.

"Congratulations on winning the championship, Yommick. It must be a great feeling."

"Yes, to feel the winning is much better than to feel the losingness that comes from the loss of not winning."

"You had good support out there today."

"Yes, I said this to myself and this is what I told myself I must do. This was my goal."

"You seemed to look over at your coach before all of the tough points."

"Yes, I must give credit to my coach. Also to my dietician, my doctor, my chef, and my pilot."

"Was today's match the toughest you've ever had?"

"Yes, but such things are relative. In tennis, much can sometimes depend on the line calls and the lateness of the courtesy car drivers."

"You were down by two sets."

"Yes, the press will say this, but in my mind, it was a different story, and this is only for me to say when I have spoken."

"Your serve brought you back."

"Yes, it was in my mind to hit a high percentage of first serves and take away his serve by coming back low and to his feet."

"Doesn't everyone try to do that?"

"Yes, but the mental aspect must come into play as well as the mind."

"In your book, you say the key to good tennis is keeping the ball on the other side of the net."

"Yes, the book is $19.95 and on sale in the boutique."

"How will you celebrate this victory?"

"Yes, Igor and I have an exo in Montreal. After that, we go to my villa in France, then to my chalet in Switzerland. If there is time before my exo tour in Japan, I will buy six cars and a diamond mine."

"Are you going to play at Wimbledon?"

"Yes, we are discussing this, but so far they have not agreed to change the dates to accomodate my busy schedule. Some people have no consideration for the competitor."

End of normal interview.

Meanwhile, my head swims with the thought that I have watched tennis progress from Don Budge and Alice Marble to Farrah Fawcett becoming John McEnroe's mother-in-law.

Multiple Choices

SLOBODAN ZIVOJINOVIC *VS.* MILOSLAV MECIR, AND SO WHAT?
That's the state of tennis nowadays. Does the sport have a bigger fan
than me? The following quiz may shed some light on this nagging
question:

1. If Martina Navratilova is going to endorse another product, it
   should be
   A. Eye shadow
   B. Nail polish
   C. A tractor
2. When you last saw Stefan Edberg, he was
   A. The waiter who brought you the mesquite-grilled salmon
   B. On the *Sports Illustrated* swimsuit cover
   C. Moving his lips in an effort to speak
3. John McEnroe is married to
   A. Madonna
   B. Molly Ringwald
   C. Kristy McNichol
4. Hana Mandlikova is
   A. Helena Sukova
   B. Sylvia Hanika
   C. Claudia Kohde-Kilsch
5. Christo Van Rensburg is
   A. The ruler of a tax-exempt principality
   B. A Formula I driver
   C. The heir to his father's detergent fortune
6. Over the past 10 years, the greatest impact on tennis has been
   made by
   A. Jimmy Connors' mother
   B. John McEnroe's father
   C. Bjorn Borg's hair

7. If you wanted to sell arms to Iran, you would deal with
    A. Todd Nelson
    B. Scott Davis
    C. Mansour Bahrami
8. If you could win any title in tennis, it would be
    A. The Nabisco Belgian-Milanese Fila Toyota Indoor-Outdoor *Grand Prix*
    B. The Nabisco Ugandan-Argentine National Clay-Sand Grand Slims
    C. The Nabisco Nigeria-Capri International Round Robin Grass-Surface Honda-Virginia International *Prix*
9. John McEnroe is married to
    A. Ally Sheedy
    B. Demi Moore
    C. Laura Dern
10. Forty-eight years ago, Boris Becker would have
    A. Flown a Messerschmitt
    B. Invaded Poland
    C. Played tennis
11. Ramesh Krishnan is
    A. A friend of Shirley MacLaine's
    B. Shirley MacLaine's other self
    C. A tennis player
12. An unseeded player comes from
    A. Behind the Iron Curtain
    B. Sweden
    C. The United States
13. Mixed doubles should be rated
    A. PG
    B. R
    C. X
14. John McEnroe is married to
    A. Sean Penn
    B. Rob Lowe
    C. Michael J. Fox
15. How many letters are missing from Ivan Lendl's name?
    A. One
    B. Two
    C. Twelve
16. Drop volley is
    A. A ski trail in Aspen
    B. A rock group from Liverpool

C. An old Southern dish made of peas, beans, and grits

17. Women's tennis will soon be dominated by
    A. Front-end loaders
    B. Grain elevators
    C. Nuclear-power plants

18. The Davis Cup is
    A. A jockstrap designed by a football player named Davis
    B. A trophy brought back to America by Dennis Conner
    C. A tennis competition that used to start again before it was over

19. Yannick Noah is
    A. A real person
    B. Not a real person
    C. South of Point Barrow, Alaska

20. John McEnroe is married to
    A. Diane Lane
    B. Daphne Zuniga
    C. Vanna White

21. Which of the following tournaments is not a Grand Slam event?
    A. Wimbledon
    B. The U.S. Open
    C. The French Open
    D. The Australian Open
    E. The Nabisco Auto Care Panama-Swiss Grand Invitational Sony Slims Grass-Seed Semi-*Prix*

22. What is more fun than spending a day at the U.S. Open in Flushing Meadow, Queens?
    A. Spending a day in Beirut
    B. Spending a day in Soweto
    C. Spending a day in Tehran

23. At Wimbledon, the duke and duchess of Kent should
    A. Shake hands with one ball boy
    B. Shake hands with two ball boys
    C. Ignore the little shits

24. Amelia Island is
    A. The site of a tennis tournament
    B. A sitcom
    C. A *Playboy* centerfold

25. Top-spin lob is
    A. A ski trail in Sun Valley
    B. Against the law of nature
    C. An overweight Oriental who tried to kill James Bond

26. Will Chris Evert
   A. Come to the net before she retires?
   B. Never come to the net?
   C. Become a network announcer and complain about players
      who don't come to the net?
27. When John McEnroe was on top of his game, would you rather
   watch him play tennis or
   A. Go to prison?
   B. Walk with a permanent limp?
   C. Eat fat meat?
28. Steffi Graf is
   A. A newspaper term
   B. The zeppelin that first flew the Atlantic
   C. Unbeatable until 2010
29. The last person to beat Steffi Graf was
   A. Alice Marble
   B. Helen Wills
   C. The 101st Airborne
30. Before Steffi Graf hits a shot, she laughs and says:
   A. "Poland!"
   B. "France!"
   C. "Rumania!"
   D. "Look! A ball!"

OTHER
GAMES

OTHER
GAMES

What Are They?

TAKE SOCCER.

Please.

A guy scores a goal, runs around the stadium shaking his fists, suddenly sinks to his knees, and everybody on the team fucks him dog-style.

What about ice hockey? The last time I looked, it was still played on ice.

Boxing. Here's a sport that now happens only in Las Vegas or Atlantic City and gives you a chance to watch every major drug dealer in the world congregate in the lobby of the same hotel, all of them wearing designer warmup suits and gold necklaces that say "Deon."

Skiing. Sane people learn quickly that if you can ride the lift up the mountain, you can ride the lift down the mountain. Otherwise, you die. I never met a gondola I didn't like.

The Olympics. Which is not a sport but several peculiar sports, none of which are football, and each of which only commands your attention every four years, like dental appointments.

Automobile racing. Campers, tattoos, and noise.

And I can't believe I left out croquet.

Futbol

FOR INDISCRIMINATE KILLING, IT'S TOUGH TO BEAT A LATIN AMERI-can country. How does this apply to sports? They take soccer seriously down there.

In fact, Latins almost take soccer as seriously as they do in England, which happens to be where the sport started, in the 11th Century, as a game called Kicking the Dane's Head. This means that Latins take the game at least as seriously as the average Brit takes his scone and clotted cream.

It's safe to say that soccer, all in all, has killed more people in Latin America than wars, terrorist raids, coups, border skirmishes, guerrilla activities, priests, and medical doctors. As I speak, another 1,300,000 are dying from soccer riots and stadium collapses in Latin America.

Ironically, however, thousands of concerned mothers in the United States today are pushing their sports-loving little boys toward soccer instead of football, believing soccer to be a safer game to play.

Most fathers would prefer to see their little boys play football, a game they can comprehend, but it's not worth arguing about. They've gone up against Magda Goebbels before and come away bruised and battered from the domestic holocaust.

You would think that American mothers would change their minds if they bothered to read the sports sections of the newspapers occasionally, but evidently they do not.

I, personally, always read soccer stories in newspapers. They can normally be found on page six, lower left-hand corner, with a headline that says, "218 DIE IN MONTEVIDEO SOCCER RIOT," OR, "STA-DIUM COLLAPSE KILLS 403 IN ECUADOR."

The stories are only one paragraph long, anyhow. Whales make bigger news.

MONTEVIDEO, URUGUAY—A riot erupted during a soccer match yesterday, killing 208 chanting, flag-waving fans and injuring many others. An eyewitness to the tragedy said the riot appeared to start when several members of the home team cheering section inadvertently began to sing off-key.

GUAYAQUIL, ECUADOR—A large area of a municipal sports stadium collapsed yesterday during a soccer match, killing 418 spectators and injuring dozens of others. Cause of the tragedy was not immediately known, but a rescue worker digging through the debris said it appeared to him that the stadium had been constructed out of balsa wood.

Don't ask me why soccer inspires such unruly passion in foreign countries, but you can ask me why it will never be a big spectator sport in the United States. The basic reasons are:

1. You can't use your hands.

For an American, it is unnatural to play a game with a ball and not be able to use your hands. The fact that people of other nations do not freely use their hands at any number of other things is a custom I lay directly at soccer's doorstep. Moreover, where foreign waiters are concerned, this custom accounts for much of the breakage in New York restaurants.

2. Nobody falls on a loose ball.

Americans see a loose ball as an object to be scooped up or dived upon. It just doesn't seem right for somebody to kick a loose ball intentionally. An American knows that if he kicks a loose ball of any kind—golf ball, tennis ball, baseball, football, basketball, bowling ball, what have you—he will either suffer a penalty in the game or, at the very least, be branded an ill-tempered motherfucker.

3. Grown men wear short pants outdoors.

In America, a man wears short pants outdoors only when he's playing tennis, mowing the lawn, or urgently leaving the home of somebody else's wife.

4. The goalie dresses funny.

On soccer teams, the goalie wears different colors from his teammates, and it causes confusion for Americans. I once tried to get to the bottom of this by discussing it with a waiter I knew in New York as Humberto Vargas Evisto de Santos.

"Humberto," I said, "why does the goalkeeper dress so funny?"

"You must understand soccer," he replied.

"I understand soccer," I said. "Maradona wins the World Cup and seventeen thousand people die in the celebration in Buenos Aires. Why does the goalkeeper wear purple when his team color is green?"

"The goalkeeper is the only one who can touch the ball with his hands. The referee must be able to recognize the goalkeeper."

"Let me suggest something," I said. "Suppose the team wears blue shirts and white shorts. Why couldn't the goalkeeper wear a white shirt and blue shorts? He would look different but he would be wearing the colors of his country."

"Not possible," Humberto said.

"Why the hell not?"

"Because he is the goalkeeper."

5. *Pelé never played for the Yankees.*

He was the greatest soccer player in history, but he didn't wear the Yankee logo, so how could "he" be taken seriously in a TV commercial?

People smoked pelé, drank pelé coladas, and vacationed in the pelé islands, but for us, he never became anything more than that little guy from down there somewhere who could bounce the ball on his head.

De-Icing the Game

MY MIND REJECTS THE FACT THAT ICE HOCKEY STARTS IN OCTOBER, before the leaves have turned, before baseball is over, before most football players have been shot up with painkillers. Ice hockey isn't supposed to start until the lakes freeze over and my car won't start. That's when Jacques puts on his new pair of skates to go with his reconstructed nose and cheekbones.

Hockey season is also supposed to end with the last howling winds of March.

This was the role that ice hockey played in my youth, back when I could name all six teams in the NHL—the Rangers, Black Hawks, Red Wings, Bruins, Canadiens, and Maple Leafs—and the season always ended with a riot up in Canada or somewhere near the Arctic Circle, and long before Easter Sunday.

Feeling that I didn't have a true appreciation of ice hockey, a friend once dragged me to Madison Square Garden to see a game between the New York Rangers and somebody else. His intention was to explain icing the puck, crossing the blue line, and why all of the players who weren't named Jacques were named Guy de Philippe de Jean-Claude de Moose.

I have to confess that the crowd in the Garden that night put me at ease instantly. For two hours or so, I felt that all of the people in the city who might otherwise have been breaking out store-front windows, mugging old ladies, or knocking off delis were there with me.

When the players came out onto the field—er, ice—I wondered why all of them looked like Quasimodo in short pants and long stockings.

My friend said it was the nature of the sport.

There was a mighty roar at one point, so I had to ask my friend what had happened.

"He scored a goal."

"Who did?"

"That guy right there."

"The Quasimodo with his stick in the air?"

"Yeah."

"What was it he did again?"

"He scored a goal."

"How?"

"He hit the puck into the net."

"What puck?"

I think this may have been when I decided to consider ways to make ice hockey more interesting and understandable to non-Canadians.

My first thought was that the sport needed a puck everybody could see, something roughly the size of a party tent that might weigh in the neighborhood of 5,000 pounds.

Next, to further simplify things, I decided that there ought to be only two teams in the NHL, the East Coast team and the West Coast team. This alone would do away with the need ever to know who Wales, Campbell, Adams, Norris, Patrick, and Smythe were, not to mention the mysterious Devils.

The season would consist of one game. With the 5,000-pound

puck situated in Lincoln, Neb., at the start, it would be a contest to see which team could get the puck into the other team's ocean first.

As a bonus attraction for the fans, it was my idea that the players wouldn't be required to wear skates. A player could wear skates if he insisted on it, of course, though he would obviously run the risk of being, say, less nimble than his teammates or opponents.

I imagined the periodic reports that the U.S. and Canada might hear during this one thrilling contest. I could see a sports announcer for network TV standing on a farm road in the Midwest at dusk, saying:

"The town you see in the distance is Springfield, Ill., and the people of this community are pretty excited about a hockey puck that's expected to arrive here in a matter of hours.

"The West Coast team has the puck moving in this direction, according to the latest report from our helicopter. The West Coast started a surprise attack back in Jefferson City, Mo., when it caught the East Coast in a vulnerable tristate defense.

"I asked Coach Jacques Jack of the East Coasters why he had gone to that defense. He said he had so many players in the penalty farm, he thought he'd better try something different.

"All along, Illinois was expected to be a key spot in the game.

"Fans of both teams remember only too well how the West Coast grabbed an early advantage in last year's game but suffered a heartbreaking loss after mistaking Lake Michigan for the Atlantic Ocean.

"Just to recap, the West Coast scored what it believed to be a victory by edging the puck into the lake near the Drake Hotel on Chicago's Near North Side.

"It was while the West Coasters were celebrating back at their homes up around Alberta and Manitoba that the East Coast retrieved the puck and drove it unchallenged all the way to Redondo Beach, where the winning goal was inched into the Pacific in the middle of a Miss Pre-Teen Surfer-Girl Contest and undercover crack bust.

"The people you see behind me are some of the sport's most passionate fans."

The announcer turns to interview two fans who are armed with machine guns and machetes.

"I understand you fellows have flown out here from the West Coast," he says.

"Yeah, we're number one!" a fan snarls at the mike. "We're goin' all the way, if the assholes can miss Lake Michigan."

The announcer politely says, "May I ask what the machine guns and machetes are for?"

The other fan answers with a wild-eyed expression and a maniacal laugh.

"It's the Midwest, ain't it?" he says. "We figured while we're out here for the game, we'd have a few beers and go kill the Clutter family."

The announcer turns to the camera.

"That's it from the world of hockey. Back to the studio."

The Last Heavyweight

ON THE NIGHT OF JUNE 18, 1941, "OUTDOORS IN THE BALL PARK," as Terry Malloy would say, a flashy young fighter named Billy Conn made an unbeatable Joe Louis look stunningly beatable for 12 smart rounds. But then, in the 13th round, as we all know, Conn inadvertently, if not cockily, danced into a boxing glove that unfortunately concealed one of Louis' fists. That punch kept Joe Louis the heavyweight champion of the world for what we came to know as the "duration," a term applied to the 10 or 15 years it was going to take for World War II to end.

A film of the first Louis-Conn fight, which was staged in New York's Polo Grounds before 54,487 people, proves that it wasn't the sporting classic it had seemed to be on the radio. Of course, no sporting classic was ever as classic as it seemed on radio, which was the charm of radio. But the Louis-Conn fight was still the last heavyweight championship that meant anything to someone like me. I happen to be a person who never saw Rocky Marciano do anything but crowd an opponent into a corner and maul him with his shoulders, who can't remember if he ever saw Muhammad Ali actually *hit* anybody, except Joe Frazier once.

In contrast, Joe Louis used to stand up and clearly punch

people, most often knocking them down, and, usually, out. I saw him do it in the newsreels, over and over.

This trait made his first fight with Billy Conn all the more memorable, for it was the closest Louis ever came to being defeated in his prime.

Billy Conn was a classy challenger. He was not a member of the Bum-of-the-Month Club, even though his fight with Louis that June followed in the wake of the champion knocking out Al McCoy in December, Red Burman in January, Gus Dorazio in February, Abe Simon in March, Tony Musto in April, and Buddy Baer in May. Conn, in fact, had been the light-heavyweight champion of the world since 1939.

Conn was a clever, stylish fighter with a pretty good punch of his own. The trouble was, he gave away reach, height, and 25 pounds to Louis. Still, he had Louis confused and far behind on points that night in the Polo Grounds, and he might well have taken the title if he hadn't grown overconfident. As Billy later said, "I had too much Pittsburgh in me. I didn't want to just win, I wanted to knock him out."

One night many years ago, I was with Billy in Pittsburgh, making the tour of his favorite saloons, as he reflected on his career.

"It wouldn't have done any good to run from Joe," he said. "Maybe I'd have won the fight, but he still would have made my life miserable for four years in the Army, knowing I had to fight the son of a bitch again when the war was over."

That particular evening, Billy told me about going up against some guys who were a lot tougher than Joe Louis.

"Mob guys," he said. "I got in a legitimate deal with 'em, but they wouldn't pay me what they owed me. They hung out in this hotel suite I knew about. So I decided to bust in there and get what I had coming. Only time in my life I ever carried a gun. I kicked the door in, pulled out the gun, and said, 'I'm Billy Conn and I'm here to get my fucking money, you assholes.'"

Billy paused long enough in his narrative for me to ask, "What happened?"

"I got laughed at," he shrugged.

I once discovered that Joe Louis had a sense of humor too.

It surfaced one night when he appeared on a cable-TV show with Muhammad Ali. According to many sportswriters, Ali was considered to be funnier than Lenny Bruce and Richard Pryor combined. I never understood why anyone thought this. All I ever heard him say was, "I'm the greatest," and the only thing he ever did that was funny was change a great name, Cassius Clay, into that of an NBA player.

On the show, Ali got around to saying to Louis, "How do you think you'd have done against me—the greatest?"

In his expressionless way, Louis said, "Oh, that's hard to say. We fought in different eras."

"You don't want to answer the question because you *know* the answer," Ali said. "You're tryin' to evade my question, ain't you?"

Calmly, Louis said, "No, it's just that we had different styles, different opponents. You fought in the Sixties and Seventies. I fought in the Thirties and Forties. You had some easy fights. I had some easy fights. I once had what they called the Bum-of-the-Month tour, and. . . ."

Ali broke in.

"You calling me a bum?"

"I didn't say that," Louis squinted.

"Yes, you did! You're callin' me a bum! Me! The greatest!"

"No, I didn't," Louis insisted.

"I heard you!" Ali yelped. "Didn't you *imply*—don't you *mean*—I'm a bum?"

A faint grin came over Louis.

"You'd have been on the tour," he said.

In that moment, Joe Louis was the heavyweight champion again—and he remains the only one I still acknowledge.

Snow Job

WINTER IS A TIME OF YEAR WHEN MILLIONS OF FASHIONABLE, FUN-loving madcaps invade the stridently quaint little Alpine villages of the world to trail-drop ("Rustler's Dip isn't nearly as crusty as Nonie's Nook"), to mountain-drop ("The back bowls at Gretchen's Gorge remind me of St. Anton"), to lodge-drop ("The chef at Heidi's

Hutch came from the Crillon"), and ultimately to lavish food and drink on Pepi, the handsome ski instructor who will teach you the heel thrust while trying to schuss your wife. I never had to worry about Pepi making it with my wife. She had already smelled a ski instructor.

I tried to learn how to ski back in the days when a new pair of Bogners left a purple ring around your waist, and still looked baggy, when the Head Standards were almost as long as the highway from Fort Worth to Waco—about 80 miles—and when every instructor on the slopes looked as if he had just stepped out of the prisoner's dock at Nuremberg.

"You vill follow me!" the instructor would shout, his quasi-Nazi voice echoing across some chic, *après*-Rockies slope, where-upon he would go *wedeln* (tail-wagging) through a corridor of fir trees, leaving me locked in a stem turn that would send me sliding 4,000 feet, head over binding, into a vat of *Gluhwein*.

And who the fuck ever drank *Gluhwein*?

"Hey, Traudl! Yeah, you—the little *Fraulein* bitch with the rosy cheeks and yellow curls who wants to grow up and marry an Austrian railroad worker and spend the rest of your life stacking firewood. Get this lemon-rind, cinnamon-stick, Burgundy shit out of my sight and bring me a Junior B., okay?"

"She is the daughter of my friend Hannes," the ski instructor would say, patting Traudl on the ass. "Hannes brought skiing to this valley. Here, the snow is always good. Over there, not so good."

"What's over there?"

"Switzerland."

Never smoke on an Alp. Skiing is a no-smoking sport, which is another thing that's wrong with it. Golf, you can smoke between shots, and tennis, you can smoke at the net, but you can't smoke on a mountain.

"I would not smoke up here," Pepi warned one day as we gazed down into a valley of chalets perfectly carved out of *raclette* cheese.

"What, are you kidding?" I smirked, flicking the Dunhill. "Here's how you smoke on the Eiger."

That first inhale turned my lungs into a tenement fire and knocked me into a bent-over, reverse-shoulder position from which I didn't recover until I got back to Heidi's Hutch and had my one and only sip of what I took to be mule piss, a drink that is known to most people as hot buttered rum.

There was a time when I actually enjoyed being around the

sport. It was in the days when I traveled with a group of maniacs known as Coach Bob Beattie and the United States Ski Team.

These were the eight or nine years which laid the groundwork for Bill Johnson finally kicking Europe's ass in the Olympic downhill at Sarajevo.

We won no gold medals in those years, from 1964 through 1972, but guys like Billy Kidd and Jimmy Huega won some big races and Rip McManus ate a lot of stemmed glasses and Spider Sabich horrified many a customer in a lodge dining room by taking a mouthful of lighter fluid, striking a match, and spewing a flame across somebody's rabbit stew.

Ski racers have nothing to do with recreational skiers, and ski racing has nothing in common with recreational skiing.

All of us hanging out with Jean-Claude Killy and Karl Schranz, we would put Volkswagens in Italian hotel lobbies for fun, dismantle discos, teach the French how to cook steak *tartare* well done and put it on a bun, and remind most Austrians of their intimate friendship with Himmler and Goebbels, and laugh most often at how witty the Swiss were.

"My sides ache," Beattie would say. "These goddamn Swiss are killing me with their one-liners."

"Yeah, I know," I would say, as we would try to load and unload about 800 pairs of racing skis from one train to another between Zug and Wengen.

Eight hundred pairs of skis and one portable typewriter.

A Switzerland person never smiled, we learned, and a German never improvised, and a Frenchman couldn't dance. But Christ, the Swiss were funny. They said chocolate, Rolex, and train—and we laughed our asses off.

I no longer try to ski but I know how to act like I do.

Not long ago, a friend was on his way to Aspen for the first time and he wanted to discuss the revolutionary rear-entry boot.

"What do you think of the SX-91s?" he asked.

I said, "Well, you've got to like the flex adjustment, but I'm still a four-buckle, crank-'em-down-tight kind of guy. Say hello to the Jerome for me and tear 'em up on Ajax."

Olympics—I

It has been said that a little blond dish named Sonja Henie invented the Winter Olympics. She won the gold medal in figure skating in 1928, 1932, and 1936. It has also been said that Sonja Henie tried to kill the Winter Olympics by becoming a movie actress.

For years, all anybody knew about winter sports was Sonja Henie, who came out of Norway to steal our hearts and, occasionally, John Payne's.

There's one thing you could be sure of when you went to see a Sonja Henie movie. She might be in the role of a shopgirl, a maid, the daughter of an innkeeper, or even a spy, but somewhere in the plot, she would happen upon this frozen pond.

A pair of ice skates would suddenly attach themselves to her dainty feet, accordion music would come out of a void, and in her platinum hair, worn like a skullcap, she would go spinning, hopping, gliding over the pond.

Part of the charm of the Winter Olympics is that ice skating and all the rest of those Olympic sports completely disappear for four years at a time.

The events haven't changed much since the first Winter Olympics in 1924. They've only multiplied.

Take speed skating. There are now 7,319 speed-skating events, which are all the same competition. People wearing leotards and shower caps, swinging one arm, skate around this oval until *Sports Illustrated* stops taking pictures.

In each Winter Olympics, 7,310 of these events are won by the same athlete, whose name is Ivar, Thun, or Eric.

Up in Lake Placid in 1980, when Eric Heiden was winning his 7,310 races, many among the press got so bored with covering it that they took to hollering at Eric each time he came around a turn.

"Fall!" more than one would shout, hoping for something different to write about.

In women's speed skating, the 7,310 events are usually won by the Beast of Buchenwald.

Bobsledding has its followers. This is a sport in which demented people sit on a sled that goes 2,000 miles per hour down an ice ditch. The same sport is often practiced without ice—when four drunks leave a fraternity party in a BMW.

Hockey leaves Canada every four years to go to the Winter Olympics, but nobody knows it's there unless the United States beats Russia.

Cross-country skiing is a sport that still mystifies me. In another life, I covered the Winter Olympics twice, once in Austria, once in France. What you do at a cross-country ski race is look for the athlete whose nose has grown the longest icicle.

These guys spend four hours in the woods, and most of the time they're going *up* something.

The winner of any cross-country ski race always has a name like Johan Sven Oddbjörn and speaks fluent salmon.

And then there's ski jumping. All of the demented people who aren't bobsledders are ski jumpers.

The athlete, whose name is Birger Viklund Saarinen Haug-Skutnabb, comes down the world's tallest playground slide and soars into the air, headfirst, hoping to land somewhere near a quaint little village below.

Beneath him, 50,000 people eagerly await his arrival, knowing that if he comes down on his head, he won't be hurt, but if he hits sideways, he can be killed.

The least watched event of a Winter Olympics is the biathlon. This is because the sport is relatively new and so misunderstood. But there is nothing complicated about the biathlon.

A Russian puts on a pair of skis, picks up a rifle, slides around in the trees, and stops every so often to shoot a West German.

Nowadays, the glamour sport of the Winter Olympics is Alpine skiing, principally because of people like Andrea Mead-Lawrence, Toni Sailer, and Jean-Claude Killy, handsome figures who won gold medals and brought racing stripes to long underwear.

Pleasure skiing, admittedly, can be a graceful, scenic, exotic sport. It has broken up a lot of marriages. But pleasure skiing has nothing to do with Alpine racing.

To be a great Alpine racer, it helps in no small way to be utterly stupid.

First, you have to feel comfortable leaning *down* a mountain. And then you have to relish such things as bumping into tree trunks at high speed, turning cart wheels down a slope for 200 yards at a whack, veering off course at a hairpin turn and winding up in St. Anton when you wanted to go to St. Moritz, and having your leg in a cast for three months out of every year.

I don't regret covering the Winter Olympics. Those were the days when the French and the Austrians were the most interesting ski racers. They gave me great quotes.

The Frenchman who would say:

"It is, for me, good, yes, but bad, not so much. I go fast, as I have learned, but the mountain is not for me to say. Yes, my skis are good, but as a child, which is what my father taught me. He was an old man, like my teacher in the Avec Saint-Raclette, you have been? Here, yes, the mountains are high but only as steep as my heart. Each man has two legs at the top. Yes, more wine. You are paying? I must have that woman over there. Is she rich?"

And the Austrian:

"Here it is not as pretty as home. Kleiner Feister Sterner is beautiful, you have been? Yes, I am great, but I lost at Bang-Platz-Henkel, a mistake. It was my mother's illness. *Fir und fumpsig, seeben und drysig.* The snow will go with my skis. Here I must win, I think. But the mountain must tell my feet. I will live here one day and take a bath."

In the end, Sonja Henie's sport turns out to make the most sense. It's elegant, it's safe, it's indoors.

You can see some great legs on the girls and a lot of guys who'd make darn fine waiters.

Olympics—II

THE NAME OF GABRIELA ANDERSEN-SCHEISS LIVES ON IN SPORTS as the person who did the most to unpollute our streets and sidewalks.

I will always be grateful to television for letting me watch
Gabriela take her final lap in the women's marathon at the 1984
Olympics in Los Angeles, wobbling, creeping, staggering—remember?—hips out of joint, a finger occasionally pointing at her nose
("Where's my vial?") and then at her head ("Where's my brain?"),
and in general looking like every dopehead I ever knew in the days
when Austin, Tex., made Berkeley look like a nursery rhyme.

As a devout anti-jogger, I was happy to see Gabriela making it
look like aimless running through the streets of neighborhoods
was the most wonderful experience you could have in this life.

Watching her, I chuckled uncontrollably as I sat comfortably at
home, smoking, drinking, overeating.

My wife came into the room and said, "What are you laughing
at?"

"Look," I said, pointing to the TV set.

"My God," she said, alarmed. "What is it?"

"A loon is trying to finish the women's marathon."

"She's going to die."

"Yes!" I cackled.

My wife stared at Gabriela on TV, then back at me.

"You're sick," she said.

"No, *she* is," I laughed.

"This is terrible," my wife said. "Why is ABC showing this?"

"Public service," I said.

As Gabriela Andersen-Scheiss trudged onward, I called a
friend in Austin.

"Are you watching this?" I asked him.

"I think I was with her last night," he said. "How'd she get to
L.A. so quick?"

We were both taping it. For this, I would have erased
Casablanca.

"It looks like she's going to make it," I said.

"Yeah, you know why? The bartender promised her Louie was
coming over with some really good shit."

We hung up and my wife said she couldn't understand anyone
laughing so hard at the spectacle, especially someone whose waist
was starting to look like a bean-receiving station.

"You don't understand," I said. "This is great. You'll be able
to get a taxi now without having to watch out for thundering
herds. You can shop without getting trampled by stockbrokers in
warmups and earphones."

I reminded my wife that you couldn't play golf or tennis on a major thoroughfare, but you could jog. That you couldn't smoke in most seats on most airplanes, but it was okay to put on shorts and a headband and sling body odor on everybody, all in the name of fitness.

Joggers needed their own stadium, I said. A place where they would be together, tromping and gasping in their pointless journeys, a place where they could munch on their crisp vegetables and bore each other.

Eugene, Oreg., I said, the running capital of the universe. They could put a dome on Eugene and sell tickets. You could sit there in comfort, smoking and drinking, and watch non-smoking joggers drop like flies from heart failure.

Gabriela Andersen-Scheiss finished the race and was carried off on a stretcher. Announcers spoke of courage, bravery, the sporting heart, the competitive instinct.

"Talk about the news!" I shouted at the TV. "Eight million people just threw their sneakers in the fucking wastebasket!"

Well, there are nutfucks who still jog today, but not as many, thanks to Gabriela.

Of course, Gabriela wasn't the only member of the female persuasion worth remembering from that Olympics. It was the Olympics that encouraged millions of people to dash out and buy a household pet, a Mary Lou Retton.

Bloomingdale's couldn't keep them in stock.

"I'm sorry, sir, we're all out of Mary Lou Rettons, but there's a cute little Commie you might enjoy."

"Does the balance beam come with her?"

"No, I'm afraid that's extra."

"Sounds too expensive. Tell you what, just sell me a pair of tights and I'll go home and hop around on my carpet."

To be honest, I must tell you that I even became a fan of Mary Lou Retton. She could do everything my Yorkshire terrier can do.

But there was a sad moment for all of Mary Lou's admirers when she blew the gold medal in the vault, supposedly her best event.

I had a friend on the scene that I expected to take it harder than anyone. Mike Lupica of the New York *Daily News* had written so much about Mary Lou for two weeks that one more column might have gotten him arrested for child molesting.

Mary Lou had won the all-around gold medal and had become America's darling before the vault, when she was suddenly outscored.

I sat in front of the TV wondering how Mike Lupica would handle the tragedy. Mary Lou had let him down.

Presently, the phone rang. It was Mike calling from the press row at Pauley Pavilion.

"Here's my lead," he said.

"She Gabrielaed," I dictated.

"No," he said. "Charming coquette becomes choking midget."

Olympics—III

WHEN THE SEOUL OLYMPICS FINALLY DISAPPEARED FROM THE TELE-vision screen, my life became empty, meaningless; I had nobody to hate for months. I could no longer hate the inscrutable East, athletes drinking steroids on the rocks, or all of those astute sports judges from the Third, Fourth, and Fifth World.

I watched and taped almost every moment from Seoul, and I often look back at the events on my VCR, but it's not the same, not nearly as much fun as those gala nights in the neighborhood bar when I stood around and rooted for the good old U.S.A. with my friends Booger Red, Gator Bill, and Cooter Joe.

It was during the opening ceremonies that Gator Bill glanced up at the TV screen and said, "Look at them silly chinks. You know why they hop around like that, don't you? The fuckers eat *dog;* it's a fact."

I didn't bother to remind Gator Bill that he had been known to eat gator tail, because I knew how Gator Bill liked to whip some-body's ass if he even honked at him too loud on Route 10.

Booger Red was disappointed that our swimmers didn't win every gold medal. He blamed it on the clean water in the pool.

"Them fuckin' East Germans swim in sewers," he said. "Think that won't make you fast? We're missin' a bet. Our swimmers ought to train in the Everglades. We got some water moccasins that'll speed their asses up."

Everybody got mad when a little Chinaman, Ling Ying Ning, or whatever his name was, kept making it hard for Greg Louganis to win another gold medal in diving.

Cooter Joe yelled at the judges through the TV screen.

"Why, hell, no, he don't make a splash! How's he gonna make a splash when he ain't no bigger than a goddamn chopstick?"

He turned to me and said, "Them judges is ignernt, is what it comes down to."

America's losing to Russia in basketball did not, of course, sit well with Booger Red, Gator Bill, and Cooter Joe.

I tried to point out that we lost because we sent a coach over there who wanted to win with defense instead of letting our best college players shoot the basketball.

"Don't make a fuck," Gator Bill said. "Them fuckin' officials from Libya is gonna let Bobby Joe Stalin take five steps ever' time he gets his hands on the damn ball—how we supposed to go up against that shit?"

"Tell you what *I* want to do," Cooter Joe said. "I want to send Magic and Michael and Isiah and the Bird over there and say, 'Awright, you Commie cocksuckers, you want to play some basketball? Here's how you play basketball, *motherfucker!*'"

"Tie their Moscow dicks in a knot," Booger Red added. "Wouldn't be nothin' else to it."

When our 4 × 100 relay team got disqualified because of a Commie complaint about a baton pass in a qualifying heat, which cost Carl Lewis a third gold medal, Booger Red couldn't do anything but shake his head sadly.

"It's the only way they could beat us," he said. "Pick out some little old pissant, obscure, shit-heel rule and call it on us. Fuckin' Russians pass microfilm inside the baton, why ain't *that* against the goddamn rules?"

"If the Olympics was run by qualified judges," Booger Red said, "the only events the Commies would win are the fifty-kilometer and the twenty-kilometer walk. Why wouldn't they be good at it?" he said. "Fuckers don't have no cars—they *have* to walk everywhere they go."

Booger Red, Gator Bill, and Cooter Joe said steroids are a minor issue compared with all the Commie guys who pass themselves off as girls so they can win more medals.

"There ought to be a tit test," Gator Bill said. "If the Commie don't have no tits, she gets disqualified."

There was nothing, however, that infuriated Booger Red, Gator

Bill, and Cooter Joe as much as the boxing decision that screwed
America's Roy Jones out of a gold medal.

They enjoyed themselves immensely as they watched Roy
Jones, the best fighter in the Olympics, beat up on a defenseless
Korean for all three rounds in the finals of the 156-pound division.

Even if you didn't know anything about boxing, it was clear
that Roy Jones had kicked the Korean's ass all the way to the DMZ
and back.

Booger Red said two motherfuckers and one sonbitch when the
referee held up the hand of the Korean, who was barely on his feet
and whose face looked like chop suey.

Gator Bill said this was the cheapest shit he'd seen since the
last time he was in Mexico.

And Cooter Joe all but climbed inside the TV set and punched
out the tubes and wires.

But what made the decision even worse was the news that the
three incompetent judges who voted against America were from
Uganda, Uruguay, and Morocco.

Booger Red, Gator Bill, and Cooter Joe said they'd never even
heard of two of them chickenshit countries, and as for Morocco, it
was Gator Bill who said he hoped ever' goddamn A-rab over there
got his dick bit off by a cobra.

Cooter Joe made the bartender turn off the TV that night. He
just couldn't watch any more of this bullshit. Made him want to
puke.

"Where's the next Olympics at?" Booger Red asked.

"Barcelona," I said.

"Near Spain, ain't it?" said Cooter Joe.

"Pretty close."

"That's great," Gator Bill said. "We'll get a big fucking break
over there too."

The Car Crowd

DARLENE STUMP, A HOUSEWIFE AND MOTHER, SAID SHE HAD NO problem with the title of her tell-all book about the life and good times of an auto racing groupie. All along, it was going to be called *Me and Harley and Ralph and Fred and Shorty and Joe Ed and Cecil and Them Others.*

The book is a paperback original and I was Darlene's first stop on her publicity tour. We met at the 7-Eleven on Route 12, halfway between Bobcat's Cleaners and Thelma's Adult Video. Not too far from the warehouse they're turning into a combination toll booth and disco.

Darlene said she wrote the book because she wanted to tell her side of the story.

"I was sick and tired of all the rumors and innuendo," she said. "It was time to set the record straight."

I asked Darlene to excuse my ignorance. I wasn't familiar with the rumors and innuendo regarding her life.

"Sue Ann Grimes started most of it," Darlene said. "She's the one who told everybody in the trailer camp that Joe Ed and me was making a baby while I was living with Shorty. Among other things, this wasn't fair to my husband Cecil."

Darlene said she got a great deal of satisfaction out of getting even with Sue Ann Grimes in the book.

"She won't be able to show her face around Daytona or Darlington anymore," Darlene said. "I put it all in there. I put it in there about Sue Ann and Royce Adcock. How she was screwing Royce Adcock and E. T. Brunson at the same time, and even Deadeye Stearns when he was home on parole. Nobody's man was safe around that woman. It's pretty much what everybody talked about in the pits."

I asked Darlene what she liked best about automobile racing.

"Well, the men are men, if you know what I mean," she said. "You don't hear an awful lot of talk about antique furniture."

While Darlene hoped her book would sell, she was mainly happy that it got published because writing a book would prove to everybody that she wasn't dumb.

"I am not dumb," she said, as we shared a sack of Chee-tos and drank a root beer and watched 7-Eleven customers buy lottery tickets. "I went to six weeks of community college like everybody else I know."

Darlene's favorite event was the 24 hours of Daytona.

"But you've got to get invited to the right parties," she said. "There's a crazy group from Fanbelt, Ind., that come down every year in their campers. They know how to get it on. They don't do nothin' but eat ribs and swap wives and husbands."

Darlene confessed that she was in the process of getting divorced again—from Joe Ed this time.

She had married Joe Ed after she married Cecil and Shorty and Ralph.

"They all worked in the pit for E. T. Brunson's racing team and they never won shit. My whole life, I'd wanted to be with a winner. That's why I married Joe Ed. He's the crew chief for Royce Adcock's team and the best tire man I ever saw. Joe Ed was the first person to shave the raised white letters off a tire to reduce wind resistance. First time I seen him doing it, I said, 'Joe Ed, I didn't know you was interested in art.' He said, 'I'm lookin' for that one-eighth of a second that's gonna get us into Victory Lane.'

"Of course, the trouble with a tire man is they don't think about nothin' but the weather."

"How so?" I asked.

Darlene said, "Baby, if you don't have the right tires on your car for the rain or the heat, you can just stay home and play with your dick."

Anybody can put the pedal to the mat and drive like a high school drunk, Darlene said. Races are won in the pits.

"But that's the trouble with being married to a pit man. They don't think about nothin' but how to invent a contraption that'll cool the fuel before it reaches the combustion chamber."

In a way, you could say that axle grease broke up Darlene's marriage to Joe Ed.

Joe Ed spent most of his time thinning it, trying to come up with a lighter lubricant to cut down on friction.

"I said, Joe Ed, why don't you put some of that axle grease on my body sometime, but he didn't even hear me," Darlene said, sadly.

It's all in her book about the night she left Joe Ed. How she kicked him in the nuts and said, "You've blocked off my radiator for the last time, butthole."

Darlene said her biggest thrill was meeting Third Turn Henderson at Indy.

"He's the only celebrity I've ever known personally," she explained. "There's a fairly intimate chapter about us in the book. It was the most wonderful three hours I've ever spent with anybody. People will say I made up some of his quotes—that I can get away with that kind of thing because he's dead now, but everything I say is true."

Darlene's interest in literature dated back to the time she read the life story of the Captain and Tennille.

Her interest in automobile racing was even older than her interest in literature, however.

In fact, she didn't understand why everybody wasn't more interested in automobile racing than any other sport.

"Cars are what people do," she said. "And everybody's a race driver, even if they aren't going nowhere but Arby's or Pizza Hut. They'll cut you off. They'll slipstream you. You just watch 'em next time you're going somewhere."

She vividly remembered the day as a young teenage girl that she became fascinated with car racing.

She and Sue Ann Grimes had driven down to Daytona.

They were overwhelmed by the excitement of it all—the trucks, the tattoos, the noise.

Then, suddenly, Darlene saw this flatbed truck and all these carefree, fun-loving guys on it.

She waved and smiled at the guys.

One of them held up a hand-lettered sign—and that was the clincher.

The sign said:

"FREE BEER IF YOU SHOW US YOUR TITS."

THE REAL WORLD

What Is It?

THE REAL WORLD ISN'T MUCH FUN AND NEVER WAS BECAUSE THERE are people in it, and anytime you get people involved in something you've got a problem.

People get to be a problem because they have these notions about what's right and what's wrong, and it almost never coincides with what other people think.

Most of the time I've found myself on the side of the other people.

This is especially true when it comes to guns, which have been known to kill people—usually the wrong people.

I've noticed it to be true when it comes to smoking too. I enjoy smoking but there's an awful lot of people who have nothing better to do than complain about it.

Why don't these people complain about guns?

Another thing people like to do is steal from other people, either through phony promotions or on Wall Street.

Lately, one of the toughest things you can do is try to ride in a New York City taxicab without getting killed.

I would kick most taxicabs if, as inanimate objects, they weren't so big. So I kick smaller inanimate objects. It's one of the most pleasurable things you can do if you live in the real world.

Of course, there was one thing that used to bind all people together. Eating food, it was called. But finding real food has become a problem because certain people went out and invented so many "creative chefs."

Right now, I think if we could solve the food problem among people, we could probably solve everything else.

Otherwise, the real world is only going to become more of a problem, and some of us don't have any way to fight back except with our typewriters.

Have Gun, Will Use

IT HAS NOW BECOME POSSIBLE, AS I UNDERSTAND IT, FOR PEOPLE IN well over half of the United States to own and carry a handgun if they simply fill out a form that says they don't particularly like Russia, they've never done time in a straitjacket, and they've almost never killed anyone who didn't deserve it.

The gentlemen who have passed these laws in various states have mostly done so on full stomachs after having been wined and dined by members of the National Rifle Association, which operates on the theory that every citizen in America has a right to defend himself, or herself, from such bodily harm as may be caused by rabbits, squirrels, deer, chipmunks, quail, and dove.

The logic of the NRA seems to be that if you take away my handgun, the next thing you'll do is take away my rifle, and then what will I use to shoot my wife or husband?

Of course, there's an upside to this. When the entire country becomes armed and dangerous, newspapers are going to be a lot more fun to read.

Here are a few of the stories I'm eagerly anticipating:

ST. PETERSBURG, FLA.—Rufus Hipple, a retired insurance executive, was shot and killed last night by a concession worker in the Pablo Plaza movie theater.

Eyewitnesses said the shooting occurred after Mr. Hipple and the concession worker had a misunderstanding over the amount of butter that belonged in a bucket of popcorn.

Gina Fay Simcox, 19, has been charged with murder.

Miss Simcox told reporters she would gladly shoot Mr. Hipple again. She only wished her .38 revolver had been fully loaded.

"The old fool hadn't ought to have talked to me in that tone of voice," Miss Simcox said.

LAKE TRACEY, GA.—Mrs. Irma Doowaddy, 54, a cashier in a drive-through bank, was shot and killed yesterday by a customer who apparently lost patience with Mrs. Doowaddy's ability to make change for a $20 bill.

Sparky Linyard, 37, a construction worker, is being held in custody and may be charged with the murder.

Rhonda Mayfort, a waitress in Leon's Diner, told law enforcement officers she overheard Mr. Linyard bragging about the killing. She quoted Mr. Linyard as saying, "That's the slowest old woman I ever saw and I been married to some fat ones."

PALM HAMMOCK, CALIF.—A crazed customer in a Cajun seafood restaurant fatally wounded three people last night. Dead are the restaurant manager, the chef, and a waiter.

Dennis Clacker, 48, a traveling salesman, surrendered to police. He was still seated in the restaurant having coffee and dessert when officers arrived on the scene.

"One of these days, people is gonna learn how to make gumbo," Mr. Clacker said.

FRUIT FLY COVE, S.C.—Violence erupted in this golf-happy resort area yesterday and at least six persons are known to be dead from gunshot wounds.

The shooting occurred when two foursomes of golfers arrived on the first tee of the Fruit Fly Country Club course and each claimed to have a 10:15 A.M. starting time.

Bobby Bent, 28, a real estate developer from North Florida, was arrested. Mortally wounded were all four members of one foursome and two members of Mr. Bent's foursome.

Mr. Bent and the other golfer played nine holes before police apprehended him.

Numerous weapons were found in Mr. Bent's golf cart.

Mr. Bent was evidently referring to the dead golfers when he said, "Six under ain't bad. Let's see what Jack Nicklaus can do with that."

AUSTIN, TEX.—Jo Carol Munson, 32, an executive secretary for Unlimited Products, Inc., confessed today to the murder of her boss, Ralph Sam Tyler, who died last week of four gunshot wounds in the chest.

Miss Munson told police she killed Mr. Tyler after an argument over her vacation dates.

"I would have confessed sooner," she said, "but it was National Fax Week."

ORLANDO, FLA.—An argument over a self-serve gas pump resulted in the death of 14 people last night.

While two out-of-town men, both said to be freelance journal-ists, were trying to figure out how to use the pump, shots began to ring out from the female passengers in three other vehicles.

Onlookers said most of the shots seemed to come from a carload of nuns.

Mrs. Emma Stickey, a survivor from one of the cars, said, "There ain't no need to go to Disney World now. Mickey can't top what I've done already saw."

Dunhills Unite!

Smoking at work or even at home will cost employees their jobs at nine USG Acoustical Products plants, and the company plans to conduct lung tests to make sure workers are complying with the ban.

—News item

THE YEAR IS IN THE NOT-SO-DISTANT FUTURE AND I'M KNOCKING on the door of Jack and Charley's smoke-easy.

A peep-hole opens.

"Who is it?" asks a tough, husky voice from inside.

"Bullets McGurn," I say.

"Who?"

"A friend of Big Sid's," I whisper.

The door opens and I enter.

Cigarette smoke is everywhere. People are smoking furiously while a jazz band plays "Potato Head Blues." Flappers are dancing on tables.

A pretty hostess greets me.

"Hi, big boy, what's your pleasure?"

"I just want to smoke."

"Table down front?"

"Wherever there's the most smoke," I say.

The hostess leads me to a table where I can hardly see the bandstand there's so much smoke in the room.

"First time here?" she asks.

"Yeah."

"What happened? They catch you smoking on the job?"

"No, I was at home," I explain. "They kicked in my door, held me down, and gave me this lung test. There were six of them in deep-sea diving suits. I didn't have a chance."

"It's tough all over," the hostess says. "I hear a lot of hard-luck stories."

The hostess leaves to dance the sugarfoot with Virginia Slim, a pretty famous racketeer around town.

A waitress comes to my table.

"Hi, big boy, what'll it be?"

I glance at the next table. Two guys in tuxedos and two dames in evening gowns are cracking open a carton of Winstons.

"Bring me the same," I tell the waitress.

"Any flint or lighter fuel on the side?"

"Why not?"

"You must be a sportswriter."

"You guessed it," I say. "What time do you close this joint?"

"Jack and Charley's never closes," she says.

"Really? You mean I can come here and have a cigarette at breakfast?"

"Sure."

"Lunch?"

"We get a very nice lunch crowd."

The waitress brings me the carton of Winstons.

I bust open a pack and sit back to enjoy the smoke and the music.

I'm not looking for company but a bimbo joins me at the table. She looks like a heavy smoker.

"Buy a lady a cigarette?" she says.

"Help yourself," I say. "There's more where these came from."

She tells me this hard-luck story. How she was the best secretary USG Acoustical Products ever had but she got caught smoking at home and they let her go.

I start to feel sorry for her, but the hostess comes back.

"Take a hike, Wanda," says the hostess to the bimbo. "Come in here again and you're dog meat."

The bimbo leaves.

"What's that all about?" I ask.

"She's a smarc."

"A what?"

"A smarc. Undercover. She works for USG. One of their top agents."

The hostess looks like a good egg. I invite her to sit down for a minute.

"It's a tough world," she says. "First it was airplanes, then restaurants, then all public places. Now it's your own home."

"The world is doomed," I say.

"Yeah, it's too bad. Look what they're doing to red meat. It's already banned in seven states."

"I know," I say through an exhale. "I go to this steak-easy when I'm in California."

I stayed through the night and came back for breakfast and ran up a pretty good tab, I suppose, just smoking and listening to the music and remembering how it used to be when the United States was a free country, before Prohibition.

Business Affairs

FOR A WHILE IN THE 1980s I TRIED TO GET RICH BY ATTEMPTING to bring sports into the New Age scam, to make sports a part of what came to be known as "psychic chic," but I failed at every turn because I could never come up with a catchy name for my cult.

First, I formed the Contented Hog Society, thinking I would surely attract thousands of golfers who would want to live in a spiritual environment near an uncrowded country club and do nothing between rounds of golf but eat sausage and biscuits with cream gravy.

It didn't work and I soon found out why. This was what all of my friends did most of the time anyhow.

Then I organized the Lifefat Movement. The idea was for my disciples to see their intellectual ferment become more significant than the Renaissance by living in the rear of a good Tex-Mex cafe and discussing the metaphysical properties of the Prince tennis racket.

This didn't work either. All anybody did was argue about who made the best chili.

I felt certain that the Actual Barbecue Forum would be a success. I took groups off to a dude ranch and tried to help them alter their state of consciousness with ribs and brisket and discussions of the instant replay.

This failed because as one deserter put it, "Hell, it's just the Sixties all over again."

My best shot came when I bought a small mountain in Northern California and opened the New Age commune. I threw in everything I could think of: reincarnation, psychic healing, spirit guides, mediums, the occult, Eastern mysticism, holistic medicine, pottery, West Coast jazz, mind control, Satanism, supernatural phenomena, Judeo-Christian rejection, cosmic isolation, biofeedback, hypnosis, meditation, neurolinguistic training, ghost intervention, and, for whatever limited use they might have, drugs.

It was a beautiful spot, with Disney rides, satellite dishes, jogging paths, and condos with Perrier squirt-guns in every room. Searching for the just-right name, something on the order of EST, I came up with TWD.

It stood for The Whole Deal.

The scheme was to lure sports-minded people out there to sit around and talk about how the world's economic and social systems and Brent Musburger had ravaged the whole planet.

With all of the pseudotherapy programs I offered, plus unrestricted chanting, I was certain my followers would develop new patterns of thought, discover their own destinies, and go away as New Age capitalists mentally equipped to resist sports on network television.

Some say TWD failed because I left out firewalking.

Others say it was because there were too many trotting races on ESPN.

I should explain that the reason I got into "psychic chic" in the first place was because of a woman named Ms. J. Z. Knight, who lived in the Pacific Northwest, passed herself off as a friend of

Shirley MacLaine's, and made a bundle by telling people that man is God and capable of creating his own divine-self person.

I read where hordes of people had actually moved from their homes, giving up everything, just to be near Ms. Knight in order to pay her $400 each time she transformed herself into a 35,000-year-old man named "Ramtha."

People did this, Ms. Knight explained, because they wanted to pull away from "fear-oriented religions."

It occurred to me immediately that a 35,000-year-old man might be a hell of a lot more frightening than a congregational religion, but who was I to knock success?

I kept it fairly simple with the last cult I tried. It was called the Homeowners Association.

For a cost of only $200 a session, I invited people to come over to my house and watch a man in his 50s transform himself into a functioning sportswriter.

I began by coughing in the morning like a 35,000-year-old man. I then lit cigarettes like a man with an extra mouth. Next, I drank two gallons of coffee while barking at the latest NCAA action on the sports pages. Finally, I washed my face in a basin of Visine and climbed a steep hill of Gelusil and moved to the typewriter.

Alas, nobody joined me but my wife and kids, but of course they'd seen it all before.

Butch Cassidy and the Arbitrage Kid

HISTORY MAY REMARK THAT THE LEADING SPORT OF THE LATE 20TH Century was insider trading, but all it proved was that crooks weren't what they used to be.

What real crook ever talked about junk bonds and arbs?

These crooks didn't even have decent names. There was no Machine Gun Kelly, no Pretty Boy Floyd, no Baby Face Nelson, no Ma Barker, and who among us would argue that Dennis and Ivan had the ring to it of Bonnie and Clyde?

Seriously, no average person ever quaked with fear when they were in a restaurant and somebody said, "See that tough-looking guy over there? He's with the Drexel Burnham Gang."

"Oh? What's his name?"

"Spurgeon Padgam-Rhinehart Shippinghorst III."

"Is he really dangerous?"

"Are you kidding? He leveraged out six whole city blocks last week."

No crook in the era excited the imagination.

Take Ivan Boesky. You'd think that a guy who admitted he stole a hundred million dollars would have had a name like Mad Dog or Scarface or Bugs or at the very least Ivan the Arb.

You'd think he would have packed a rod and left Wall Street in a getaway car instead of a limo.

"Look out, here comes Ivan the Arb!"

"Who's he with?"

"Duck! It's Big Boyd the Warehouser!"

In the good old days, Ma Barker and her boys would knock off a bank in Terre Haute and it would be front-page news everywhere.

In the '80s when a guy stole a whole corporation it was a sidebar in the business section.

He wasn't even called a mobster.

Sometimes he was called a manipulator who parked stocks illegally, and sometimes he was called an inside trader who circumvented the disclosure laws.

They stole their millions, "cooperated with the investigation," did a few months in a suntan joint, and the next thing you knew, they'd lowered their handicaps to three and were winning Pro-Ams.

They never went on tri-crime sprees, rubbed out G-men with their heaters, and went to prize fights with platinum-haired gun molls.

No character, no individuality. What, a guy in a Brooks Brothers suit with a calculator in his pocket has glamour?

I say they should have been sent to a tough joint, thrown in there with Benny, Rocko, and C.W.

Benny would be in there for plugging four cops. Rocko would be doing life for poisoning six dozen 10-year-olds with heroin. C.W. would be in there for the mass murder of 37 people at a take-out pizza franchise.

And here would come Spurgeon Padgam-Rhinehart Shippinghorst III.

"What are you in for?" Rocko would ask.

"Well, uh, basically, I tried to park some stocks."

"You did *what?*"

"It was all a misunderstanding. They accused me of trying to hide some inadequate capital levels. You see, there was this firm that was in a weak financial condition but we wanted to conceal its position in order for that company to make a corporate raid on this other company, so. . . ."

Spurgeon wouldn't like the way Benny, Rocko, and C.W. were looking at him, moving in on him.

"Try again or bend over," Benny would say.

"All right, all right!" Spurgeon would whimper. "You can have the house in Palm Beach, the property in Haiti, the cabin in New Hampshire, the resort in Oregon, everything!"

"Say it," Rocko would sneer.

"Okay, okay," Spurgeon would whimper again. "I got nabbed by the Feds because I was an insider kingpin."

"That's more like it," Rocko would grin. "Welcome to the club."

Death and Taxis

THE QUESTION OF WHICH SPORT IS THE MOST DANGEROUS HAS BEEN argued for years. You hear votes for skiing, mountain climbing, powerboating, car racing, boxing, eating fried food, smoking. The answer comes easily for me. The most dangerous sport in the world is riding in a New York City taxi.

Nowadays, six blocks through Manhattan with Mhambed or Cadeeb at the wheel is guaranteed to make you squeal like a wounded animal and curl up in a knot. You're thankful just to get out of the cab safely; never mind the wrong address. Never mind that you're going to shit water for the next 24 hours.

It happened overnight. Nine out of every 10 New York City cabdrivers are suddenly maniac terrorists of no ascertainable nationality. And no one can explain how this has occurred. Not Mayor Koch. Not Governor Cuomo. Nobody.

All I know is, I got into a cab one day, and before I could tell the driver my destination, we were going 80 miles an hour up Third Avenue, swerving to scare pedestrians.

When I said something to the driver, his reply was, "*Carrock ahmgamma posta meglock!*"

"Stop here!" I yelled.

He ignored me.

"Now!" I cried.

"You speak?"

"Yes!"

"What you want, maybe?"

"I want out!"

"Where?"

"Here!"

He slammed on the brakes.

"*Yebbis onga gish rackem!*" he snarled at a city bus.

I handed him a wad of bills and leaped to safety.

That was four years ago. Now they've added refinements. They have NO SMOKING signs all over the car and they play loud, horrifying, tuneless music at full treble.

The other day, I got into Mhambed's cab and tried to shout out the address over the music.

"Seventy-fifth and Third!" I bellowed.

He hadn't waited to hear it. We were going 60 down Park Avenue, barging through red lights.

"Sheekonga dababa rackemba dar!" was what I think he said, which I took to mean that he didn't care if he lived or died.

"Sir?" I said. *"Excuse* me!"

We were racing toward the most dangerous intersection in Manhattan, 86th and Park, a four-way jungle at which every Mhambed in town flirts with death.

"Kadash po-yamman deck!" howled Mhambed, as the intersection went by in a blur.

I think I heard a crash behind us, above the screeching of the music; but I didn't glance back, because I was trying to light a cigarette while sliding back and forth across the seat.

Before I knew it, we were dashing through the 60s.

"Too far!" I yelled.

"No!" the driver said.

"No?"

"You say Fifty-seven!"

He sped past a limo. *"Slobba din spicelam!"* he sputtered out the window at the limo driver.

"Let me out!" I called. "Stop, damn it!"

"No!"

He didn't stop until 57th, like he said.

"Get out," he sneered. "You crazy man."

I gave him a 10.

"No change."

"Keep it," I said, adoring the pavement under my feet. "Buy a grenade."

It doesn't seem like all that long ago that New York cabdrivers were as much fun as they were safe.

They were all named Mike or Gus, and they understood something. No matter how fast or slowly you drove, everybody wound up on 59th Street at the same time. And they were entertaining, because they spoke, by and large, English.

You got into one of these cabs and the driver crept away at a sane speed. Presently, he would say, "Jesus, that Carter." And you had a political discussion if you felt like it.

Or he would say, "Jesus, the Yankees. My toilet looks better."
And you could talk sports if you felt like it.

But you didn't have to say anything. You could just smoke and
listen to Mike or Gus.

Recently, I thought I had a guy like that. A throwback to the old
days—Nick or Tony. I felt good about getting into his cab. I thanked
him for stopping for me and gave him the address.

"Just fucking great," he said—and floored it.

We went 80 for two blocks and got caught by a light and some
other cars. He glanced over at the cab next to us.

"Fuck you, asshole!" he shouted at the other driver.

"Go fuck yourself," came the reply.

"I'm sayin' fuck you!"

"Yeah? Well, fuck you!"

"Listen," I said, interrupting. "Do you mind if . . . ?"

But we sped away, side by side with the other cab.

And then we both skidded to a stop at another light.

"Fuckin' asshole!" my driver called out.

I looked at the passenger in the other cab. Somebody's
grandmother.

The other driver yelled, "You know who you're fuckin' with
here? You're fuckin' with *me,* you fuckhead. You want to fuck with
me? Come on! Fuck with me!"

My driver said to him, "Hey, look at me! I'm tryin' to make a
fuckin' livin' here, you fuckin' asshole."

"So make your fuckin' living; I don't give a fuck!"

"Aw, fuck you."

"Fuck you."

"Go fuck yourself."

"In your ass."

"My dick!"

"Fuckin' cocksucker. Fuck off!"

"Yeah, well, fuck this!"

That's pretty much the way I left it. In Manhattan, I can take
only so much intellectual conversation in one day. Somehow I
missed Mhambed.

Object Lesson

A COAT HANGER THAT WOULDN'T PROMPTLY COME OUT OF A CLOSET reminded me that my own, personal favorite sport, for my whole life, has been torturing, punishing, and cussing inanimate objects.

It's good for you. Look at me. I'm a healthy, well-adjusted person of upper middle age because I've tortured, punished, and cussed inanimate objects for years.

One or two moments of heated violence and you feel great.

You can say and do things to an inanimate object that you can never say or do to a human being. Not if you're as well adjusted as I am.

The coat hanger in the Boston hotel room can tell you about it. It didn't want to come off the bar and release my slacks. I pulled. It clung. I pulled harder. It still clung.

I jerked at it and something snapped.

Not only did something snap, a tiny piece of metal hit me in the forehead.

The son of a bitch could have put my eye out.

"What the fuck is this shit?" I said to the coat hanger, which had by then been dislodged from the closet. I was holding it at arm's length, along with the pair of slacks.

"You trying to put a man's eye out?" I continued. "Are you trying to put a man's *goddamn eye out?*"

I slammed the coat hanger and the pair of slacks to the floor and kicked at them.

"Motherfuckin' cocksucker! Try to put a man's eye out. That is some load of shit is what *that* is!"

I picked up the wire hanger and bent it into a peculiar art form, and bent it again, and stuffed it into a wastebasket.

The slacks were an accomplice, I decided, so I crumpled them up and put them into the wastebasket on top of the bent hanger. The idea was to smother the hanger to death, just in case there was an ounce of life left in it.

It was to the pair of slacks that I said, with great satisfaction, "I don't need any of *your* shit, either!"

The biggest battle I ever fought was against a Thermos.

That was years ago, when I was working for a newspaper in Texas. I had driven to Augusta, Ga., to cover The Masters. My wife had gone along. We'd had a swell time. It had been a terrific golf tournament. And now it was time to start the drive home.

But first we stopped for breakfast at a Toddle House. And in the middle of breakfast, I remembered I had a Thermos in the trunk of the car.

"Don't let them take my plate," I said to my wife. "I'll go get the Thermos and have it filled up with coffee for the road."

The car was parked on the street, right in front of the restaurant.

Two scenes now, one outside, one inside.

Outside, I opened the trunk and picked up the Thermos, which had been rotting in there for a week. I barely turned the lid when it exploded.

Yeah. It blew up.

Now my face and shirt and pants were covered with week-old coffee.

I don't have to take this from a Thermos, never.

"You miserable cocksucker!" I yelled, bashing the Thermos on the sidewalk. "Blow up in a man's face, goddamn you!"

I kicked at it.

I picked it up and threw it against the side of the car. I kicked at it again and stubbed my toe and hopped around in a circle.

Then I grabbed the bastard and broke the modern-day record for long-distance Thermos throwing by a sportswriter.

"Have a good life, you son of a cocksucking bitch!"

Inside, my wife had noticed that all the other customers and the two fry cooks were staring out the windows with amazement.

"Isn't that the man who was in here with you a while ago?" my wife was asked by a restaurant employee.

"No," she said. "The man who was with me was my husband and had on a white shirt and was sane. The man outside has on a brown shirt and is *in*sane."

I say a tooth counts as an inanimate object.

About four years ago, on a Friday night, I got one of those all-time toothaches, the kind that comes on you only when you can't get to a dentist until Monday.

Over the weekend, I bought up, and used, all the oil of clove that was available in Manhattan. I also set an Anacin record.

I spent Saturday and Sunday with tears in my eyes and everything throbbing from the top of my head through my shoulder blades. I might add that I have about as low a threshold for pain as I do for any minor inconvenience.

I finally got to the dentist on Monday morning, still in pain, still tearful, still in pain, blinded with hate.

"This is an upper-jaw tooth," Dr. Klein said. "I think I can save it."

"I want it out," I said. "I want that fucker out and I want it out *now.*"

"You really can't afford to lose it," he said.

"I don't care if I have to eat Cream of Wheat the rest of my life, get that son of a bitch out of my goddamn mouth!"

He pulled the tooth.

I took it from the tray.

Leaving, I walked a few calm steps down 50th Street, but I couldn't wait any longer. I stopped, removed the tooth from my pocket, and placed it on the sidewalk.

I leaned over to speak to the tooth.

"Had some fun, did you?" I said. "Well, your fun's over, pal."

With that, I stomped on the tooth with my right heel.

And again, for good measure.

Passersby might have heard what I then said to the dust particles on the pavement.

"*Now* hurt somebody, you lousy motherfucker," I said, and walked on up the street, as happy and self-satisfied as I've ever been in my life.

The Deal on Food

FOOD HAS ALWAYS RATED VERY HIGH ON THE LIST OF THINGS PEOPLE like to eat. You would think, therefore, that in this plentiful country of ours, food would be in evidence on almost every dinner table. Sadly, this is no longer true. The fact is, there are now only two days out of the year, Thanksgiving and Christmas, when we can be assured of seeing food on a dinner table—and that's because our grandmothers have stubbornly held the line and manage to serve food on these holidays in bitter opposition to Duane, Colin, Trevor, Randall, and America's other precious chefs who plan to stamp out food by the year 1990. This being the case, I look forward more than ever to Thanksgiving and Christmas dinner, because I know I can count on something to eat: a nice roasted turkey without kiwi, dressing without *radicchio,* giblet gravy without prawns, mashed potatoes without grapes, and green beans cooked in salt pork instead of Giorgio perfume. Real food, in other words. Food, hold the fag.

Yeah, I get angry about food today. That's because I grew up on food. I never ate a peanut-butter-and-carambola sandwich, okay? I never said, "Meemaw, can I have some more of that jicama-and-*babaco* salad you do so well?" And if a wrinkled, purple leaf—a salad savoy, they call it—had ever made its way into my grandmother's kitchen, it would have had its ass kicked by a good old American head of lettuce.

It's clearly time for food eaters to take a tough stand on the issue of food. If we don't, a hearty meal in another couple of years will consist of a mesquite-smoked quail's egg sitting on a little bed of tomato ice. Which brings to mind an important question: Who the fuck ever ate a tomato snow cone?

When I say we should take a tough stand on food, I mean murder. I urge every food eater in the United States to go out and kill one precious chef immediately.

There would still be thousands of precious chefs around, but they might get the idea that food eaters were serious about retaliation and go back to their old, familiar pleasures: mounting campaigns against smokers in San Francisco, designing clothes that don't fit anyone who weighs more than 98 pounds, selling new draperies and Victorian chairs to people who don't need them, and keeping the Broadway musical in a state of tuneless, pretentious incoherence.

These pursuits used to be enough to keep the precious people occupied. Of course, this was before they came out of the closet, which is where they were happiest—and so were we. Out of the closet, however, they've grown restless. They've obviously decided to devote their energies to making all food look like Monet's lilies. It's not entirely coincidental that the gay-rights movement started about the same time as the public's unwitting acceptance of green pasta, *arugula*, anchovy paste, and blood orange, the "connoisseur's citrus." It was during those lurid days that I happened to gag on a piece of zucchini that some precious chef had cleverly disguised as a French fry.

"What the fuck was *that*?" I said, spitting on the floor of a homey Manhattan hangout that a Texas friend insists on referring to as "Ilene's."

"Zucchini," somebody said, smiling and reaching for a zucchini.

"It looks like a French fry."

"It's summer squash."

"You're shitting me."

The nearest disinfectant was my glass of J&B. I poured it down my neck. Moments later, I sampled the platter of onion rings.

"Jesus Christ!" I blurted out, trying to swallow. "What happened to the onion rings?"

"This is calamari," I was informed by the adventuress who had ordered it.

"Who . . . ?"

"Squid."

I stared at the woman incredulously. Two friends at the table noticed the look on my face and began digging foxholes.

"Squid . . . ?"

"Try some; it's good."

"Squid?" I said again, glaring. "Like in octopus squid? Like that thing it took John Wayne and Ray Milland an hour to kill in *Reap the Wild Wind*?"

"It's not the same thing."

"The fuckers eat submarines!"

I looked around the table. Two of my companions were motioning for the check. The others sank deeper into their chairs.

"That's it for fags," I said. "I mean, fuck it. They've got Broadway. They've got half of Hollywood. They've got books, museums, fashion. They've got furniture. What is it, antiques don't keep 'em busy? Now they want French fries and onion rings? They're gonna take *squash* and *squid* and make 'em look like *my* French fries and onion rings? I'm gonna go chip all their fucking antique vases."

In the next breath, I'm afraid I unleashed a dialogue.

" 'What are your plans, Colin—after we come out of the closet, I mean?' 'I'm not sure, Randall. I've been giving some thought to food.' 'In what sense?' 'Oh, just various ways to fuck it up, generally.' 'Sounds like fun. With mousse alone, the possibilities are limitless.' 'Actually, I've been thinking a lot about colors. Yellow, orange, green, mauve—a few mottled tones, perhaps.' 'With food, you mean?' 'Yes.' 'Now that you mention it, food has never, *never* kept pace with the four-color process of magazine printing.' 'Well, one of the problems, of course, is that it comes in so many odd shapes. If food could be confined to stringy little things or small ovals, let's say, preferably those with a soft, creamy texture, there wouldn't be any real need to change it. Veggies, for instance—they should all have a green skin and a yellowy flesh.' 'Heaven, Colin. Absolute heaven! Do you *know,* can you *imagine* how many people we can piss off if we really get heavy into food?' "

I suppose my eyes were ablaze as I then said in my own voice, "Yeah, I know *one,* you tender-crisp, goat-cheese, zucchini-squid, no-smoking assholes!"

A woman idly said, "I didn't know you did drugs."

"I don't do that shit!" I snapped. "I hate that shit! This is *me* talking—a food guy! A guy who doesn't drink skim milk and wear those fucking Everlast weights around his ankles when he goes to the deli, all right? Let me tell you about food. Food is brown and white and not crinkly. Okay, it's orange sometimes—if it's cheese. Maybe maroon—if it's pinto beans. I'll give you two kinds of green. Lettuce green—and none of that Bibb or romaine shit—and dark green for green beans, which you cook in lard if you don't have a ham bone or a slab of bacon around. Don't get the white mixed up with cheese. You want Swiss cheese on a cheeseburger, go to the West Side! The only time cheese can be white is when it's on a goddamn pizza! Food don't make noise, either. Like when you bite into some kind of vegetable that's been steamed and you hear a crack, that's bullshit! Only four kinds of food can make noise. A taco makes noise. A potato chip makes noise. Corn on the cob makes noise. And the lower half of an ice-cream cone makes noise. You want to gimme popcorn, don't you? Wrong. Popcorn don't make noise if it's got enough butter on it. The key to good food is grease. Grease got us through the Depression; grease is coming back. You know the first thing grease is gonna do? Go round up aspic and start kicking ass. That'll be some fucking blood bath, man, and I don't want to miss it. Who needs a drink?"

Nobody. I'd cleared the room.

I'm sorry my friends didn't get to hear about the prison plans. In a better world, precious chefs would do time for the following crimes:

1. Putting sugar in corn bread.
2. Putting tomatoes and/or kidney beans in chili.
3. Putting anchovies in anything.
4. Cooking fried chicken in cornmeal batter like it's some kind of fucking fish.
5. Putting mushrooms in anything.
6. Using seed buns for cheeseburgers.
7. Not using enough salt and pepper on everything but the Haägen-Dazs.
8. Saying bad things about grease.
9. Not frying bacon crispy-chewy.
10. Not frying eggs runny-hard.
11. Not cooking meat well-done pink.
12. Getting the spaghetti sauce too fucking red and splattering it over your plate.
13. Leaving strangers in the chicken and dumplings.
14. Pushing mousse.
15. Inventing trout pizza.
16. Serving tomatoes that have cancer in the center.
17. Sneering at cold meatloaf sandwiches.
18. Trying to "liven up" the tuna salad with weird crap.
19. Putting sweet sauce on meat.
20. Fat omelettes.
21. Putting sour cream on enchiladas.
22. Calling it barbecue if it doesn't come from Texas.
23. Fucking around with aspic.

24. Sneering at Navy beans and thinking they're supposed to be blue.
25. Making any dessert that's not strawberry shortcake or peach cobbler.

It would be remiss of me not to comment on some foods of the world.

Chinese food: That pork stuff you roll up in a leaf of straight lettuce is okay, but the rest is shoelaces and sweet-and-sour coat buttons.

Japanese food: Some guy throws knives up in the air and a raw thing crawls out of your bean sprouts.

Indian food: Curry makes your armpits glow.

French food: Omelettes, soup, French fries, bread. Otherwise, you're looking at fat duck and puréed rabbit.

Italian food: If you haven't been to Italy or New York City, you haven't eaten it.

Mexican food: Tex-Mex is the only kind that's worth a damn, so if you can't go to Texas, go to Juanita's in New York or Jacksonville Beach, Fla., where my wife knows how to do it right.

Deli food: If you haven't been to New York City, you haven't eaten it.

California cuisine: "I'll just have a little dish of *feijoas* with fern on the side and perhaps a glass of *babaco*—and get me out of here quick, asshole, so I can go get something to eat."

The last thing you need to know about food is how to fix a good cheeseburger, which is mostly what you're going to eat, anyhow.

First, don't charcoal the meat unless you want it to taste like charcoal and remind you of your neighbor's backyard in the '50s.

Cook the meat in a skillet with plenty of grease. This is after you've chopped up onions and mashed them into the meat and showered the meat with salt and pepper.

Put mustard *and* mayonnaise on the bun, and dill chips, straight lettuce, and a slice of tomato that doesn't have a malignancy in the middle.

Put double cheese (orange, American) on the meat while it sizzles in the skillet. Put the bun on top of the cheese. Mash down on the bun two or three times with the spatula while the meat is cooking.

If you do all this right, juice will run down your wrist when you bite into the cheeseburger.

I guess by now you get the idea that I don't buy that myth about how you can't be too rich or too thin. People who like precious chefs fall for that shit. The line that suits me best is the one about the perfect Englishman. The food I don't eat, I wear.

SPORTS
MOVIES

What Are They?

SPORTS MOVIES FOR THE MOST PART TEND TO BE EMBARRASSING, disappointing, naive, silly, nowhere close to reality, and simple-minded, but this doesn't make them different from most movies about most other subjects.

Sports movies are also considered to be bad box office, which again doesn't make them different from most movies.

It would be interesting someday to see what a sports movie would do at the box office if it weren't embarrassing, disappointing, naive, silly, nowhere close to reality, and simple-minded, but it's not likely that this will ever be tried because Hollywood knows best.

In this context, the term Hollywood applies to the people in Hollywood who have power—the power to say yes to a project and give you the money—and those directors who are deemed to be reliable by the studios because, for one odd reason or another, they have presided over "hits," or at least pictures that didn't lose a great sum of money.

A director who has presided over a picture that was only an "artistic success" is pure fucking dog meat and may never work again.

One of these days, Hollywood is going to make the all-time sports movie. A baseball pitcher with only one leg will turn to football before he catches an incurable disease, brought on by his marriage to Teresa Wright. He will grow another leg and become a quarterback, but he will get kidnapped before the big game by the statue of Tecumseh at Annapolis, which will have strangely come to life. He will fight Tecumseh for the heavyweight title, in slow motion, to the sound of the *Rocky* theme, and win, and thus earn the right to go to the big game, which will turn out to be a combination surfing contest and automobile race. No characters connected with the film will bear any resemblance to persons living or dead, except for the brain-dead audience.

Semi-Tough *Goes to Hollywood*

IT ALL BEGAN WITH A PIECE OF PAPER IN A TYPEWRITER AND A MAN staring at it, wondering where a character named Billy Clyde Puckett would go after the first paragraph. It ended a few years later with Burt Reynolds zigzagging his way to a touchdown on a play that a script girl labeled, "117 apple, 28 frame."

Semi-Tough, the novel, went to Hollywood about four years after I wrote it, and about a year and a half after David Merrick tried to make it into a Broadway musical.

I was in favor of the Broadway musical idea, intrigued with what type of melody Cole Porter or Irving Berlin would set to a ballad called *Niggers Go Long.*

But it didn't work, and I vividly remember the day that David Merrick and I decided that it wouldn't work.

We were in David's office, eagerly looking forward to hearing the first four songs that had been written by a modestly successful song-writing team, whose names I will withhold as a favor to their close friends and kin.

I had begun to worry about one of them, frankly, a few weeks earlier when he had handed me a newspaper clipping about Evel Knievel, saying he thought it would be "very valuable" when I started the rewrite of the libretto, "the book," for the musical.

This surprised and troubled me on two counts. One, I didn't know the libretto needed rewriting, and two, I didn't know what Evel Knievel had to do with pro football.

One of the men sat down at the piano in Merrick's office, and the other stood next to it.

We heard a song about apples.

We heard a song about acorns.

We heard a song about homesickness.

And finally we heard a song I didn't really listen to all that closely because one of the song-writing team introduced it to us as a number that Billy *Jack* Puckett and the leading lady would sing to each other as they roller-skated through Bloomingdale's.

David Merrick thanked them graciously while I lit a cigarette, but as soon as they were out of the door, he turned to me and said:

"I think we'd better make a movie."

I passed up an opportunity to take a shot at the screenplay. Busy going to sports events. But I liked the screenplay that Ring Lardner Jr. wrote. So did Merrick. So did everybody but a man named Michael Ritchie, who was hired by United Artists to direct the film.

Nobody knows more about life, death, divorce, laughter, sorrow, or even pro football than a movie director, even though nobody knows how you get to be a movie director in the first place.

There is an old story about a writer trying to become a director for Sam Goldwyn.

Goldwyn balked, saying to the man, "You're a writer, not a director."

The man pointed out that Frank Capra, John Ford, King Vidor, they all had to start somewhere.

"Don't you believe it," Goldwyn said.

There is also an old saying around Hollywood, which goes like this: It doesn't matter whether you like the director's work or not—if he can get the goddamn project off the ground, go with him.

Michael Ritchie was a nice guy and he had done some films I liked, but I knew he was going to be wrong for *Semi-Tough* when I discovered he had gone to Harvard (trouble), lived near San Francisco (more trouble), had read a book titled *Powers of Mind* (big trouble), and was interested in the consciousness movement (bigger trouble).

Ritchie promptly dumped Ring Lardner Jr.'s script and ordered a new one by Walter Bernstein, one that the director practically dictated.

He then explained to me, "The screenplay has to transcend the episodic nature of the novel. All I've done is take a relationship hinted at in the final pages of the book and expand on them. Think of it as a few years later in the lives of your characters."

I said I would do that as soon as I stopped thinking of it as a movie that could have been about pro football instead of consciousness-raising.

I added, "I don't know how to break this to you, Michael, but they've already made *Bob and Carol and Ted and Alice*."

Along about here, Burt Reynolds and Kris Kristofferson were signed to play Billy Clyde and Shake Tiller, or Butch Gifford and Sundance Meredith, or even Butch Jurgensen and Sundance Hawkins, as some people thought of them, including me.

Good choices, I felt.

As for Barbara Jane Bookman, everybody wanted Candy Bergen—Burt, Kris, Merrick, me.

So Michael Ritchie picked Jill Clayburgh.

Nothing against Jill Clayburgh. She's a wonderful actress and a nifty lady; she just wasn't the Barbara Jane that all of us had envisioned, though she gave it the old college try.

The NFL, of course, refused to cooperate with the movie, taking the position that America didn't need to see athletes using naughty language or discussing the economy with ladies on barstools.

One NFL owner was delighted to cooperate, however. He was Joe Robbie, owner of the Miami Dolphins. Which was why Billy Clyde and Shake wound up playing for a Miami team instead of a New York team, as in the novel.

People who later saw the movie asked, as I did at the time of the filming, how it was possible for Miami of the American Conference to be in a play-off game with Green Bay of the National Conference.

Michael Ritchie only smiled and said, "Let's say there's been a realignment."

The day they shot a scene in the movie where Burt, Kris, and Jill discussed the "rating list" of women was one of the most depressing days of my life.

They are sitting around a swimming pool. Kris thought he spotted a Nine, the nearest thing to perfection. Jill claimed to be a Ten.

"No such thing as a Ten," Burt said.

Jill: "In college, you said Emily Kirkland was a Ten."

Burt: "No, I said Emily Kirkland and her sister *together* were a Ten."

In the novel, a One was the best, not a Ten. It was based on things that made sense: who's Number One in college football, what was Number One on the best-seller lists, the record charts.

I had been lobbying to get the dialogue changed ever since the production began.

I said to the director, "If a Ten is supposed to be the best, what's an Eleven?"

"Good question," he said. "I've heard it both ways. One to ten, ten to one. I think it's something we can't win either way."

"So why not go with the novel?" I said.

"This is the movie," he smiled.

There was more than one moment on location when I thought of the old Hollywood joke: World War II would never have happened if somebody had let Hitler direct movies.

In the end, *Semi-Tough* wasn't a horrible movie in my opinion, although it should have been called *Son of Semi.*

The final result reminded me of a conversation I once had with a group of friends about which movie had been more faithful to the novel than any movie any of us had ever seen.

Gone With the Wind got the consensus vote.

"That's right," somebody said. "In *Gone With the Wind,* they only left out two of Scarlett's children."

Dead Solid Perfect *Goes to Hollywood*

FOR A FEW NAIVE AND FOOLISH WEEKS IN 1988, THE YEAR OF THE Gerbil, plus Deane Beman, I went around thinking that everybody I had ever known in golf would be happy with the news that Hollywood was in serious danger of making a feature film, a romantic comedy, about the pro golf tour. After all, Hollywood hadn't exactly been making movies about the tour every day; in fact, there hadn't been one in 37 years, not since *Follow the Sun,* a film in which

Glenn Ford, portraying Ben Hogan, wore a cap too big for him and swung the club like me. Actually, not as good as me.

The movie going into production at HBO Pictures was called *Dead Solid Perfect.* This title pleased me greatly since it happened to be the title of the novel I had written back in 1974. I was also pleased that the movie would try to be about pro golfers instead of laser beams, robo-creatures, and teenage nightmares on Rambo Street. It would attempt to be, substantially, the same story as *Dead Solid Perfect,* the book. An unknown touring pro finds love and laughter on and off the fairways, as well as in various bedrooms, and finally conquers his self-doubt and wins a big tournament, and wins back his wife, the end.

The director was a talented filmmaker named Bobby Roth, who, by happy coincidence, was a golf nut. Despite his beard and sneakers, Bobby traveled with a good golf swing and played to a 5-handicap at Brentwood Country Club in Los Angeles.

The novel had been sold for a movie 10 years earlier, and although a lot of James Garners, Nick Noltes, and Roy Scheiders had expressed an interest to star in it, no director would ever attach himself to it because he felt insecure about trying to shoot the golf stuff, and no studio was overly enthusiastic about making a "sports movie."

"Sports don't do foreign" is my favorite thing a studio mogul ever said to me.

No matter who buys a property from you—in this case it was David Merrick again—you still need a studio.

In Hollywood, you can point out to the studio bosses that *Chariots of Fire* was an artistic and commercial success, but they will say, "*Chariots of Fire* wasn't a sports movie, it was about people."

You can tell them that *Slap Shot* was the funniest sports movie ever made, and made money, but they will say, "*Slap Shot* wasn't a sports movie, it was about Paul Newman."

After acquiring a director, the next thing *DSP* needed was a couple of leading men who could swing a golf club without looking like interior decorators on the takeaway and hammer throwers on the follow-through.

Hollywood can perform incredible magic. It can take us into outer space, re-create bloody wars, make midgets appear to be six feet tall, pass off one actor after another as a raging heterosexual, and make us fall in love with women who in real life are the most conniving, insecure, self-serving bitches God ever put on earth, but

Hollywood magic can't give a man a golf swing if he doesn't have one.

Bobby Roth assured me of this.

That's why it was a nice thing that we got Randy Quaid to play Kenny and Brett Cullen to play Donny. They both looked, acted, and could swing the club like pros—Randy was even a 6-handicapper.

Another lucky break was getting Jack Warden to play Bad Hair, Randy's sponsor on the tour.

I knew that certain touring pros would laugh at a specific grillroom scene when they heard the following dialogue:

Bad Hair: "It's too bad your wife don't like golf, Kenny. Want my advice?"

Kenny: "I'll take any advice I can get where Beverly's concerned."

Bad Hair: "Get rid of her."

Actually, I'm not sure the pros laughed at all at this—it may have hit too close to home.

The women in the movie, in the unbiased opinion of the screenwriter and executive producer, both of whom happened to be me, were more perfect than dead solid.

The luscious Kathryn Harrold *was* Beverly, Randy Quaid's gorgeous, cynical, wisecracking wife. Corinne Bohrer *was* Janie Ruth, the cute and wicked bimbo who takes up with Randy for a while. And DeLane Matthews *was* Katie Beth, the most understanding tour wife who was ever married to a cocky, gallivanting, big-name golf star.

While the cast and crew were being assembled, we were also looking for locations to film and begging for as much cooperation as we could get from the golfing "establishment."

Enter Deane Beman.

The commissioner of the PGA Tour glanced at an early draft of the script and decided that it wasn't in what he called "the best interest of the Tour" for anyone associated with the tour—players, sponsors, golf courses, country clubs, tour staff, TV people—to cooperate with us.

Egad, Deane noted, there were four-letter words in the script, and a touring pro was even going to wind up in bed with a lady who wasn't his wife.

"That's not the image we want to project," Deane said.

I said, "Well, Deane, we all know touring pros never cuss or get divorced."

Terry Hanson, the Tour's director of communications, sought

me out and said, "Surely, you can appreciate Deane's position. He doesn't think Pete Rozelle would cooperate with a movie like this about the National Football League."

"I guess commissioners have a problem with humor," I said. "I remember how Rozelle wouldn't cooperate with *Semi-Tough,* a comedy, but he cooperated with *Black Sunday,* a movie about a terrorist who tries to blow up the Super Bowl. Tell Deane I'll write in a part for a lunatic to blow up the back nine at TPC."

Beman didn't institute an official boycott of the movie—there are limits to what he can tell the big-name players they can do, anyhow—but he let certain sponsors know that if they allowed our cameras on the premises, he might seriously have to reexamine their tournament dates and futures.

The movie lost a considerable amount of authenticity, or what Hollywood calls "texture," because Deane Beman didn't want to see the pros humanized. He liked them better as Nabisco robots.

We were already shooting around Fort Worth and Dallas when I got a surprising phone call from my friend Ben Crenshaw.

Ben had agreed to give us a half day of his time, playing himself in a cameo role at Colonial Country Club. All he was expected to do was hit a few golf shots and say whatever came to him naturally as he appeared in a threesome with Peter Jacobson, also playing himself, and Randy Quaid. In the script, this was the last round of a fictitious Colonial tournament.

But now Ben was calling to say he had changed his mind.

He had gone over the three pages of the script I had shown him, to put him at ease, and noticed there were some naughty words that would be spoken by the Jack Warden character, who would be in the gallery consisting of Colonial members and hired extras.

"There's some bad language in there," Ben said.

"Yeah, it's sort of the way people talk."

"I feel bad about letting you down," he said, "but, dang, there's these little old ladies, you know?"

"What little old ladies?"

"My fans."

"I remember when your fans were all nineteen-year-old showstoppers. Are they little old ladies now?"

"Those little old ladies are going to wonder why in the world I'm in this movie. I feel like a heel, but I just can't do it."

The next day on location, Peter Jacobson had some fun at Crenshaw's expense, in Crenshaw's absence.

Off-camera, Peter would say to the crowd, "Hi, I'm Ben Cren-shaw. I used to cuss a lot but now I'm pure."

About a week later we got the cheery news that ABC-TV would not permit my friends Jack Whitaker, Dave Marr, and Ed Sneed to appear in the movie as themselves, as the announcers at our fictitious U.S. Open. Conflict of interest, it was ordained by the network, by one of those striving, ass-kissing tap-dancers who always manage to gain a foothold in upper management in corporate America.

Happily, there *was* cooperation on the part of countless people or the movie could never have been made.

Colonial Country Club in Fort Worth, where many of the members are old friends of mine, doubled as both the Colonial National Invitational and the "Gulf Coast Classic." Glen Garden Country Club in Fort Worth, where Ben Hogan and Byron Nelson caddied as kids, became "Shady Creek" in West Texas, the site of a hustling game. Mira Vista Country Club in Fort Worth hosted the "Titleist Invitational." PGA West in Palm Springs hosted the "Palm Springs Open" as well as a Las Vegas tournament. And our fictitious U.S. Open was played over three different courses, from Industry Hills near L.A. to La Cumbre and Montecito in Santa Barbara, with crowd shots blended in from the real U.S. Open at the Country Club in Brookline, Mass. Upset of the decade. The United States Golf Association cooperated with us when the PGA Tour would not.

Scattering our fictitious Open over three courses in two cities enabled Randy Quaid to hit the longest tee shot in the history of golf. He once swung at the ball in L.A. and it landed in a fairway in Santa Barbara. Hollywood magic.

Randy spent three agonizing hours on another day trying to make a 25-foot putt that broke about 16 inches to the right.

I went over to Jimmy Simons, the assistant director, at one point and said, "Nobody can make a putt that breaks right. Why can't it break left?"

"Talk to him," said Jimmy, nodding at Bobby Roth. "All I say is, 'Roll,' 'Lunch,' and 'Wrap.' He says, 'Action.' "

Randy finally sank the putt and the extras, for the 33rd time, leaped and shouted.

Kathryn Harrold gave us all a battle cry for the movie.

There was this tender scene where she was supposed to leave Randy, fed up with the tour. Her parting line was an old tour expression: "Fairways and greens, Kenny."

On the first take, she looked at him sadly and said, "Freeways and tees, Ken." Cut!

Movie-making is a tedious, torturous business. It can seem pretty boring to the casual observer. Up at dawn. Shoot till dark. Have meetings. Deal with tomorrow's problems. Babysit a performer. Look at dailies. Sneak a pizza. Sleep a few hours. Go at it again.

You stand there and watch a scene played that seems to go fairly well, but they do it again—and again. Over his shoulder. Over her shoulder. From a distance. In close. More accent on this word or that phrase. "Go again, please—back to one."

A truth about Hollywood is that most directors hate writers. They don't want them on the set. A writer is apt to talk to the actors and actresses and get them confused.

This wasn't the case with Bobby Roth. He wanted me around as much as I cared to be. "These are your people," he would say. I would thank him but accuse him of trying to shift the blame.

He even insisted on my wife and me doing a Hitchcock thing.

Interior, hallway, motel, night.

Kenny and Janie Ruth have been having a swell time in their room but now they're thirsty and out of ice.

Unclad, Janie Ruth walks briskly down the hall to refill the ice bucket. I should mention that this particular Janie Ruth, unclad, would not have to apologize to any centerfold you had ever seen.

On her way back down the hall, she passes my wife and me—the startled couple.

"Hi," said Corinne Bohrer, or Janie, cheerfully, whereupon she leaped into Randy's arms and they vanished into the motel room.

This was Take One.

"What was *that?*" June Jenkins asked.

"Somebody's daughter," I shrugged, and we walked away.

Ad-libs.

Bobby Roth cleared his throat and said, "Uh . . . can we try it again—but without the dialogue?"

After all of this came the months of editing, patching, scoring, mixing, and looping, those processes by which all of the rehearsing and shooting becomes the actual movie you see on the screen.

When I first viewed the final product, I wished it had benefited from more "texture," but I wasn't ashamed to be associated with it.

And I had only one thing to say to anyone who didn't like it.

They would just have to wait for Deane Beman to write, produce, and direct his own movie about golf: *Follow the Logo,* the heart-warming story of a big-name pro who falls in love with his Nabisco visor, drowns in obscurity on the all-exempt tour, but achieves immortality in a thrilling series of corporate outings.

TRAVEL

What Is It?

IN SPORTS, TRAVEL MEANS NEVER HAVING TO PAY YOUR OWN WAY. IT also means somebody is always giving you money to go to another town and get drunk.

The main thing to know about travel is how to handle your expense account.

Without a receipt, breakfast is $24.99, lunch is $24.99, dinner is $24.99.

With a receipt, breakfast is $56.27, lunch is $89.42, and dinner is $237.40.

That's in Shreveport.

Anywhere else, the figures double and often triple.

The sports personality you most generally entertain at breakfast, lunch, or dinner is Red Strafalino, who has been known to play every sport but polo.

Red Strafalino would never play polo.

T. Phillip de Menil plays polo.

Most sports travel will take you to a Marriott somewhere, usually on the opposite side of town from the stadium, fieldhouse, ball park, or golf course.

If at all possible, never let a travel department in the company book your plane reservations. The lady in the travel department will make you depart on a prop jet at midnight in a blizzard and route you through Cincinnati with three more stops before you reach your destination, in any direction.

A tip about turning in your first expense report: Start them out big. You have nowhere to go but up.

Dateline Erotica

LONDON

I TYPE THIS DATELINE WITH GREAT ENTHUSIASM FOR IT WAS IN MY
journalistic youth that datelines seemed more important than food,
drink, women, cars—everything but cigarettes.

Back then, working on a paper in Fort Worth, Tex., a fellow
rarely got to travel so most of us were convinced that when we *were*
sent somewhere on an assignment, it could only enhance the quality of our prose.

Datelines demanded great literary efforts, we thought. Datelines made you try harder.

But the results, as I remember them, were often calamitous.
They ran along these lines:

BEAUMONT—He was an old man who pitched alone in a ball
park only 28 miles from the sea.

WACO—Call me Ishmael, but only if you can't reach me at the
Southwest Conference Track & Field meet.

WICHITA FALLS—If Red Grange was poetry and symphony on
the football field, what can you say about Billy Don Vogel?

SAN ANTONIO—They marched through the old city like a
river of steel. You never saw so many golfers in town for the State
Junior.

HOUSTON—It wasn't a particularly warm day if you were a fruit
fly, but for a Dallas Cowboy. . . .

For those of us who stuck with typing for a living, we would
see the datelines grow more exotic. Alas, a chance to display our
sense of history.

ROME—I looked up at the balcony where Mussolini had stood
so often and thought to myself, "That's a seafood restaurant?"

PARIS—We landed at dawn and went straight to the broad
boulevard lined with chestnut trees, but there were no seats left at
any of the sidewalk cafes. They had landed two hours ahead of us.

Some of them were from Stanford and some of them were from Middlebury.

Believe it or not, there was a time in this world when nobody went anywhere except on business or a troop ship. This was in a dark age known as BBAT—Before Bonus Air Travel.

I speak of that period in history when it was possible for a kid to reach the age of 17 without spending a summer in the south of France.

It was a giddy time. You could walk into almost any airline terminal and not have to wade through 700 Duke sophomores just to stand in line at a check-in counter behind the entire population of Okinawa.

As for London, it is a pleasure to report that it's still my favorite city despite the fact that there are no English here.

If you want to see Dallas, for example, go to Harrods.

I decided to look for an English person this week so I went to this little, out-of-the-way Italian restaurant on the Chelsea Embankment near the Battersea Bridge. For years, it had been a hangout for Fleet Street scribes and American journalists.

Not now. All of the tables were occupied by people from Columbus, Ga.

Next, I tried my favorite secluded pub, the Grenadier in Knightsbridge. No English in sight. But everybody from New York City was there. I suggested a name change to the management: P. J. Grenadier's.

Finally, it came to me. I would find some English people at Motcomb's, down in a cellar, a French bistro in Belgravia. Nobody knew about Motcomb's but me and the English.

"Hey, old buddy," a voice said as I walked in.

The voice had a Texas ring to it.

I turned to see a vaguely familiar person.

"What in the world are you doing here?" I asked.

The man said, "Remember the night we got drunk in Fort Worth? You told us where to go in London. Well, here we are! Come meet our group!"

Bay Area Blues

AMAZING THAT I HAVE BEEN THE ONE TO DISCOVER WHAT HAPPENED to Ambrose Bierce after all these years and all of the academic discussion on the subject. He walked out of John's Grill one day and got swallowed by this huge, psychopathic fern.

The fern had gone berserk, escaped from its hanging pot, and was attacking innocent people on the street, all because some San Francisco restaurateur had spoken to it too harshly.

Ferns do that out here. If somebody doesn't recite avant-garde poetry to a fern twice daily, the fern loses control, grabs up a total stranger, and dangles him by his heels over a table of "California cuisine," which is the next best thing to eating astronaut food through a straw.

But Ambrose Bierce could have suffered a worse fate. Had he stood around idly on the sidewalk outside John's Grill, which is a short stagger from the *Chronicle* and *Examiner,* a joint first made famous by Bierce and then by Dashiell Hammett, he might have succumbed to death by wine discussion.

A new survey, soon to be made public, will confirm that wine discussion has become San Francisco's No. 1 killer.

Serious wine-discussers are everywhere in San Francisco, even in the media, and of course there's nothing sadder than a journalist who's serious about wine.

Newshounds are supposed to drink whiskey and beer, and usually out of vats.

It never seems to do any good, but I keep telling my San Francisco friends that there are only two things you need to know about wine.

1. It's red or white.
2. The more it tastes like water, the more it costs.

People can suffer other horrible fates in San Francisco, I've learned.

There are many depressing tales of writers and artists who turned to carpentry after discovering that no one had heard of them once they crossed a bridge.

In this city where the martini was said to have been invented, there is the lurid story of a man who drank so many of them at one of the countless Martini Festivals that are held annually, he wound up in a decorative center in Sausalito being sold as a piece of driftwood.

Also distressing is the story of a man who died a few years ago during one of the great natural disasters of our time, a phenomenon that could only have occurred in San Francisco.

I speak of that day when everybody in the city, all at once, removed the umbrellas from their drinks. The city suddenly dropped 50 feet, straight down—as did the man.

Though trapped in the rubble, he might have been saved, except that his screams for help were interpreted by passersby as the words of another North Beach poet, reading his work aloud.

A majority of San Franciscans, I've noticed over the years, take it far too personally that San Francisco is not New York. A moment after you say hello to them, they begin to brag about their opera, their symphony, their art galleries, their writers-at-work, their wine, their climate, and the latest advances in their spinach salads.

What I generally do in self-defense is call it Dallas with bridges, a city culturally linked by the dots that lead from one Herb Caen item to the next.

The San Francisco natives I number among my friends know that I secretly like the place, that I always enjoy hanging out at the Washington Square Bar & Grill, which has become press headquarters for anything that happens in town.

In there, we pretend that Ambrose Bierce and Robert Louis Stevenson and Jack London and Dashiell Hammett are still around somewhere, and that the city is still what Will Irwin once described as the gateway to the untamed Pacific, the back eddy of European civilization.

It's just that I have to keep reminding my friends that their city isn't *that* great. After all, it hasn't had a really good gold rush in 140 years and it hasn't shown us a really good earthquake in over 80 years and it hasn't invented a decade since the '60s, so what's the big deal?

Where Drooling Is Optional

IT'S ALWAYS FUN TO SEE FOO FOO AND NONNIE AND STUDY THEIR rare collection of Euro-trash yuppies. They are really what Palm Beach is all about, give or take a lisp.

I hadn't seen Foo Foo since her eighth divorce, and I hadn't seen Nonnie since she had gone to the Porsche plant to have the cracks in her face filled in with metallic paint.

The first thing I noticed was that Foo Foo and Nonnie had both had their knees done so they could wear miniskirts again.

Being too rich and too thin, their knees had started to look like a dog's head.

Dog's head knees on a rich skeleton are pretty unsightly, even in Palm Beach, where you can see almost anything imaginable when it comes to wealthy deformity.

The heavy burden of being rich and aimless has taken its toll on the gentlemen friends of Foo Foo and Nonnie. The men stand like question marks normally, but they take on the appearance of a giraffe when they attempt to speak, not that any of them have ever spoken an interesting sentence.

Foo Foo and Nonnie know how to keep themselves up. Now in their new knees and their miniskirts, they didn't look a day over 63 although both of them must be pushing 45 now.

I caught up with them on Worth Avenue, the main shopping street, where they were looking for some of those new blouses made out of alimony documents.

Foo Foo was buying Istanbul for her backyard, and Nonnie was buying Greece for her patio.

They took me to tea at this chic little place called the Euro-trash Cafe. Foo Foo drank six double martinis. Nonnie drank a quart of tequila.

I had a cup of something the waitress called coffee and I called molten amphetamine.

I observed that the ladies looked very happy.

"Of course we are," said Foo Foo. "We live in Palm Beach."

"But don't you ever yearn for an interesting conversation?"

"Heavens, no," Foo Foo said. "That's the beauty of Palm Beach. You don't have to *know* anything, you don't have to *do* anything, you just have to be here."

"What about the drooling?" I said. "I noticed a lot of drooling the last time I was here."

"It's still optional," Nonnie reported. "Most of the older men drool. That's why Euro-trash yuppies are so much in demand now. They're handsome, totally empty-headed, but they're too young to drool."

"How do you get around the furry legs?"

"Darling," Foo Foo explained, "they're only for evenings, for parties and balls. You wouldn't allow one in your pool."

Nonnie asked what I was doing in town.

"Golf tournament," I said.

"Oh, dear," she said. "I had forgotten they're still doing that sort of thing."

I wanted to get back to the Euro-trash yuppies. I asked if I could see some of them.

"Wrong time of year," Foo Foo said. "They're all in Provence."

"They'll be back in the fall," Nonnie said. "That's when things start to pick up. More funerals. More divorces. More fraud. More liposuction surgery."

I said, "I guess that would be the best time to come back and hear a conversation."

"About what?" Foo Foo asked.

"I don't know," I shrugged. "Anything."

Foo Foo smiled and said, "Darling, this is the most anyone in Palm Beach has talked for years."

Umlauts Vs. Hyphens

SOMEWHERE IN THE SWISS ALPS

A NIFTY WAR WOULD BE THE ONE WHERE THE SWISS GO UP AGAINST the Swedes. If it were truly bloody, if they could fire enough umlauts and hyphens at each other, we could get rid of 50 percent of the dullest people in the world.

The Swiss and Swedes can't help it because they're dull, of course. It has to do with geography.

Sweden is off over there somewhere near the Northern Lights, a bunch of reindeer, and Nobel Prizes. There have never been more than 22 people in Sweden at one time, except during World War II when several dozen Nazis were in and out of Stockholm on business and pleasure.

Ten of the 22 Swedes can't speak at all, owing to the fact that they are cross-country skiers and their tongues are frozen to their mustaches.

Of the other 12, six are blondes named Ingrid who spend most of their time making free love to two guys named Lars, which means they are all too busy to speak as well.

Groaning does not count as speaking in most civilized countries.

The other four Swedes are all named Sven. They are large, jovial businessmen who like to pound their fists on tables when they aren't brooding about life or an Ingmar Bergman movie.

I once had dinner with one of these jovial Svens. Between courses, he broke six pieces of furniture and three window panes as he said, jovially, "Ha-ho! Yes! Goot! Love! Fish! Sleep!"

It only seems that the Swiss are slightly more interesting than the Swedes. This is because of the terrain. Here in the Alps, a Swiss person has to hike up or down in order to go anywhere. The Swiss are always leaning, in other words.

There are no more Swiss than there are Swedes, actually. Twenty-two in all. Everyone else in Switzerland is a tourist.

It is also a lie that half of the Swiss speak French and the other half speak German. In fact, all 22 Swiss speak four languages: fondue, chocolate, wrist watch, and numbered account.

I conversed in all four of these languages one day after a ski race when I was trying to find my way back to the quaint little chalet I had rented in a quaint little village.

"Excuse me," I said to a Swiss person in a village that was quaint but wasn't mine. "Can you tell me how to get to Something-sur-le-Steep?"

"Fondue?"

"No, thank you."

"Chocolate?"

"No, thank you."

"Rolex?"

"Thanks, anyhow."

"Numbered account?"

"Another time, maybe. Where is Something-sur-le-Steep? I know it's around here somewhere. It's about this big. It has Alps, a steeple, some cows on a hill, a great deal of firewood, and people yodeling."

The Swiss person pointed straight up.

"Is that it?" I asked, staring at a ledge on a tall Alp.

"No, Raclette-sur-le-Steep is down here."

The Swiss person pointed to a dot at the bottom of a valley, and said, "But you must go up there to get down there. It is the way of the mountains."

"Where can I get a taxi?" I inquired.

"There are no taxis."

"I came here in a taxi."

"He is dead. The roads are treacherous."

"Is there a train?"

"Yes, every three minutes, but they all go to Montreux."

"Can I buy a car? How much is this one?"

"That is not a car."

"What is it?"

"My Rolex."

"It looks like it would carry two people to Something-sur-le-Steep."

"It is possible, yes."

"I'll take it—how much?"

"Are you on an expense account?"

"Yes."

"It is seven hundred thousand dollars."

"It's a deal," I said. "Fill it up with unleaded fondue and I'm outta here."

Vacation Spot

TO ME, A VACATION HAS ALWAYS BEEN SOMETHING YOU WENT ON and did nothing but eat, sleep, read, stroll, smoke, and not think about anything. Certainly you can imagine my surprise, then, when I came over here with my wife and a few American friends to watch Seve Ballesteros win another golf tournament and found out that I was also on a vacation.

No problem to combine work and play, it was decided by the Foreign Country Vacation Law.

I'll skip the part about the fact that it cost $400,000 for two weeks, not counting tips, and just take you through a typical day.

Up at dawn so the light would be just right for the Nikons when we went to see the castle where the king slaughtered four of his wives for taking too long to play the back nine at North Berwick.

But not to linger. We had to go to the antique shops in the old part of the city where a friend from Dallas could buy a chest and have it shipped home by bagpipe for only $12,765.

But not to linger there either. We had to go to the cashmere factory where all of us could buy $76,419 worth of sweaters, a saving of 12 cents off the price we would have paid in a country club pro shop in America.

Lunch was reserved in the most exquisite restaurant in Scotland. This was booked months in advance and we couldn't be late because the restaurant didn't serve past 1:57 P.M. We got there at 1:52 and enjoyed a nice, leisurely lunch that lasted until 2:30.

By 3:42 we had toured the museum and seen the heads of all wives the king had chopped off, and this meant it was time to seek out the loft where the little old lady could duplicate all of the jewelry that Lady McTavish ever wore to a sheep-shearing.

Time then for tea at the quaint country inn where we were staying, tea being the only reason to stay there, according to all the guide books.

Six watercress sandwiches later, we were on our way to five stately homes, one graveyard, and two abbeys.

This was pretty much of a mad dash because our dinner reservation at the second most exquisite restaurant in Scotland was for 8 o'clock sharp, booked months ahead of time.

The restaurant was in a rural part of Scotland, so dinner had to be finished by 10:17 in order to catch the last train back to the city.

It was essential to get back to the city by midnight because there would still be time to play 18 holes of golf at Old Dungeon, the course where Mary Queen of Scots invented the rut iron — and used it on a group of Scottish lords who had invented body odor.

The hours between 3 A.M. and 5 A.M. were spent hiring a limo and driver to retrace our steps and try to find the three passports and two books of travelers' checks that some of our friends had lost.

It was getting light again about 5:16 A.M., so it was decided that there could be no better time to go see another castle, the one where a king had beheaded three of his Pro-Am partners.

I could only stare wistfully at the guillotine and wish I had been one of them.

Vacations killed far too slowly for my taste.

Which Way to L.A.?

IT OCCURRED TO ME IN THE MIDDLE OF A COCKTAIL IN THE POLO Lounge one spring evening that I had been coming out to the Coast for over 30 years on the business of journalism and I had never seen Los Angeles. All I had ever seen were a few golf courses, the L.A. Coliseum, a restaurant in Santa Monica, another restaurant in Malibu, a handful of hideouts in Hollywood, and most of what is generally thought of as Beverly Hills, which is several rows of mansions and shops and an equally long row of maitre d's who somehow always seem to know when my expense account is due to land at LAX.

The only time I ever came close to seeing Los Angeles was on a Saturday back in 1967 when, after leaving the Coliseum and a football game, I got forced into the wrong lane on a freeway.

Six different freeways and three hours later, I was back at the Beverly Hills Hotel, proclaiming it to be what everybody refers to when they say they're going out to L.A.

I have rarely left since, for there is very little driving required if you stay at the Beverly Hills Hotel—it all comes to you, if not at poolside, where you can watch music company executives pretend to talk on the phone, then surely in the Polo Lounge, where you can watch producers and agents pretend to talk on the phone.

Actors and actresses used to frequent the Beverly Hills Hotel, but this was before they got overrun by shoe company owners from New Jersey and dentists from Cleveland.

From time to time, an actor or actress will still appear in the Polo Lounge, but the actor is usually an ex-actor who now owns a piece of a clothing store or a deli, and the actress is usually an ex-actress who has gone into real estate or facelifts.

Still it's fun to wallow in, or why else would I have become so intimate with Dino, Walter, and Nino, three gentlemen I personally helped enter the Hall of Fame of maitre d's?

Dino, Walter, and Nino ran the Polo Lounge like Hitler ran Germany, and this was as it should be or Beverly Hills wouldn't have been Los Angeles.

All three of them had the uncanny sense to know that there was a $20 bill in my hand as we greeted each other warmly.

What this did was always make sure that I got a booth on the left side of the room as you enter, one of only six precious booths on the left side, which was only four in actuality because Dino, Walter, and Nino liked to hold two open in case Clark Gable or Greg Bautzer came back to life.

It was always a pleasure to be hugged by Dino, Walter, or Nino.

"Ah, Mr. Jenson, how are you?" Dino would say. "I have your booth ready."

Out would come the guacamole and cheese dip.

Dino would ask how the picture was going.

"Fine," I would smile.

I became the only man in Los Angeles who ever produced a picture for $20.

"Ah, Mr. Jessup, how are you?" Walter would say in later years. "I have your booth ready."

Out would come a phone I didn't need.

"How is the series going?" Walter would ask.

"Fine," I would smile.

I became the only man in Los Angeles who ever produced a TV series for $20.

"Ah, Mr. Jennings, how are you?" Nino would say—or still says. "I have your booth ready."

Out would come a cigarette girl I didn't need.

"How is the pilot going?" Nino would ask, or will ask.

"Fine."

I became the only man in Los Angeles who ever produced a $20 pilot.

You may ask why anyone would enjoy sitting in the Polo Lounge for seven or eight hours at a time.

It's the overheards.

There is absolutely nowhere else in the world where you can hear a person say:

"Call it art if you want to, but I say *Romeo and Juliet* is just another fucking buddy picture."

Europe's Fun Couple

IN THIS CITY WHERE ELEGANT LADIES ONCE WORE DIAMOND swastikas on their evening gowns to embassy functions, there are no Nazis anywhere today, and according to the Man on the Street, there were never any Nazis here—they were all over there somewhere.

Shame on history, is all I can say about it. History should have perfected television sooner.

If TV had been around 50 years ago, we could have seen Nazis live and on tape at the height of their social season, which has often been referred to as 1939.

We could have watched old Doc Goebbels and his charming wife, Magda, dipping into the sauerbraten at a party old Herm Goering was throwing for Germany's Olympic hopefuls, who in 1940 would be going for the gold in dive-bombing and blitzkrieg.

But the biggest treat we missed was what could have been the best *Barbara Walters Special* ever taped. America's favorite hard-hitting interviewer would surely have visited with Europe's most talked-about couple, Adolf Hitler and Eva Braun, and asked them important questions about their likes, dislikes, hobbies, goals, future plans.

I like to think I know how it would have gone, so . . .

Here, now, are Barbara and tonight's guests in the Reich Chancellor's gaily decorated living room at Wilhelmstrasse 77, Berlin, W.8.

"Adolf, you and Eva have had a storybook romance. You, the busy dictator. She, the lowly photographer's assistant. Do you still have a warm relationship? Is there much touching?"

The Fuehrer glances at Eva, who sits next to him on a sofa. "Want to take that one?"

Eva blushes but says, "Yes, Barbara, we're still very much in love. I couldn't be happy with any other dictator."

Eva continues, saying, "The Fuehrer and I hold hands when we go for walks. He is a kind, thoughtful person. He gives me wonderful presents."

"What has he given you lately?" Barbara asks.

"Czechoslovakia."

The Fuehrer smiles as Eva gives him a peck on the cheek.

Barbara leans forward in her chair, leveling a stern gaze at the Fuehrer.

"Still," she says, "there are other women in your life. May I ask about Winifred Wagner?"

"Ah, yes, the composer's daughter-in-law," Hitler chuckles. "She is an aristocratic friend, nothing more. Joe Goebbels thinks it looks good, PR-wise, if we're seen together in public occasionally."

Eva pokes Hitler in the ribs.

"You took her to Goering's party last week!"

"That was business," Hitler frowns.

"Fine," says Eva, "but if that bimbo turns up at Berchtesgaden again, you're in big trouble, buddy."

Barbara bores in with another indelicate question.

"What about Leni Riefenstahl?"

"Yuk!" says Eva. "She thinks she's Marlene Dietrich."

"A brilliant filmmaker," Hitler replies. "I thought there might have been more closeups of me in *Triumph of the Will,* but, hey, it worked—you can't believe the grosses."

Barbara says, "I hear Leni has a two-picture deal to shoot the 1940 Tokyo Olympics and the 1944 London Olympics."

Hitler thinks for a moment.

"I wouldn't bet a lot of money on the Olympics being held in '40 and '44," he says.

Barbara leans forward again, leveling an even sterner gaze at the Fuehrer, as if she's going to hit him with her most penetrating question.

"Adolf, if you were a tree, what kind of tree would you be?"

Hitler looks at Eva worriedly. Eva looks at the Fuehrer with nervous uncertainty.

"I'm afraid that's too personal," Hitler says. "I must insist we go on to something else."

Barbara consults her notes. She then says, "Are you still close friends with Rudolph Hess?"

"Not as close as we were," Hitler says. "Not since he started bugging me so much for an 'as told to' credit on *Mein Kampf.*"

"Rudolph looks unhappy and restless, if you ask me," Eva says idly.

"Tell me about Joseph Stalin," says Barbara.

Hitler shrugs. "He's just a guy who's five-foot-one and has a withered arm—what's to tell?"

"I only ask because it's rumored that you don't much care for Bolsheviks and might have something in store for them in the future."

The Fuehrer mulls over Barbara's comment as he removes a vial from his pocket. He sprinkles a line of white powder on the coffee table. Eva hands the Fuehrer a straw. Holding the straw to his nostril, Hitler sniffs the line of white powder.

A brief sneezing fit follows, after which the Fuehrer looks wildly alert, even a little mischievous.

Suddenly, he leaps to his feet with a cocky grin.

"Russia?" he shouts. "WHY NOT?"

Texas Chic

FORT WORTH, TEX.

SHOCKING IS A WORD I TRY TO USE SPARINGLY, LIKE LYMPHO-granuloma, or yurt, which are neither here nor there, but it seems to be the right word to describe a discovery in the 1980s that was made by *W,* a simply-named publication that reaches an elite, world-wide audience of, I think, 26 people.

This is not to say that *W* isn't vital. *W* is extremely vital because those 26 people have a combined wealth of 879 trillion dollars, which they spend freely on helicopter skiing, interior decorators, designer clothes, and being naughty at lunch.

I should add that *W* is also vital because it is put out by *Women's Wear Daily,* which is read by more people who eat mesquite-grilled fish than any other newspaper.

But to get back to shocking. What *W* did that was so shocking was come out with one of those In and Out lists in which it proclaimed that Fort Worth, Tex., was In.

Yes. New York City was Out, Australia was Out, Hawaii was Out, Atlanta was Out, St. Moritz and Gstaad were Out, even Sigourney Weaver was Out, but Forth Worth was In.

Well, of course, there was nothing to do but come back here to my old hometown and try to find out why it was In after 140 years of being Out, except on those occasions when Sam Baugh and Davey O'Brien were throwing passes, and when Ben Hogan and Byron Nelson were winning golf tournaments.

I looked around for a week and found that nothing had changed, so I could only conclude that *W* had taken certain unusual characteristics of the city into consideration.

1. Fort Worth still does not have an ocean.

Evidently, *W* saw this as a big plus. We all know how it is when there's an ocean nearby. Salt spray gets on the window panes and the doors won't slide easily. Patio furniture gets stolen by surfers. There is the necessity of bug lamps and the constant threat of hurricanes. None of that in Fort Worth.

Fort Worth has sensible water, an assortment of country club swimming pools, and a Trinity River that's much too narrow for an ostentatious rowboat.

2. Fort Worth still does not have mountains.

Evidently, *W* saw this as another plus. We all know how it is when there are mountains nearby. Always the threat of melting glaciers, mud slides, roads clogged with tourists, people virtually skiing into your living room.

Fort Worth is flat, thus there is nothing to slow down the wind, which is either hot or cold and can never be accused of being in-between.

3. Fort Worth does not have a professional sports team.

Evidently, *W* saw this as a very large plus, inasmuch as almost any city that wants one can have a professional sports team. San Antonio has one, for example. Foxboro, Mass., has one. Anaheim, Calif., has one. East Rutherford, N.J., has two.

Not having a professional sports team keeps the people of Fort Worth calmer and makes it unimportant that very few of them have any money.

4. Fort Worth invented Western swing, the ice-cream drum-stick, and the washateria.

Evidently, *W* placed a high value on this.

5. Fort Worth still has railroad crossings.

I conducted an experiment and found that it's near impossible to go get any barbecue anywhere without stopping for two freight trains.

Fort Worth obviously got high marks from *W* for this facet of its old-world charm.

I noticed one thing about Fort Worth that might have cost it dearly, had *W*'s editors been more alert.

Happily, it's still a town where you can find an enchilada without duck sauce on it.

LITERATURE

What Is It?

LITERATURE IS WRITING THAT USUALLY APPEARS IN BOOKS, BUT IT can also appear in magazines and newspapers, although this is over the objection of most college English professors, who do not believe that magazine and newspaper writing is as vague, oblique, pretentious, or experimental as it should be.

Literature comes in two basic forms. Profound literature was written a long time ago and is generally avoided at all cost by most college students, except for some books that were written by a Russian, a German, a Frenchman, and an Englishman. Entertaining literature is written by everybody else and it can be read on most toilet seats, or even in a chair or a bed.

Some literature has been written for the stage, as when Shakespeare did it, and some has been written for motion pictures, as when Paddy Chayefsky did it.

Molière, the French playwright, said the best thing I ever read about literature, which was:

"Writing is like prostitution. First you do it for the love of it. Then you do it for a few friends. And finally you do it for money."

One of those best-selling lady novelists—I forget which one— said the second best thing I ever read about it, which was:

"I don't consider a big advance on a book to be outrageous. I consider it damages for the misfortune of having been born a writer in the first place."

Where sportswriting figures in all this was best summed up by the great John Lardner, who said:

"It beats working."

Obscure Lit

IT'S BEEN SAID THAT NO SPORT IS REALLY WORTHWHILE UNLESS IT has a literature. I've always thought the person who said this first was probably thinking about whale fishing and *Moby Dick* rather than football, baseball, boxing, horse racing, and golf, which are the sports that have the most literature. Personally, I think every sport is worth while to one group or another. It's just that certain sports have a more obscure literature than others.

Take bowling. Is it bowling's fault that so few people have ever read *A Farewell to Akron*, by Bubba Hemingway?

> *I went to the door of the diner.*
> *"Stay out of here, asshole," one of the bimbos said.*
> *"Fuck you, Denna," I said.*
> *"Fuck you, Frederick."*
> *"I'm gonna get some eggs," I said, "and I don't give a fuck what you or Catherine think about it."*
> *The sorry bitches left me alone while I had my eggs, but it wasn't any good. It was like saying goodbye to Cleveland. After a while, I went out and rolled up my pack of cigarettes in the sleeve of my T-shirt and walked back to my truck in the rain.*

Take surfing. Is it surfing's fault that so few people have ever read *The Naked and the Drugs*, by Skip Mailer?

> *Nobody could sleep. When morning came, the speed would wear off and the first wave of honeys would hit the beach at Laguna. All over town, all through the head shops, there was the knowledge that in a few more hours some of the dudes would be fucked up again.*

Cycling is a sport that takes a lot of abuse, even though an American won the Tour de France in the 1980s. Why? It's because so darn few people have discovered Herman Walter's classic, *The Winds of Cycling.*

> *Byron Henry pedaled his bike through a gusty gray rainstorm and reached the top of the hill where Natalie was waiting for him.*
> *"Briny, let's go to France," she said eagerly.*
> *"We just left France," said Byron, gasping for breath.*
> *"That was France? Gee, it sure went by fast. Okay, let's go to Poland."*
> *Byron wondered if Natalie would ever get tired of pedaling across Europe, especially during a war, when the roads were so bad. If they kept on darting around like this, he felt they were bound to wind up in some kind of trouble.*
> *"Natalie, that's the German border!" he yelled. "We'd better turn around."*
> *"Oh, Briny, you're such a worrywart," she said, speeding down the hill toward the village.*
> *Byron tried to keep up with her as she pedaled hard through the village, tossing her hair and winking at all of the Gestapo agents sitting at the sidewalk cafes.*

While it may seem that tennis is still bereft of literature, it is only because Maggie Meacham's *Gone With Wimbledon* has yet to be discovered.

> *Scarlett O'Hair was not beautiful, but women seldom realized it when caught by her charm, as the Tarleton sisters were.*
> *Scarlett made a pretty picture as she stood at center court, and the Tarleton sisters stared at her pale-green eyes, seeing in them a turbulent, willful lust for life. Dared they approach her after the match to suggest a three-way?*

Consider the plight of skiing. Sadly, it gets attention only every four years, during the Winter Olympics. But what if, by now, everyone had read *Of Human Bunk Beds,* by Billy Maugham?

> *The day broke gray and dull. The clouds hung heavily, and there was a rawness in the air that suggested snow. A woman came into the lodge and saw them all sleeping on top of each other. She went over to the pile.*
> *"Wake up, Philip," she said. "It's time for you and these other bums to pay your bill or get the fuck out!"*

Gymnastics is in the same category as skiing. It is only during a Summer Olympics that it catches anyone's attention, but this would not be so today if Irene Dinesen's fabulous *Out of Amarillo* had caught on the way it should have.

I had a farm in Amarillo, at the foot of a Denny's and a Taco Bell. You want to talk about somebody doing flip-flops and cart wheels? You should have seen me the day I left that chickenshit place for good.

It's hard to guess how much stock-car racing would benefit from a wider public acceptance of *A Tale of Two Throttles*, by Red Dickens, but it certainly couldn't hurt.

It was the best of cars; it was the worst of cars. It was the age of fuel consumption; it was the age of tire changes. It was the spring of pricks; it was the winter of cocksuckers. We were all going direct to Darlington, or we were all going direct to Daytona. Either way, we had lots of pussy.

Only those who follow wrestling as closely as I do can know how much it would have meant if *The Great Patsy*, by Scotty Fitz, had become a best-seller.

In my younger days and more vulnerable years, I wore a gold cape with sequins, and my father gave me some advice that I've been turning over in my mind ever since.
"Whenever you feel like wearing that cape," he told me, "just remember that there are plumbers and construction workers in this world who don't have a sense of humor."
But I believed in the gold cape, so I beat on, heads against the mat, borne back ceaselessly into the ring.

Amazing Tales

I WAS RAISED ON WHAT WAS ONCE CALLED "LITERATURE OF THE air," which was radio, and much of what I learned about sports at an early age, and subsequently had to unlearn, came to me in segments of 15 riveting moments every week from Bill Stern, the Colgate shave-cream man, who dealt in heroes and legends and seldom let facts get in the way of either one.

Of course, in those days I never heard that part of the show where Bill Stern got himself off the hook by saying that some of his stories were based on hearsay.

If I did, I must have assumed that Hearsay was a sportswriter who hung out with Bill Stern, Grantland Rice, Bill Corum, Bob Considine, and the rest of the boys. Buster Hearsay, columnist.

Bill Stern was a man from Rochester, N.Y., who got his big break in Gotham by becoming the stage director of Radio City Music Hall. From there, he went to announcing college football games with Graham McNamee, to broadcasting Friday night fights for Adam Hats, to appearing in MGM's *News of the Day* newsreel, but he became best known for *The Colgate Sports Newsreel,* which aired on NBC from 1939 through 1951 and blended crazed, bizarre non-facts with melodramatic organ music.

The show opened with his theme, sung in barbershop-quartet style, to the tune of *Mademoiselle from Armentieres:* "Bill Stern, the Colgate shave-cream man, is on the air/Bill Stern, the Colgate shave-cream man, with stories rare."

You heard that theme and you knew you were in for something pretty doggone exciting.

He always ended the show the same way, by saying, "That's the three-oh mark for tonight."

I found out quickly that this was a newspaper term, but it was years before I learned that Bill Stern had never worked on a newspaper.

No matter. His stories were what was important. Only on

The Colgate Sports Newsreel could you hear something like the following:

"Army against Navy. The big game. As big as the two academies had ever played. And out there on the field was Army's gutsy little quarterback, a kid who had sworn he'd never lose to the Middies. His name: Douglas MacArthur.

"But on the other side was a fullback who swore he'd never lose to the Cadets. His name: Chester W. Nimitz.

"It was a tough scrap, all right. A tie game all the way until late in the fourth quarter. That's when a skinny kid came off the Army bench and said he'd throw a key block for Mac. That kid's name: Omar Bradley.

"But at the same time, a tough little Middie had come off the bench and sworn to stop 'em. His name: William F. "Bull" Halsey.

"Still tied with a minute to go. And what's this? Another skinny kid coming in off the Army bench. He called a special play the Cadets had been saving, and lugged the ball across for the winning touchdown.

"That skinny kid's name: Dwight D. Eisenhower!

"But that's not the end of the story.

"Sitting in the Polo Grounds that day were a couple of foreigners watching their first American football game. Their names wouldn't have meant much to the boys on the field, but they do *now*.

"Those two men were Hermann Goering and Field Marshal Karl von Rundstedt!"

Then would come reel two:

"The old brickyard was ready for a great Indy—maybe the greatest. And a plucky guy named Eddie Rickenbacker was all set to win it.

"Eddie had the nerve and he had the best car.

"And most of the way, that Indy belonged to Eddie Rickenbacker. But it was on the final lap that fate stepped in.

"As Eddie bore down on the checkered flag, a little boy suddenly wandered onto the track. He had slipped out of his mother's grasp.

"To save the kid's life, Eddie slammed on his brakes and skidded across the infield.

"A race lost but a life saved!

"But that's not the end of the story.

"That little boy's name?

"Fred MacMurray—who would grow up to *play* Eddie Rickenbacker in the movie *Captain Eddie!*"

In today's world of sports scandals, Bill Stern might come up with a reel three like this:

"He was a big, tough kid who only wanted to play football. He made all-America for a team down South, then he went high in the NFL draft.

"But fate stepped in. On a tour of New York, the big city, the kid decided to have his picture made for the folks back home. He put his face down on the glass surface of an NP-270 F copy machine and pressed the button.

"Tragically, the big kid was blinded to such an extent that he could never play football again.

"The owner of that copy machine? Pete Rozelle, commissioner of the NFL.

"But that's not the end of the story.

"The kid's eyesight was partially restored through the miracles of surgery, and he is, today, one of the finest referees in pro football.

"That's the three-oh mark for tonight."

Colorful Pages

WHENEVER I SEE A MAN WEARING A PINK AND GREEN HAWAIIAN shirt, a pair of lavender slacks, a yellow golf cap, and bright blue sneakers, I assume he's a reader of *USA Today* and he's only trying to dress like his favorite newspaper.

This "Nation's newspaper" has affected us in other ways, of course, apart from brightening up our closets, coffee tables, car seats, what have you. It has narrowed our interest in vital issues down to two paragraphs or one chart, caused many of the country's other papers to be drenched in water colors, and has even made some of us begin to talk in strange ways.

I discovered the change in language one day when I called a friend long distance.

"How's the weather?" I asked.

"It's still pretty red down here," he said, "but we're expecting it to orange up by the weekend."

"No golf, huh?"

"Not till it yellows up. By God, it greened so much the other night, we had to put on sweaters."

I thought he then said he hadn't had any dots down there, none to speak of. A few dots the other night and it even dashed for an hour or so but no slashes to be concerned about.

"I guess the country club can use some yellow," I said.

"Oh, boy, can it? Our bent greens are about blued to pieces."

A day or two later I met another friend at a lunch counter, and as I was preparing to order, he said, "Sixty-seven percent of all people over the age of fifty like meatloaf."

I said I had planned to have the chicken and dumplings.

"Thirty-two percent of all people raised in the South have eaten cream gravy before their seventh birthday," he said.

I asked how his job was going.

"Good," he said, "given the fact that twenty-eight percent of us will be in a new profession by 1993."

I asked how his sister was getting along.

"She's forty-two," he said, sadly.

"What's wrong with that?"

He said, "Fifty-three percent of all single women her age have a better chance of getting killed by terrorists than they do of finding a man."

He handed me the sports section of his *USA Today.*

I noticed that in a weekend poll of pro football fans, only three percent could name an offensive lineman in the NFL.

I read where 36 percent of all baseball managers would not want to be Tommy Lasorda, owing to their dislike of Italian food.

The lead news story was about Pete Rose increasing his autograph fee from $7 to $8.95.

I traded my friend the sports section for the front section and turned to a daily feature called "Voices From Across the USA." The day's question was:

"Should Death Be Permanent?"

Kathy Lurch, 38, pediatrics nurse, Crevice, Utah, said, "I don't want to come out on the side of death altogether, but it does create openings in the job market."

Max Bosko, 58, salesman, Green Glitter, Calif., said: "I wish death would get around to some purchasing agents."

Jack Hergsperch, 31, corporate executive, New Canaan, Conn., said: "My Harvard degree guaranteed me a high-level position, which is as it should be, but there has been very little permanent death at the top of this company. I don't know how much longer I'm going to be happy here with the non-permanent death ratio this corporation is maintaining."

Suzy Coucher, 27, waitress, Blithe Farm, Md., said: "Death in movies or books is all right, but when it gets around to real life or rock music, I get very depressed. I just wish death would stay in Russia and leave the United States alone."

I paid for lunch, which was okay with my friend. He said that people in his age group only eat 27 percent of what is on their plates anyhow.

Reading the Classifieds

I HAVE AN IDEA THAT THE PEOPLE WHO RUN SINGLES ADS IN THESE give-away weeklies, which have names like *Beach Gazette, Reflections,* and *Folio,* are not having much luck because none of them seem to be sports fans. I'm certainly not anti-fucking, but isn't there a place for Wimbledon, or a Yankee–Red Sox series, or a Notre Dame–USC game in their lives?

I submit the following suggestions for ads and wish everybody good hunting!

WRITE TO ME
Single white female, 35, seeks professional man, humorous, adventurous, high-principled, and has a dick like an outside linebacker. Box T417.

BIG SCREEN FANATIC
Attractive 43-year-old gentleman seeks woman with VCR. I am five-seven, 165 pounds, brown hair, blue eyes, outgoing, success-

ful, and have wonderful collection of football highlights on Betamax. Need to transfer immediately. No children, pets, or foreign travel involved. Box B187.

LAUGHTER LOVER
Fantastically funny white male, 32, requires friendship with delusional schizophrenic who follows Chicago Cubs and has body of goddess. I am very much into pain. Box L440.

SOCCER FAN
European-born white male seeks slim, attractive, honest, sensuous lady for romantic relationship leading to marriage. Prefer Hispanic or Arabic descent and must be familiar with World Cup history. Box H139.

NEED NYMPHET
Man born to life of crime desires fetching nymphet with poor memory and knowledge of six-point teasers in college football. Send photo. Box A998.

SEX SLAVE
Morally corrupt woman, 32, intelligent, career-oriented, smoker, social drinker, seeks married man who is gentleman in public, deviate in private. Must be fan of Dallas Cowboys. Box M763.

DIVORCED MALE
I am 62 years old, very wealthy, pleasant, outgoing, and sensitive. My dream is to meet a non-professional female, preferably under 50, who enjoys dining out, good wine, travel, and buying football players for Notre Dame. No photo required. Box B688.

NEW TO AREA
White male just turned 40 but I look younger. I am physically fit, non-smoker, non-drinker, non-reader, non-talker, but vitally interested in making it with woman instead of some rather beastly tennis pros whose names I won't mention. Box N130.

ONE OF A KIND
Guaranteed to bring out the best in you! I am cute, quiet, passionate female, 25, who is sick and tired of relief pitchers and desires permanent relationship with outfielder who bats over .300 and plays for team on West Coast. Box F330.

ATTRACTIVE BLONDE

Educated, romantic, sexy woman, 52, seeks handsome silver-haired gentleman to pamper and spoil, provided he is a 3-handicapper from the back tees and has season tickets to Masters. Box M980.

FUTURE LOTTERY WINNER

I am not quite middle-aged, not quite divorced, and not quite financially solvent, but I keep a hard-on throughout football season and most of basketball season, and would like to share it with a fun-loving blonde under 30 who believes in the future. Preference given if your name is Melissa. Box C221.

NEW BEGINNER

Single white female with sparkling eyes, under 30, must meet this wonderful man who wants to provide home and family like the Waltons and enjoys the wonder of life's simple things. Take a chance on a dream. Take Auburn with 6½ over Alabama. Box D119.

FORGOTTEN LADY

Yes, I do exist. I am 29, blond, trim, vivacious, a dancer, smoker, drinker, dopehead, and collector's edition nymphomaniac, but I am tired of sucking cock in the American League West and wish to settle down to simple friendship and dating. Box E776.

COMPLETELY FREE

Single male who has undergone sex operation wishes relationship with normal human being. I am 36, unselfish, respectful, resourceful, affectionate, generous, and willing to adjust to any situation. Very experienced, stemming from seven years on the ladies' golf tour. Both men and women are invited to respond. Box D888.

TALL IN SADDLE

Man six-ten, capable of reverse, hang time, slam dunk, heavily into recreational drugs, seeks companionship with all good-looking bitches under 21. Send photos. I ain't interested in no motherfucking grandmothers, you hear this shit? Box F101.

The Book Shelf

SOMEDAY WHEN HISTORIANS SPEAK OF THE 1980S, AND THEY WILL, I hope they point out that it was an age in which "sports books" carved out a niche for themselves on the best-seller lists. I hadn't given much thought to this sociological phenomenon until it was called to my attention by Sam Niche, a freelance writer, who co-authored six books on psycho linebackers, three books on drug-reliant outfielders, and two autobiographies of volleyball coaches.

Here are some excerpts from a few of the most popular sports books of the decade:

From *Wilbur: The Story of a Linebacker's Dick That Wouldn't Stay in His Pants*, by Mike "Wagon Tongue" Thompson as told to Sam Niche:

"I shouldn't have diddled the coach's wife. I shouldn't have diddled the preacher's wife. I shouldn't have diddled my brother-in-law's daughter or any of them other little girls in the ninth grade, but shit—how's a man supposed to know who to diddle and who not to diddle when he's a football stud and there's all that pussy being throwed at him?"

From *Blades: Confessions of a Gay Speed Skater*, by Richie Pemberton as told to Crew Slammer:

"God, I love to look at men in Lycra."

From *Everything You Always Wanted to Know About Slam Dunks but Were Afraid to Ask a Black Person*, by Shek-el Hadeeb Abdul Mustafa as told to Chip Typer:

"I've searched my brain, when I wasn't playing backgammock, and I just don't know how all this bad shit got started about cocaine."

From *One Wife at a Time, or, How I Made It Big on the Pro Golf Tour*, by Billy Don Edgar as told to Biff Roberts:

"I decided to dump Sara Beth the day I three-putted the six-teenth at Pebble Beach for the second goddamn day in a row. A man's got no chance to play this game if he's married to a

killer bitch from hell—you can write that down on your memo pad."

From *Hey, Look at Me, I Tricked a Sportswriter Into Writing Another Book for Me,* by Big Boy Mattern as told to Dave Palestine:

"I knew TV was where I belonged when I started getting all these fan letters about my animal noises."

From *Screaming Headphones: My Life as an Offensive Coordinator Who Worked for the Dumbest Head Coach in College Football,* by Bones McCauley as told to Bernie Glotzer:

"Veer left, no gain. Veer right, no gain. Veer fumble. Punt. You think I got tired of seeing that crap? Tell me about it."

From *Hangin' Out With the Humper,* by Jack "The Humper" Vickorick as told to Blaine Fromm:

"I got the wheels. I got the dope. I got the clothes. I got the broads. Who wouldn't want to be me?"

From *The Man Above the Rim,* by Tomsk Vasilievich as told to Harlan Trimble:

"In Communist country they make fun of boy seven foot tall and bald-headed, but I discover basketball in Olympics and make life for myself in American university.

"My story begins in Murmansk where. . . ."

From *Grits for Brains: Confessions of an NFL Referee,* by Red Farrington as told to Brick Stoddard:

"Around my house, you hear a lot of talk about judgment calls."

From *Mrs. October: The Inside Story of a Home Run Hitter's Third Ex-Wife,* by Barbara Ann Clutch as told to Thornton Wilks:

"Call me naive but I had honestly never heard of the clap in Idaho."

From *Backhands and Barbie Dolls,* by Amy Colette as told to Bud Shepherd:

"My goal is to win Wimbledon before I'm fourteen years old. Really. I mean, like, my Mom thinks I can do it, you know?"

From *The Koz: A Scholar-Athlete's Journey to Three Orange Bowls,* by Barney Kozinski as told to Rank Rickert:

"All of the nights before a home game are the same: the chicks come over and get naked and start carving up the coke while me and Buster load the guns."

From *I'm X, You're O: The Odyssey of an All-Pro Middle Guard,* by Scratch Timmons as told to the heavily edited Paul Zucker:

"The Giants.

"The Packers.

"The Rams.

"The Steelers.

"And all the others. Every Sunday. Sometimes Monday night. They're on my turf. And they stink. That's how it is in the trenches. I live in the stink."

From *Beer and Comforts: An Investigation Into America's Preoccupation With Sports on Television,* by Dr. Jerome F. Klingman and Prof. Hamilton W. Fracker:

"In the beginning there was the universe, though not necessarily."

From *Up for Grabs,* by Coach Bobby "Grab Your Ankles" Blight as told to John Kleinstern:

"Any kid who's ever played basketball for me will tell you that grades come first. Then good citizenship. Then church. Then dress code. Then cleanliness.

"If a kid gets all this down, he's ready to play basketball for the Big Red—and he better not fuck up or the cocksucker's outta here."

The World of MTV

IT OCCURRED TO ME DURING AN ULCER ATTACK THAT MUSIC VIDEOS might be the easiest things in the world to write, seeing as how they largely appeal to the warped and brainless, and it further occurred to me that sports had yet to tap into this lucrative market. That's why I made a phone call to Ennui & Languor, the agency that represents me in Hollywood, and somebody in their office suggested I submit the following treatment to MTV:

Eric Derek

Gimme All of Your Drugs

(Greed Records)

OPEN ON girl in slinky evening gown coming out of warehouse. She licks her lips, gazes sexily at camera. Is she a black chick? Is she white? Is she, in fact, a girl? And why is she holding a tennis racquet?

DISSOLVE TO a gorilla paddling a gondola down a Venice canal. But it's not a gorilla. It's an America's Cup skipper, as we learn when he takes off his gorilla head.

A strong wind comes up, a spinnaker is unfurled, and the gondola goes speeding across an ocean toward a Pepsi Cola plant.

CUT TO a group of street punks. They have jagged hair and steel balls in their eyes. They are eating Big Macs along with the arms and legs of a small child.

DISSOLVE TO girl again. She sits in a rowboat in the Everglades and holds a microphone, hosting a pre–Super Bowl talent contest for NFL players.

A football player chews a handful of amphetamines and slobbers on microphone. This is his act in the talent contest.

CAMERA GOES TO audience, which consists of 4,000 teenage girls, begging for amphetamines.

CUT TO one of the street punks. He moon-walks on the stomach of a fat man, who turns out to be a wrestler who wandered into the wrong TV channel.

BRING ON Eric Derek.

He does not look altogether like a female, although his dress and high heels are confusing at first.

Eric sings *Gimme All of Your Drugs* to a cluster of priests, who go dancing across the Notre Dame campus.

CUT BACK TO the girl. She is totally naked and climbing the north wall of the Eiger in a pantyhose commercial.

The girl tosses her hair, closes her eyes, and dreams.

CUT TO slide show.

We see black-and-white shots of:

Janis Joplin, dead.

Jim Morrison, dead.

John Lennon, dead.

Jimi Hendrix, dead.

Elvis Presley, dead but still alive, and trying to lift his huge frame out of a coffin.

CLOSEUP OF girl, who now sits at a table in a vast desert and is suddenly approached by Arnold Palmer and O. J. Simpson in a Hertz car.

CUT TO a Miller Lite party where John Madden is punching his fist through a sheetrock wall.

BACK TO Eric Derek. He scrapes up the sheetrock dust and puts it in several clear plastic bags.

Out of nowhere come dozens of NBA players, who start throwing money at Eric Derek.

CUT TO 7,000 teenage boys with straws in their noses. They remove the straws, snarl viciously, and begin to leap off tall buildings.

Eric Derek sings over this, and we hear:

"They don't get no more . . .

"They don't get no more . . .

"They don't get no more. . . ."

DISSOLVE TO a whole city being destroyed by a single electric guitar.

CUT TO the warehouse of the opening scene.

A dinosaur stares at it, moodily. It is either a dinosaur or an offensive lineman for the Chicago Bears—you can't be sure because of the face mask.

CAMERA takes us inside the warehouse where Eric Derek and the girl are cutting this song for an album. The street punks we saw earlier are the band.

BACK TO dinosaur. We watch it eat the warehouse and everything inside it.

(Note to MTV producers: This would be the only known happy ending to a music video.)

Gone With the Sequel

IF ONLY I HAD RECOGNIZED THE NEED FOR A SEQUEL TO *GONE WITH the Wind* in time, the project might have been turned over to me instead of Ms. Alexandra Ripley and it could have become the sports book that America was waiting for, or not.

I already had the outline prepared, I just didn't make the phone call soon enough.

CHAPTER ONE
"On second thought, I do give a damn," Rhett Butler said, coming back into the house with his golf clubs over his shoulder.

CHAPTER TWO
Scarlett said she would think about it today, after all. Tomorrow was another day, but it was also Saturday and Notre Dame–USC would be on Channel 8.

CHAPTER THREE
Scarlett stared at her surprise dinner guest. "Melanie," she said. "What are you doing here? You're supposed to be dead."

"Dear Scarlett," Melanie smiled sweetly. "Didn't Ashley tell you? I came back for the sequel."

CHAPTER FOUR
Ashley Wilkes sat on the porch at Twelve Oaks and remembered the day he came home from the war, how he limped up the path in his ragged Confederate uniform, and how Scarlett had raced to meet him.

"Ashley, you're home!" she had cried out.

"Yes, Scarlett, I'm home."

"What was the score?"

"Forty-eight to thirteen, Penn State," he said wearily.

CHAPTER FIVE

Melanie was heartbroken. How dare those Pi Phis at LSU not pledge her daughter?

CHAPTER SIX

Scarlett and Rhett were having tea on the lawn at Tara when Scarlett finally asked him a question that had been nagging at her for years.

"Rhett Butler, you Will o' the Wisp of the Bounding Main, I know you're rich but I've never known what business you're in. What is it?"

"Didn't I tell you? Several years ago, I played tennis."

CHAPTER SEVEN

Ashley and Scarlett sat on the veranda at Twelve Oaks and watched the last foursome come up the 18th fairway.

"One day, Scarlett," said Ashley, "there'll be thirty-six holes and condos as far as you can see."

CHAPTER EIGHT

Rhett Butler was leaving Scarlett, and this time for good.

Pausing at the front door, he said, "Frankly, my dear, I'm in love with a Dallas Cowboy cheerleader."

EPILOGUE

Scarlett O'Hara stood knee-deep in the rough and held a Titleist 3 up to the sky.

"As God is my witness," she said, "I'll never play golf again."

The Old Listmaker

I GUESS I'VE NEVER MET A LIST I DIDN'T LIKE, INCLUDING THE ONES I take with me to Hank's One-Stop Stereo Center & Country Hams at the mall.

A friend pointed out to me one day that I had never written a novel that didn't have a list in it somewhere.

That came as no surprise to this reporter.

For years, or ever since I got into the dodge of novel-writing, loyal readers have come up to me and said the thing they liked best about my latest book was "that list—you know what I mean. How'd it go?"

I can't ever remember, so I've looked them up, and I hereby reprint them as a public service.

In *Baja Oklahoma*, it was the character of Slick Henderson who came up with mankind's 10 stages of drunkenness:

- Witty and Charming.
- Rich and Powerful.
- Benevolent.
- Clairvoyant.
- Fuck Dinner.
- Patriotic.
- Crank Up the *Enola Gay.*
- Witty and Charming, Part II.
- Invisible.
- Bulletproof.

In *Limo,* which I co-wrote with Bud Shrake, the character of Stanley Coffman, president of a TV network, came up with an idea for a show called *Super Assholes* in which the 10 events would be:

1. Wine-Discussing.
2. Maitre d'–Handling.
3. Name-Dropping.
4. Subject-Evading.
5. Credit Card–Fondling.
6. Spinnaker-Flying.
7. Entree-Ordering.
8. Blazer-Wearing.
9. Chairman of the Board–Sucking.
10. Paddle Tennis.

It was in *Fast Copy* that Betsy Throckmorton gave her sports editor some tips on how to write a better game story.

1. Most readers already know who won. See how many para-

graphs you can write without putting in the score. This may force you to think of other elements.

2. There is a key moment in every contest, a big play. Hammer it. Kick it to death.
3. When you have a strong angle, weave it all through the piece, reinforcing it with quotes and your own observations.
4. Write shorter. Nobody reads a garden hose.
5. Sights, sounds, and smells. Take the reader to the event with you.
6. Don't strain. Use the descriptions that come naturally to you, even if they're clichés.
7. Don't try to force in things that simply don't fit. Save the fascinating anecdote for another story where it does fit.
8. Never begin a story with a quote.
9. Avoid jargon. A game is a game, not a clash or a melee.
10. Be confident. After all, you were there and saw what happened; you interviewed the athletes involved; you are the professional who's been hired to tell the readers what happened, and why. I tend to take the position that if the readers don't like what I write, it's their problem, not mine.

Life Its Ownself went overboard on lists.

At one point, Billy Clyde Puckett dwelled on the Enemies of Love, some of which were:

* The insane cost of living.
* The stranglehold of analysts.
* Male-chauvinist jerks.
* Male-chauvinist feminists.
* Liberated wenches.
* Bizarre sexual demands.
* No sex at all.
* Whiskey.
* Recreational drugs.
* Born-again.
* Overly familiar barmaids.
* Porsche overhauls.
* People who change.
* People who refuse to change.
* Office flirtations.
* Business travel.
* Jogging.

- VCRs.
- Perrier.
- Bumper stickers ("NUKE THE FAG WHALES FOR JESUS").
- Men "preoccupied with success."
- Women "suffocating" for undisclosed reasons.
- She's too "assertive."
- He's not "supportive."
- Bloomingdale's.
- "I'm a person, too, you selfish mutant!"

Then Jim Tom Pinch, the sportswriter, wrote down his Top 10 favorite morning-after lines that he was accustomed to hearing from a shapely adorable who had slept over:

1. "Hey, it's Saturday—I have the whole day free!"
2. "Are these clean towels?"
3. "That's a neat picture—your wife is really pretty."
4. "It's actually in remission."
5. "You probably shouldn't drink so much—it would help."
6. "Don't worry, I would never pick up your phone."
7. "What were you doing with that pinlight last night?"
8. "Is it hard to get back on the freeway from here?"
9. "Richie will answer if I'm not there, but it's cool, he's just a good friend."
10. "In the bar, I thought you were the most cynical person I had ever met."

Before the last round of the U.S. Open golf championship in *Dead Solid Perfect,* Kenny made out his List of Woes, some of which were:

- Self-doubt sucks.
- I'm already choking.
- I have to drive to Dallas.
- I haven't shit in two days.
- My lighter is out of fuel.
- I'm going to hit it sideways in front of 30,000 people.
- The pills are all gone.
- At this moment, Janie Ruth is writing a check for the balance of my account.
- I never tried to understand my wife.
- MasterCard has a hit out on me.
- The Skipper is laughing.

Finally, there was Billy Clyde Puckett and Shake Tiller's girl-rating system from *Semi-Tough*. From the bottom up, it went like this:

"A Ten was a Healing Scab. Had a bad complexion but was hung and could turn into a barracuda in the rack.

"A Nine was a Head Cold. Good-looking but sort of proper and didn't know what a man liked.

"An Eight was a Young Dose of the Clap, but pretty in a dime-store kind of way, and not bad for an hour.

"A Seven was just rich.

"A Six was a Stove, or a Stovette. A Stove was over thirty and usually married. A Stovette was just under thirty, divorced, talked filthy, and tried to make up for all the studs she never got to eat because she got married so young.

"A Five was a Dirty Leg. She wore lots of cheap wigs, waited tables, was truly hung, might chew gum, posed for pictures, and got most of her fun in groups.

"A Four was a Homecoming Queen and a hard-hitting dumb-ass. Fours married insurance salesmen and got fat and later in life stayed sick a lot.

"A Three was a Semi, which is pronounced sem-eye by a Texan. You had to beware of Semis because you might marry them in a weak minute. Threes had it all put together in looks and style and sophistication. They could drink a lot and dance good and hang around and make conversation.

"A Two was a Her. If a Semi was tough, a Her was tougher. You might marry the same Her twice. Barbara Jane was a Her, or a Two.

"A One was extremely gorgeous in all ways from the minute she woke up in the morning until she fixed a man his cold meatloaf sandwich after love practice at four A.M.

"A One never got mad at anything a man might accidentally do, no matter how thoughtless or careless it might be.

"A One didn't care about having a lot of money.

"A One was good-natured and laughed a lot. Words like fuck and shit and piss and tit and fart and spick didn't bother a One.

"A One was a lady at all times.

"A One could cook anything a man wanted fixed, such as biscuits and cream gravy, fried chicken, enchiladas, navy beans, tunafish salad, barbecued ribs, and strawberry shortcake.

"A One tanned easily and never had a blemish on her whole body.

"A One was well-read and smart and witty, but not as well-read and smart and witty as the guys she hung out with.

"A One was a happy drunk and never aggressive.

"A One had no hangups and enjoyed every kind of normal sexual adventure, but she didn't particularly care about getting married.

"And of course there had never been a One. Ever."

Real Men Eat Clichés

IT'S TIME FOR ALL OF US INTERESTED IN LITERATURE TO STOP SMILing cordially and nodding agreeably when a coach or athlete says, "It's not over till the fat lady sings." Why? Because the expression is now older than Egypt and wasn't even accurate in the first place. Operas are never over.

Years ago, the statement was mildly amusing when the first football coach said it—Darrell Royal, John McKay, Duffy Daugherty, some wit like that—but it lost its charm when everybody in sports, in politics, on Wall Street, and in the oil business started saying it.

Today, at no extra cost, I offer the following alternatives:

It's not over till the fat lady remarries.
It's not over till they break through the "Star Wars" shield.
It's not over till the TV announcers shut up.
It's not over till they stop making Anacin.
It's not over till the Arabs bathe.
It's not over till you get the bill from the lawyer.
It's not over till Mother Teresa goes punk.
It's not over till they scramble every channel.
It's not over till they can't let out the waist.
It's not over till all the banks collapse.

It's not over till they find a treatment for nouvelle cuisine.

It's not over till the ambassador burns the files.

It's not over till your shoes don't match.

It's not over till they start selling beachfront property in Nebraska.

It's not over till you're on 60 Minutes.

It's not over till your fax machine starts editing.

It's not over till you're wearing a Nehru jacket again.

It's not over till you've tried to collect on the insurance.

Meanwhile, there's another shopworn saying that needs to be dealt with: "We took what they gave us."

Football coaches say this a lot, and have for years, and I've always thought I knew what it meant, but maybe not.

It doesn't necessarily mean that the coach had somebody outsmarted going in and wound up with more than he hoped for. It could very well mean that somebody had *him* outsmarted and he didn't come away with enough of whatever it was.

In any case, I think "We took what they gave us" needs to be clearer. A few suggestions:

We took what they gave us, which is why we wound up with all the slow white guys.

We took what they gave us, which is why we've moved from the 34th floor to the sub-basement.

We took what they gave us, and we still can't figure out why anybody hired them in the first place.

We took what they gave us, and now it's in the hands of the Grand Jury.

We took what they gave us, and we can only hope it won't be transmitted to our wives.

We took what they gave us, which means they got the bank and all we got was a postcard from Monaco.

We took what they gave us, which is how we wound up with nothing but this book.

Afterword:

"Sports Is My Life"

"SPORTS IS MY LIFE" IS A CRY THAT HAS BEEN KNOWN TO RING OUT IN press boxes at the conclusion of athletic events for as long as publications have had deadlines, which makes the expression a lot older than the forward pass, not to mention several coherent sentences.

The cry is usually intoned with an inflection of cynicism, or sarcasm, or a high degree of irritability.

The deadline itself was popularized by an editor in 1923 who believed that the only obligation of a daily newspaper was to come out every day. It is accepted theory that the man became an editor in the first place because he couldn't write a lick.

Deadlines wormed their way into magazines about the same time as the four-color printing process, which was how I found out that the New York Yankees wore blue and the Germans wore gray.

Red Smith, one of the most celebrated sportswriters who ever lived, along with Grantland Rice, Ring Lardner, and Damon Runyon, and one of the two best sportswriters who ever lived, along with John Lardner, once explained how he handled deadlines.

"I open a vein and bleed," he said.

All of the stories that have been presented here were written on deadlines that were dictated by the business or were self-imposed—I wanted to get back to the saloon.

By the clock, these deadlines ranged from one hour and 22 minutes to two days, 39 cups of coffee, and eight packs of Winstons.

The last time I looked, however, this display of lightning speed at the manual typewriter had not increased their resale value at Rita's Thrift Shop.

But that's not news. No sportswriter is ever going to be as rich as a dead artist. In fact, nobody is ever going to be as rich as a dead artist, including an NFL owner.

"Sports is my life" is something I hope to be saying a while longer in press boxes or press tents, but right now, an impatient Yorkshire terrier named "Barbara Jane Bookman" is staring up at me wistfully, telling me it's time to go for her walk.

Dan Jenkins
New York City
Spring 1989

368

DAN JENKINS has been a sportswriter all his life and in 1972 he became a best-selling novelist as well. His writing career began on *The Fort Worth Press* in 1948. He became sports editor of the *Press* in 1957. He moved to *The Dallas Times Herald* as sports editor and columnist in 1960. He joined the staff of *Sports Illustrated* in New York in 1962 and wrote over 500 articles for the magazine through 1984. He now writes a monthly sports column for *Playboy* and contributes essays and covers major golf championships for *Golf Digest*.

His best-selling novels are *Semi-Tough* (1972), *Dead Solid Perfect* (1974), *Limo* (with Bud Shrake, 1976), *Baja Oklahoma* (1981), *Life Its Ownself* (1984), and *Fast Copy* (1988). Jenkins also co-wrote the screenplays for the HBO productions of *Baja Oklahoma* and *Dead Solid Perfect*.

A native Texan, Jenkins is currently at work on a new novel for Simon & Schuster and divides his time between New York City and Ponte Vedra, Fla.